OMOO: ADVENTURES IN THE SOUTH SEAS

Herman Melville

Omoo: Adventures in the South Seas

By

Herman Melville

PART I

CHAPTER I. MY RECEPTION ABOARD

CHAPTER II. SOME ACCOUNT OF THE SHIP

CHAPTER III. FURTHER ACCOUNT OF THE JULIA

CHAPTER IV. A SCENE IN THE FORECASTLE

CHAPTER V. WHAT HAPPENED AT HYTYHOO

CHAPTER VI. WE TOUCH AT LA DOMINICA

CHAPTER VII. WHAT HAPPENED AT HANNAMANOO

CHAPTER VIII. THE TATTOOERS OF LA DOMINICA

CHAPTER IX. WE STEER TO THE WESTWARD--STATE OF AFFAIRS

CHAPTER X. A SEA-PARLOUR DESCRIBED, WITH SOME OF ITS TENANTS

CHAPTER XI. DOCTOR LONG GHOST A WAG--ONE OF HIS CAPERS

CHAPTER XII. DEATH AND BURIAL OF TWO OF THE CREW

CHAPTER XIII. OUR DESTINATION CHANGED

CHAPTER XIV. ROPE YARN

CHAPTER XV. CHIPS AND BUNGS

CHAPTER XVI. WE ENCOUNTER A GALE

CHAPTER XVII. THE CORAL ISLANDS

CHAPTER XVIII. TAHITI

CHAPTER XIX. A SURPRISE--MORE ABOUT BEMBO

CHAPTER XX. THE ROUND ROBIN--VISITORS FROM SHORE

CHAPTER XXI. PROCEEDINGS OF THE CONSUL

CHAPTER XXII. THE CONSUL'S DEPARTURE

CHAPTER XXIII. THE SECOND NIGHT OFF PAPEETEE

CHAPTER XXIV. OUTBREAK OF THE CREW

CHAPTER XXV. JERMIN ENCOUNTERS AN OLD SHIPMATE

CHAPTER XXVI. WE ENTER THE HARBOUR--JIM THE PILOT

CHAPTER XXVII. A GLANCE AT PAPEETEE--WE ARE SENT ABOARD THE FRIGATE

CHAPTER XXVIII. RECEPTION FROM THE FRENCHMAN

CHAPTER XXIX. THE REINE BLANCHE

CHAPTER XXX. THEY TAKE US ASHORE--WHAT HAPPENED THERE

CHAPTER XXXI. THE CALABOOZA BERETANEE

CHAPTER XXXII. PROCEEDINGS OF THE FRENCH AT TAHITI

CHAPTER XXXIII. WE RECEIVE CALLS AT THE HOTEL DE CALABOOZA

CHAPTER XXXIV. LIFE AT THE CALABOOZA

CHAPTER XXXV. VISIT FROM AN OLD ACQUAINTANCE

CHAPTER XXXVI. WE ARE CARRIED BEFORE THE CONSUL AND CAPTAIN

CHAPTER XXXVII. THE FRENCH PRIESTS PAY THEIR RESPECTS

CHAPTER XXXVIII. LITTLE JULIA SAILS WITHOUT US

CHAPTER XXXIX. JERMIN SERVES US A GOOD TURN--FRIENDSHIPS IN POLYNESIA

PART II

CHAPTER XL. WE TAKE UNTO OURSELVES FRIENDS

CHAPTER XLI. WE LEVY CONTRIBUTIONS ON THE SHIPPING

CHAPTER XLII. MOTOO-OTOO A TAHITIAN CASUIST

CHAPTER XLIII. ONE IS JUDGED BY THE COMPANY HE KEEPS

CHAPTER XLIV. CATHEDRAL OF PAPOAR--THE CHURCH OP THE COCOA-NUTS

CHAPTER XLV. MISSIONARY'S SERMON; WITH SOME REFLECTIONS

CHAPTER XLVI. SOMETHING ABOUT THE KANNAKIPPERS

CHAPTER XLVII. HOW THEY DRESS IN TAHITI

CHAPTER XLVIII. TAHITI AS IT IS

CHAPTER XLIX. SAME SUBJECT CONTINUED

CHAPTER L. SOMETHING HAPPENS TO LONG GHOST

CHAPTER LI. WILSON GIVES US THE CUT--DEPARTURE FOR IMEEO

CHAPTER LII. THE VALLEY OF MARTAIR

CHAPTER LIII. FARMING IN POLYNESIA

CHAPTER LIV. SOME ACCOUNT OF THE WILD CATTLE IN POLYNESIA

CHAPTER LV. A HUNTING RAMBLE WITH ZEKE

CHAPTER LVI. MOSQUITOES

CHAPTER LVII. THE SECOND HUNT IN THE MOUNTAINS

CHAPTER LVIII. THE HUNTING-FEAST; AND A VISIT TO AFREHITOO

CHAPTER LIX. THE MURPHIES

CHAPTER LX. WHAT THEY THOUGHT OF US IN MARTAIR

CHAPTER LXI. PREPARING FOR THE JOURNEY

CHAPTER LXII. TAMAI

CHAPTER LXIII. A DANCE IN THE VALLEY

CHAPTER LXIV. MYSTERIOUS

CHAPTER LXV. THE HEGIRA, OR FLIGHT

CHAPTER LXVI. HOW WE WERE TO GET TO TALOO

CHAPTER LXVII. THE JOURNEY ROUND THE BEACH

CHAPTER LXVIII. A DINNER-PARTY IN IMEEO

CHAPTER LXIX. THE COCOA-PALM

CHAPTER LXX. LIFE AT LOOHOOLOO

CHAPTER LXXI. WE START FOR TALOO

CHAPTER LXXII. A DEALER IN THE CONTRABAND

CHAPTER LXXIII. OUR RECEPTION IN PARTOOWYE

CHAPTER LXXIV. RETIRING FOR THE NIGHT--THE DOCTOR GROWS DEVOUT

CHAPTER LXXV. A RAMBLE THROUGH THE SETTLEMENT

CHAPTER LXXVI. AN ISLAND JILT--WE VISIT THE SHIP

CHAPTER LXXVII. A PARTY OF ROVERS--LITTLE LOO AND THE DOCTOR

CHAPTER LXXVIII. MRS. BELL

CHAPTER LXXIX. TALOO CHAPEL--HOLDING COURT IN POLYNESIA

CHAPTER LXXX. QUEEN POMAREE

CHAPTER LXXXI. WE VISIT THE COURT

CHAPTER LXXXII. WHICH ENDS THE BOOK

PART I

CHAPTER I.

MY RECEPTION ABOARD

IT WAS the middle of a bright tropical afternoon that we made good our escape from the bay. The vessel we sought lay with her main-topsail aback about a league from the land, and was the only object that broke the broad expanse of the ocean.

On approaching, she turned out to be a small, slatternly-looking craft, her hull and spars a dingy black, rigging all slack and bleached nearly white, and everything denoting an ill state of affairs aboard. The four boats hanging from her sides proclaimed her a whaler. Leaning carelessly over the bulwarks were the sailors, wild, haggard-looking fellows in Scotch caps and faded blue frocks; some of them with cheeks of a mottled bronze, to which sickness soon changes the rich berry-brown of a seaman's complexion in the tropics.

On the quarter-deck was one whom I took for the chief mate. He wore a broad-brimmed Panama hat, and his spy-glass was levelled as we advanced.

When we came alongside, a low cry ran fore and aft the deck, and everybody gazed at us with inquiring eyes. And well they might. To say nothing of the savage boat's crew, panting with excitement, all gesture and vociferation, my own appearance was calculated to excite curiosity. A robe of the native cloth was thrown over my shoulders, my hair and beard were uncut, and I betrayed other evidences of my recent adventure. Immediately on gaining the deck, they beset me on all sides with questions, the half of which I could not answer, so incessantly were they put.

As an instance of the curious coincidences which often befall the sailor, I must here mention that two countenances before me were familiar. One was that of an old man-of-war's-man, whose acquaintance I had made in Rio de Janeiro, at which place touched the ship in which I sailed from home. The other was a young man whom, four years previous, I had frequently met in a sailor boarding-house in Liverpool. I remembered parting with him at Prince's Dock Gates, in the midst of a swarm of police-officers, trackmen, stevedores, beggars, and the like. And here we were again:--years had rolled by, many a league of ocean had been traversed, and we were thrown together under circumstances which almost made me doubt my own existence.

But a few moments passed ere I was sent for into the cabin by the captain.

He was quite a young man, pale and slender, more like a sickly counting-house clerk than a bluff sea-captain. Bidding me be seated, he ordered the steward to hand me a glass of Pisco. In the state I was, this stimulus almost made me delirious; so that of all I then went on to relate concerning my residence on the island I can scarcely remember a word. After this I was asked whether I desired to "ship"; of course I said yes; that is, if he would allow me to enter for one cruise, engaging to discharge me, if I so desired, at the next port. In this way men are frequently shipped on board whalemen in the South Seas. My stipulation was acceded to, and the ship's articles handed me to sign.

The mate was now called below, and charged to make a "well man" of me; not, let it be borne in mind, that the captain felt any great compassion for me, he only desired to have the benefit of my services as soon as possible.

Helping me on deck, the mate stretched me out on the windlass and commenced examining my limb; and then doctoring it after a fashion with something from the medicine-chest, rolled it up in a piece of an old sail, making so big a bundle that, with my feet resting on the windlass, I might have been taken for a sailor with the gout. While this was going on, someone removing my tappa cloak slipped on a blue frock in its place, and another, actuated by the same desire to make a civilized mortal of me, flourished about my head a great pair lie imminent jeopardy of both ears, and the certain destruction of hair and beard.

The day was now drawing to a close, and, as the land faded from my sight, I was all alive to the change in my condition. But how far short of our expectations is oftentimes the fulfilment of the most ardent hopes. Safe aboard of a ship--so long my earnest prayer--with home and friends once more in prospect, I nevertheless felt weighed down by a melancholy that could not be shaken off. It was the thought of never more seeing those who, notwithstanding their desire to retain me a captive, had, upon the whole, treated me so kindly. I was leaving them for ever.

So unforeseen and sudden had been my escape, so excited had I been through it all, and so great the contrast between the luxurious repose of the valley, and the wild noise and motion of a ship at sea, that at times my recent adventures had all the strangeness of a dream; and I could scarcely believe that the same sun now setting over a waste of waters, had that very morning risen above the mountains and peered in upon me as I lay on my mat in Typee.

Going below into the forecastle just after dark, I was inducted into a wretched "bunk" or sleeping-box built over another. The rickety bottoms of both were spread with several pieces of a blanket. A battered tin can was then handed me, containing about half a pint of "tea"--so called by courtesy, though whether the juice of such stalks as one finds floating therein deserves that title, is a matter all shipowners must settle with their consciences. A cube of salt beef, on a hard round biscuit by way of platter, was also handed up; and without more ado, I made a meal, the salt flavour of which, after the Nebuchadnezzar fare of the valley, was positively delicious.

While thus engaged, an old sailor on a chest just under me was puffing out volumes of tobacco smoke. My supper finished, he brushed the stem of his sooty pipe against the sleeve of his frock, and politely waved it toward me. The attention was sailor-like; as for the nicety of the thing, no man who has lived in forecastles is at all fastidious; and so, after a few vigorous whiffs to induce repose, I turned over and tried my best to forget myself. But in vain. My crib, instead of extending fore and aft, as it should have done, was placed athwart ships, that is, at right angles to the keel, and the vessel, going before the wind, rolled to such a degree, that-every time my heels went up and my head went down, I thought I was on the point of turning a somerset. Beside this, there were still more annoying causes of inquietude; and every once in a while a splash of water came down the open scuttle, and flung the spray in my face.

At last, after a sleepless night, broken twice by the merciless call of the watch, a peep of daylight struggled into view from above, and someone came below. It was my old friend with the pipe.

"Here, shipmate," said I, "help me out of this place, and let me go on deck."

"Halloa, who's that croaking?" was the rejoinder, as he peered into the obscurity where I lay. "Ay, Typee, my king of the cannibals, is it you I But I say, my lad, how's that spar of your'n? the mate says it's in a devil of a way; and last night set the steward to sharpening the handsaw: hope he won't have the carving of ye."

Long before daylight we arrived off the bay of Nukuheva, and making short tacks until morning, we then ran in and sent a boat ashore with the natives who had brought me to the ship. Upon its return, we made sail again, and stood off from the land. There was a fine breeze; and notwithstanding my bad night's rest, the cool, fresh air of a morning at sea was so bracing, mat, as soon as I breathed it, my spirits rose at once.

Seated upon the windlass the greater portion of the day, and chatting freely with the men, I learned the history of the voyage thus far, and everything respecting the ship and its present condition.

These matters I will now throw together in the next.

CHAPTER II.

SOME ACCOUNT OF THE SHIP

FIRST AND foremost, I must give some account of the Julia herself; or "Little Jule," as the sailors familiarly styled her.

She was a small barque of a beautiful model, something more than two hundred tons, Yankee-built and very old. Fitted for a privateer out of a New England port during the war of 1812, she had been captured at sea by a British cruiser, and, after seeing all sorts of service, was at last employed as a government packet in the Australian seas. Being condemned, however, about two years previous, she was purchased at auction by a house in Sydney, who, after some slight repairs, dispatched her on the present voyage.

Notwithstanding the repairs, she was still in a miserable plight. The lower masts were said to be unsound; the standing rigging was much worn; and, in some places, even the bulwarks were quite rotten. Still, she was tolerably tight, and but little more than the ordinary pumping of a morning served to keep her free.

But all this had nothing to do with her sailing; at that, brave Little Jule, plump Little Jule, was a witch. Blow high, or blow low, she was always ready for the breeze; and when she dashed the waves from her prow, and pranced, and pawed the sea, you never thought of her

patched sails and blistered hull. How the fleet creature would fly
before the wind! rolling, now and then, to be sure, but in very
playfulness. Sailing to windward, no gale could bow her over: with
spars erect, she looked right up into the wind's eye, and so she went.

But after all, Little Jule was not to be confided in. Lively enough,
and playful she was, but on that very account the more to be
distrusted. Who knew, but that like some vivacious old mortal all at
once sinking into a decline, she might, some dark night, spring a
leak and carry us all to the bottom. However, she played us no such
ugly trick, and therefore, I wrong Little Jule in supposing it.

She had a free roving commission. According to her papers she might go
whither she pleased--whaling, sealing, or anything else. Sperm
whaling, however, was what she relied upon; though, as yet, only two
fish had been brought alongside.

The day they sailed out of Sydney Heads, the ship's company, all told,
numbered some thirty-two souls; now, they mustered about twenty; the
rest had deserted. Even the three junior mates who had headed the
whaleboats were gone: and of the four harpooners, only one was left,
a wild New Zealander, or "Mowree" as his countrymen are more commonly
called in the Pacific. But this was not all. More than half the
seamen remaining were more or less unwell from a long sojourn in a
dissipated port; some of them wholly unfit for duty, one or two
dangerously ill, and the rest managing to stand their watch though

they could do but little.

The captain was a young cockney, who, a few years before, had emigrated to Australia, and, by some favouritism or other, had procured the command of the vessel, though in no wise competent. He was essentially a landsman, and though a man of education, no more meant for the sea than a hairdresser. Hence everybody made fun of him. They called him "The Cabin Boy," "Paper Jack," and half a dozen other undignified names. In truth, the men made no secret of the derision in which they held him; and as for the slender gentleman himself, he knew it all very well, and bore himself with becoming meekness. Holding as little intercourse with them as possible, he left everything to the chief mate, who, as the story went, had been given his captain in charge. Yet, despite his apparent unobtrusiveness, the silent captain had more to do with the men than they thought. In short, although one of your sheepish-looking fellows, he had a sort of still, timid cunning, which no one would have suspected, and which, for that very reason, was all the more active. So the bluff mate, who always thought he did what he pleased, was occasionally made a fool of; and some obnoxious measures which he carried out, in spite of all growlings, were little thought to originate with the dapper little fellow in nankeen jacket and white canvas pumps. But, to all appearance, at least, the mate had everything his own way; indeed, in most things this was actually the case; and it was quite plain that the captain stood in awe of him.

So far as courage, seamanship, and a natural aptitude for keeping riotous spirits in subjection were concerned, no man was better qualified for his vocation than John Jermin. He was the very beau-ideal of the efficient race of short, thick-set men. His hair curled in little rings of iron gray all over his round bullet head. As for his countenance, it was strongly marked, deeply pitted with the small-pox. For the rest, there was a fierce little squint out of one eye; the nose had a rakish twist to one side; while his large mouth, and great white teeth, looked absolutely sharkish when he laughed. In a word, no one, after getting a fair look at him, would ever think of improving the shape of his nose, wanting in symmetry as it was. Notwithstanding his pugnacious looks, however, Jermin had a heart as big as a bullock's; that you saw at a glance.

Such was our mate; but he had one failing: he abhorred all weak infusions, and cleaved manfully to strong drink.. At all times he was more or less under the influence of it. Taken in moderate quantities, I believe, in my soul, it did a man like him good; brightened his eyes, swept the cobwebs out of his brain, and regulated his pulse. But the worst of it was, that sometimes he drank too much, and a more obstreperous fellow than Jermin in his cups, you seldom came across. He was always for having a fight; but the very men he flogged loved him as a brother, for he had such an irresistibly good-natured way of knocking them down, that no one could find it in his heart to bear malice against him. So much for stout little Jermin.

All English whalemen are bound by-law to carry a physician, who, of course, is rated a gentleman, and lives in the cabin, with nothing but his professional duties to attend to; but incidentally he drinks "flip" and plays cards with the captain. There was such a worthy aboard of the Julia; but, curious to tell, he lived in the forecastle with the men. And this was the way it happened.

In the early part of the voyage the doctor and the captain lived together as pleasantly as could be. To say nothing of many a can they drank over the cabin transom, both of them had read books, and one of them had travelled; so their stories never flagged. But once on a time they got into a dispute about politics, and the doctor, moreover, getting into a rage, drove home an argument with his fist, and left the captain on the floor literally silenced. This was carrying it with a high hand; so he was shut up in his state-room for ten days, and left to meditate on bread and water, and the impropriety of flying into a passion. Smarting under his disgrace, he undertook, a short time after his liberation, to leave the vessel clandestinely at one of the islands, but was brought back ignominiously, and again shut up. Being set at large for the second time, he vowed he would not live any longer with the captain, and went forward with his chests among the sailors, where he was received with open arms as a good fellow and an injured man.

I must give some further account of him, for he figures largely in the narrative. His early history, like that of many other heroes, was enveloped in the profoundest obscurity; though he threw out hints of a patrimonial estate, a nabob uncle, and an unfortunate affair which sent him a-roving. All that was known, however, was this. He had gone out to Sydney as assistant-surgeon of an emigrant ship. On his arrival there, he went back into the country, and after a few months' wanderings, returned to Sydney penniless, and entered as doctor aboard of the Julia.

His personal appearance was remarkable. He was over six feet high--a tower of bones, with a complexion absolutely colourless, fair hair, and a light unscrupulous gray eye, twinkling occasionally at the very devil of mischief. Among the crew, he went by the name of the Long Doctor, or more frequently still, Doctor Long Ghost. And from whatever high estate Doctor Long Ghost might have fallen, he had certainly at some time or other spent money, drunk Burgundy, and associated with gentlemen.

As for his learning, he quoted Virgil, and talked of Hobbs of Malmsbury, beside repeating poetry by the canto, especially Hudibras. He was, moreover, a man who had seen the world. In the easiest way imaginable, he could refer to an amour he had in Palermo, his lion-hunting before breakfast among the Caffres, and the quality of the coffee to be drunk in Muscat; and about these places, and a hundred others, he had more anecdotes than I can tell of. Then such mellow old songs as he sang, in a voice so round and racy, the real juice of sound. How such notes came forth from his lank body was a constant marvel.

Upon the whole, Long Ghost was as entertaining a companion as one could wish; and to me in the Julia, an absolute godsend.

CHAPTER III.

FURTHER ACCOUNT OF THE JULIA

OWING to the absence of anything like regular discipline, the vessel was in a state of the greatest uproar. The captain, having for some time past been more or less confined to the cabin from sickness, was seldom seen. The mate, however, was as hearty as a young lion, and ran about the decks making himself heard at all hours. Bembo, the New Zealand harpooner, held little intercourse with anybody but the mate, who could talk to him freely in his own lingo. Part of his time he spent out on the bowsprit, fishing for albicores with a bone hook; and occasionally he waked all hands up of a dark night dancing some cannibal fandango all by himself on the forecastle. But, upon the whole, he was remarkably quiet, though something in his eye showed he was far from being harmless.

Doctor Long Ghost, having sent in a written resignation as the ship's doctor, gave himself out as a passenger for Sydney, and took the world quite easy. As for the crew, those who were sick seemed marvellously contented for men in their condition; and the rest, not displeased with the general licence, gave themselves little thought of the morrow.

The Julia's provisions were very poor. When opened, the barrels of pork looked as if preserved in iron rust, and diffused an odour like a stale ragout. The beef was worse yet; a mahogany-coloured fibrous substance, so tough and tasteless, that I almost believed the cook's story of a horse's hoof with the shoe on having been fished up out of the pickle of one of the casks. Nor was the biscuit much better; nearly all of it was broken into hard, little gunflints, honeycombed through and through, as if the worms usually infesting this article in long tropical voyages had, in boring after nutriment, come out at the antipodes without finding anything.

Of what sailors call "small stores," we had but little. "Tea," however, we had in abundance; though, I dare say, the Hong merchants never had the shipping of it. Beside this, every other day we had what English seamen call "shot soup"--great round peas, polishing themselves like pebbles by rolling about in tepid water.

It was afterward told me, that all our provisions had been purchased by the owners at an auction sale of condemned navy stores in Sydney.

But notwithstanding the wateriness of the first course of soup, and the saline flavour of the beef and pork, a sailor might have made a satisfactory meal aboard of the Julia had there been any side dishes--a potato or two, a yam, or a plantain. But there was nothing of the kind. Still, there was something else, which, in the estimation of the men, made up for all deficiencies; and that was the regular allowance of Pisco.

It may seem strange that in such a state of affairs the captain should be willing to keep the sea with his ship. But the truth was, that by lying in harbour, he ran the risk of losing the remainder of his men by desertion; and as it was, he still feared that, in some outlandish bay or other, he might one day find his anchor down, and no crew to weigh it.

With judicious officers the most unruly seamen can at sea be kept in some sort of subjection; but once get them within a cable's length of the land, and it is hard restraining them. It is for this reason that many South Sea whalemen do not come to anchor for eighteen or twenty months on a stretch. When fresh provisions are needed, they run for the nearest land--heave to eight or ten miles off, and send a boat ashore to trade. The crews manning vessels like these are for the most part villains of all nations and dyes; picked up in the lawless ports of the Spanish Main, and among the savages of the islands. Like galley-slaves, they are only to be governed by scourges and chains. Their officers go among them with dirk and pistol--concealed, but ready at a grasp.

Not a few of our own crew were men of this stamp; but, riotous at times as they were, the bluff drunken energies of Jennin were just the thing to hold them in some sort of noisy subjection. Upon an emergency, he flew in among them, showering his kicks and cuffs right and left, and "creating a sensation" in every direction. And as hinted before, they bore this knock-down authority with great good-humour. A sober, discreet, dignified officer could have done nothing with them; such a set would have thrown him and his dignity overboard.

Matters being thus, there was nothing for the ship but to keep the sea. Nor was the captain without hope that the invalid portion of his crew, as well as himself, would soon recover; and then there was no telling what luck in the fishery might yet be in store for us. At any rate, at the time of my coming aboard, the report was, that Captain Guy was resolved upon retrieving the past and filling the vessel with oil in the shortest space possible.

With this intention, we were now shaping our course for Hytyhoo, a village on the island of St. Christina--one of the Marquesas, and so named by Mendanna--for the purpose of obtaining eight seamen, who, some weeks before, had stepped ashore there from the Julia. It was supposed that, by this time, they must have recreated themselves sufficiently, and would be glad to return to their duty.

So to Hytyhoo, with all our canvas spread, and coquetting with the warm, breezy Trades, we bowled along; gliding up and down the long, slow swells, the bonettas and albicores frolicking round us.

CHAPTER IV.

A SCENE IN THE FORECASTLE

I HAD scarcely been aboard of the ship twenty-four hours, when a circumstance occurred, which, although noways picturesque, is so significant of the state of affairs that I cannot forbear relating it.

In the first place, however, it must be known, that among the crew was a man so excessively ugly, that he went by the ironical appellation of "Beauty." He was the ship's carpenter; and for that reason was sometimes known by his nautical cognomen of "Chips." There was no absolute deformity about the man; he was symmetrically ugly. But ill favoured as he was in person, Beauty was none the less ugly in temper; but no one could blame him; his countenance had soured his heart. Now Jermin and Beauty were always at swords' points. The truth was, the latter was the only man in the ship whom the mate had never decidedly got the better of; and hence the grudge he bore him. As for Beauty, he prided himself upon talking up to the mate, as we shall soon see.

Toward evening there was something to be done on deck, and the carpenter who belonged to the watch was missing. "Where's that skulk, Chips?" shouted Jermin down the forecastle scuttle.

"Taking his ease, d'ye see, down here on a chest, if you want to know," replied that worthy himself, quietly withdrawing his pipe from his mouth. This insolence flung the fiery little mate into a mighty rage; but Beauty said nothing, puffing away with all the tranquillity imaginable. Here it must be remembered that, never mind what may be the provocation, no prudent officer ever dreams of entering a ship's forecastle on a hostile visit. If he wants to see anybody who happens to be there, and refuses to come up, why he must wait patiently until the sailor is willing. The reason is this. The place is very dark: and nothing is easier than to knock one descending on the head, before he knows where he is, and a very long while before he ever finds out who did it.

Nobody knew this better than Jermin, and so he contented himself with looking down the scuttle and storming. At last Beauty made some cool observation which set him half wild.

"Tumble on deck," he then bellowed--"come, up with you, or I'll jump down and make you." The carpenter begged him to go about it at once.

No sooner said than done: prudence forgotten, Jermin was there; and by a sort of instinct, had his man by the throat before he could well see him. One of the men now made a rush at him, but the rest dragged him off, protesting that they should have fair play.

"Now come on deck," shouted the mate, struggling like a good fellow to hold the carpenter fast.

"Take me there," was the dogged answer, and Beauty wriggled about in the nervous grasp of the other like a couple of yards of boa-constrictor.

His assailant now undertook to make him up into a compact bundle, the more easily to transport him. While thus occupied, Beauty got his arms loose, and threw him over backward. But Jermin quickly recovered himself, when for a time they had it every way, dragging each other about, bumping their heads against the projecting beams, and returning each other's blows the first favourable opportunity that offered. Unfortunately, Jermin at last slipped and fell; his foe seating himself on his chest, and keeping him down. Now this was one of those situations in which the voice of counsel, or reproof, comes with peculiar unction. Nor did Beauty let the opportunity slip. But the mate said nothing in reply, only foaming at the mouth and struggling to rise.

Just then a thin tremor of a voice was heard from above. It was the captain; who, happening to ascend to the quarter-deck at the commencement of the scuffle, would gladly have returned to the cabin, but was prevented by the fear of ridicule. As the din increased, and it became evident that his officer was in serious trouble, he thought it would never do to stand leaning over the bulwarks, so he made his appearance on the forecastle, resolved, as his best policy, to treat the matter lightly.

"Why, why," he begun, speaking pettishly, and very fast, "what's all this about?--Mr. Jermin, Mr. Jermin--carpenter, carpenter; what are you doing down there? Come on deck; come on deck."

Whereupon Doctor Long Ghost cries out in a squeak, "Ah! Miss Guy, is that you? Now, my dear, go right home, or you'll get hurt."

"Pooh, pooh! you, sir, whoever you are, I was not speaking to you; none of your nonsense. Mr. Jermin, I was talking to you; have the kindness to come on deck, sir; I want to see you."

"And how, in the devil's name, am I to get there?" cried the mate, furiously. "Jump down here, Captain Guy, and show yourself a man. Let me up, you Chips! unhand me, I say! Oh! I'll pay you for this, some day! Come on, Captain Guy!"

At this appeal, the poor man was seized with a perfect spasm of fidgets. "Pooh, pooh, carpenter; have done with your nonsense! Let him up, sir; let him up! Do you hear? Let Mr. Jermm come on deck!"

"Go along with you, Paper Jack," replied Beauty; "this quarrel's between the mate and me; so go aft, where you belong!"

As the captain once more dipped his head down the scuttle to make answer, from an unseen hand he received, full in the face, the contents of a tin can of soaked biscuit and tea-leaves. The doctor was not far off just then. Without waiting for anything more, the discomfited gentleman, with both hands to his streaming face, retreated to the quarter-deck.

A few moments more, and Jermin, forced to a compromise, followed after, in his torn frock and scarred face, looking for all the world as if he had just disentangled himself from some intricate piece of machinery. For about half an hour both remained in the cabin, where the mate's rough tones were heard high above the low, smooth voice of the captain.

Of all his conflicts with the men, this was the first in which Jermin had been worsted; and he was proportionably enraged. Upon going below--as the steward afterward told us--he bluntly informed Guy that, for the future, he might look out for his ship himself; for his part, he had done with her, if that was the way he allowed his officers to be treated. After many high words, the captain finally assured him that, the first fitting opportunity, the carpenter should be cordially flogged; though, as matters stood, the experiment would be a hazardous one. Upon this Jermin reluctantly consented to drop the matter for the present; and he soon drowned all thoughts of it in a can of flip, which Guy had previously instructed the steward to prepare, as a sop to allay his wrath.

Nothing more ever came of this.

CHAPTER V.

WHAT HAPPENED AT HYTYHOO

LESS than forty-eight hours after leaving Nukuheva, the blue, looming island of St. Christina greeted us from afar. Drawing near the shore, the grim, black spars and waspish hull of a small man-of-war craft crept into view; the masts and yards lined distinctly against the sky. She was riding to her anchor in the bay, and proved to be a French corvette.

This pleased our captain exceedingly, and, coming on deck, he examined her from the mizzen rigging with his glass. His original intention was not to let go an anchor; but, counting upon the assistance of the corvette in case of any difficulty, he now changed his mind, and anchored alongside of her. As soon as a boat could be lowered, he then went off to pay his respects to the commander, and, moreover, as we supposed, to concert measures for the apprehension of the runaways.

Returning in the course of twenty minutes, he brought along with him two officers in undress and whiskers, and three or four drunken obstreperous old chiefs; one with his legs thrust into the armholes of a scarlet vest, another with a pair of spurs on his heels, and a third in a cocked hat and feather. In addition to these articles, they merely wore the ordinary costume of their race--a slip of native cloth about the loins. Indecorous as their behaviour was, these worthies turned out to be a deputation from the reverend the clergy of the island; and the object of their visit was to put our ship under a rigorous "Taboo," to prevent the disorderly scenes and facilities for desertion which would ensue, were the natives--men and women--allowed to come off to us freely.

There was little ceremony about the matter. The priests went aside for a moment, laid their shaven old crowns together, and went over a little mummery. Whereupon, their leader tore a long strip from his girdle of white tappa, and handed it to one of the French officers, who, after explaining what was to be done, gave it to Jermin. The mate at once went out to the end of the flying jib boom, and fastened there the mystic symbol of the ban. This put to flight a party of girls who had been observed swimming toward us. Tossing their arms about, and splashing the water like porpoises, with loud cries of "taboo! taboo!" they turned about and made for the shore.

The night of our arrival, the mate and the Mowree were to stand "watch and watch," relieving each other every four hours; the crew, as is sometimes customary when lying at an anchor, being allowed to remain all night below. A distrust of the men, however, was, in the present instance, the principal reason for this proceeding. Indeed, it was all but certain, that some kind of attempt would be made at desertion; and therefore, when Jermin's first watch came on at eight bells (midnight)--by which time all was quiet--he mounted to the deck with a flask of spirits in one hand, and the other in readiness to assail the first countenance that showed itself above the forecastle scuttle.

Thus prepared, he doubtless meant to stay awake; but for all that, he before long fell asleep; and slept with such hearty good-will too, that the men who left us that night might have been waked up by his snoring. Certain it was, the mate snored most strangely; and no wonder, with that crooked bugle of his. When he came to himself it was just dawn, but quite light enough to show two boats gone from the side. In an instant he knew what had happened.

Dragging the Mowree out of an old sail where he was napping, he ordered him to clear away another boat, and then darted into the cabin to tell the captain the news. Springing on deck again, he drove down into the forecastle for a couple of oarsmen, but hardly got there before there was a cry, and a loud splash heard over the side. It was the Mowree and the boat--into which he had just leaped to get ready for lowering--rolling over and over in the water.

The boat having at nightfall been hoisted up to its place over the starboard quarter, someone had so cut the tackles which held it there, that a moderate strain would at once part them. Bembo's weight had answered the purpose, showing that the deserters must have ascertained his specific gravity to a fibre of hemp. There was another boat remaining; but it was as well to examine it before attempting to lower. And it was well they did; for there was a hole in the bottom large enough to drop a barrel through: she had been scuttled most ruthlessly.

Jermin was frantic. Dashing his hat upon deck, he was about to plunge overboard and swim to the corvette for a cutter, when Captain Guy made his appearance and begged him to stay where he was. By this time the officer of the deck aboard the Frenchman had noticed our movements, and hailed to know what had happened. Guy informed him through his trumpet, and men to go in pursuit were instantly promised. There was a whistling of a boatswain's pipe, an order or two, and then a large cutter pulled out from the man-of-war's stern, and in half a dozen strokes was alongside. The mate leaped into her, and they pulled rapidly ashore.

Another cutter, carrying an armed crew, soon followed.

In an hour's time the first returned, towing the two whale-boats, which had been found turned up like tortoises on the beach.

Noon came, and nothing more was heard from the deserters. Meanwhile Doctor Long Ghost and myself lounged about, cultivating an acquaintance, and gazing upon the shore scenery. The bay was as calm as death; the sun high and hot; and occasionally a still gliding canoe stole out from behind the headlands, and shot across the water.

And all the morning long our sick men limped about the deck, casting wistful glances inland, where the palm-trees waved and beckoned them into their reviving shades. Poor invalid rascals! How conducive to the restoration of their shattered health would have been those delicious groves! But hard-hearted Jermin assured them, with an oath, that foot of theirs should never touch the beach.

Toward sunset a crowd was seen coming down to the water. In advance of all were the fugitives--bareheaded--their frocks and trousers hanging in tatters, every face covered with blood and dust, and their arms pinioned behind them with green thongs. Following them up, was a shouting rabble of islanders, pricking them with the points of their long spears, the party from the corvette menacing them in flank with their naked cutlasses.

The bonus of a musket to the King of the Bay, and the promise of a tumblerful of powder for every man caught, had set the whole population on their track; and so successful was the hunt, that not only were that morning's deserters brought back, but five of those left behind on a former visit. The natives, however, were the mere hounds of the chase, raising the game in their coverts, but leaving the securing of it to the Frenchmen. Here, as elsewhere, the islanders have no idea of taking part in such a scuffle as ensues upon the capture of a party of desperate seamen.

The runaways were at once brought aboard, and, though they looked rather sulky, soon came round, and treated the whole affair as a frolicsome adventure.

CHAPTER VI.

WE TOUCH AT LA DOMINICA

FEARFUL of spending another night at Hytyhoo, Captain Guy caused the ship to be got under way shortly after dark.

The next morning, when all supposed that we were fairly embarked for a long cruise, our course was suddenly altered for La Dominica, or Hivarhoo, an island just north of the one we had quitted. The object of this, as we learned, was to procure, if possible, several English sailors, who, according to the commander of the corvette, had recently gone ashore there from an American whaler, and were desirous of shipping aboard one of their own country vessels.

We made the land in the afternoon, coming abreast of a shady glen opening from a deep bay, and winding by green denies far out of sight. "Hands by the weather-main-brace!" roared the mate, jumping up on the bulwarks; and in a moment the prancing Julia, suddenly arrested in her course, bridled her head like a steed reined in, while the foam flaked under her bows.

This was the place where we expected to obtain the men; so a boat was at once got in readiness to go ashore. Now it was necessary to provide a picked crew--men the least likely to abscond. After considerable deliberation on the part of the captain and mate, four of the seamen were pitched upon as the most trustworthy; or rather they were selected from a choice assortment of suspicious characters as being of an inferior order of rascality.

Armed with cutlasses all round--the natives were said to be an ugly set--they were followed over the side by the invalid captain, who, on this occasion, it seems, was determined to signalize himself. Accordingly, in addition to his cutlass, he wore an old boarding belt, in which was thrust a brace of pistols. They at once shoved off.

My friend Long Ghost had, among other things which looked somewhat strange in a ship's forecastle, a capital spy-glass, and on the present occasion we had it in use.

When the boat neared the head of the inlet, though invisible to the naked eye, it was plainly revealed by the glass; looking no bigger than an egg-shell, and the men diminished to pigmies.

At last, borne on what seemed a long flake of foam, the tiny craft shot up the beach amid a shower of sparkles. Not a soul was there. Leaving one of their number by the water, the rest of the pigmies stepped ashore, looking about them very circumspectly, pausing now and then hand to ear, and peering under a dense grove which swept down within a few paces of the sea. No one came, and to all appearances everything was as still as the grave. Presently he with the pistols, followed by the rest flourishing their bodkins, entered the wood and were soon lost to view. They did not stay long; probably anticipating some inhospitable ambush were they to stray any distance up the glen.

In a few moments they embarked again, and were soon riding pertly over the waves of the bay. All of a sudden the captain started to his feet--the boat spun round, and again made for the shore. Some twenty or thirty natives armed with spears which through the glass looked like reeds, had just come out of the grove, and were apparently shouting to the strangers not to be in such a hurry, but return and be sociable. But they were somewhat distrusted, for the boat paused about its length from the beach, when the captain standing up in its head delivered an address in pantomime, the object of which seemed to be, that the islanders should draw near. One of them stepped forward and made answer, seemingly again urging the strangers not to be diffident, but beach their boat. The captain declined, tossing his arms about in another pantomime. In the end he said something which made them shake their spears; whereupon he fired a pistol among them, which set the whole party running; while one poor little fellow, dropping his spear and clapping his hand behind him, limped away in a manner which almost made me itch to get a shot at his assailant.

Wanton acts of cruelty like this are not unusual on the part of sea captains landing at islands comparatively unknown. Even at the Pomotu group, but a day's sail from Tahiti, the islanders coming down to the shore have several times been fired at by trading schooners passing through their narrow channels; and this too as a mere amusement on the part of the ruffians.

Indeed, it is almost incredible, the light in which many sailors regard these naked heathens. They hardly consider them human. But it is a curious fact, that the more ignorant and degraded men are, the more contemptuously they look upon those whom they deem their inferiors.

All powers of persuasion being thus lost upon these foolish savages, and no hope left of holding further intercourse, the boat returned to the ship.

CHAPTER VII.

WHAT HAPPENED AT HANNAMANOO

ON the other side of the island was the large and populous bay of Hannamanoo, where the men sought might yet be found. But as the sun was setting by the time the boat came alongside, we got our offshore tacks aboard and stood away for an offing. About daybreak we wore, and ran in, and by the time the sun was well up, entered the long, narrow channel dividing the islands of La Dominica and St. Christina.

On one hand was a range of steep green bluffs hundreds of feet high, the white huts of the natives here and there nestling like birds' nests in deep clefts gushing with verdure. Across the water, the land rolled away in bright hillsides, so warm and undulating that they seemed almost to palpitate in the sun. On we swept, past bluff and grove, wooded glen and valley, and dark ravines lighted up far inland with wild falls of water. A fresh land-breeze filled our sails, the embayed waters were gentle as a lake, and every wave broke with a tinkle against our coppered prow.

On gaining the end of the channel we rounded a point, and came full upon the bay of Hannamanoo. This is the only harbour of any note about the island, though as far as a safe anchorage is concerned it hardly deserves the title.

Before we held any communication with the shore, an incident occurred which may convey some further idea of the character of our crew.

Having approached as near the land as we could prudently, our headway was stopped, and we awaited the arrival of a canoe which was coming out of the bay. All at once we got into a strong current, which swept us rapidly toward a rocky promontory forming one side of the harbour. The wind had died away; so two boats were at once lowered for the purpose of pulling the ship's head round. Before this could be done, the eddies were whirling upon all sides, and the rock so near that it seemed as if one might leap upon it from the masthead. Notwithstanding the speechless fright of the captain, and the hoarse shouts of the unappalled Jennin, the men handled the ropes as deliberately as possible, some of them chuckling at the prospect of going ashore, and others so eager for the vessel to strike, that they could hardly contain themselves. Unexpectedly a countercurrent befriended us, and assisted by the boats we were soon out of danger.

What a disappointment for our crew! All their little plans for swimming ashore from the wreck, and having a fine time of it for the rest of their days, thus cruelly nipped in the bud.

Soon after, the canoe came alongside. In it were eight or ten natives, comely, vivacious-looking youths, all gesture and exclamation; the red feathers in their head-bands perpetually nodding. With them also came a stranger, a renegade from Christendom and humanity--a white man, in the South Sea girdle, and tattooed in the face. A broad blue band stretched across his face from ear to ear, and on his forehead was the taper figure of a blue shark, nothing but fins from head to tail.

Some of us gazed upon this man with a feeling akin to horror, no ways abated when informed that he had voluntarily submitted to this embellishment of his countenance. What an impress! Far worse than Cain's--his was perhaps a wrinkle, or a freckle, which some of our modern cosmetics might have effaced; but the blue shark was a mark indelible, which all the waters of Abana and Pharpar, rivers of Damascus, could never wash out. He was an Englishman, Lem Hardy he called himself, who had deserted from a trading brig touching at the island for wood and water some ten years previous. He had gone ashore as a sovereign power armed with a musket and a bag of ammunition, and ready if need were, to prosecute war on his own account. The country was divided by the hostile kings of several large valleys. With one of them, from whom he first received overtures, he formed an alliance, and became what he now was, the military leader of the tribe, and war-god of the entire island.

His campaigns beat Napoleon's. In one night attack, his invincible musket, backed by the light infantry of spears and javelins, vanquished two clans, and the next morning brought all the others to the feet of his royal ally.

Nor was the rise of his domestic fortunes at all behind the Corsican's: three days after landing, the exquisitely tattooed hand of a princess was his; receiving along with the damsel as her portion, one thousand fathoms of fine tappa, fifty double-braided mats of split grass, four hundred hogs, ten houses in different parts of her native valley, and the sacred protection of an express edict of the Taboo, declaring his person inviolable for ever.

Now, this man was settled for life, perfectly satisfied with his circumstances, and feeling no desire to return to his friends.

"Friends," indeed, he had none. He told me his history. Thrown upon the world a foundling, his paternal origin was as much a mystery to him as the genealogy of Odin; and, scorned by everybody, he fled the parish workhouse when a boy, and launched upon the sea. He had followed it for several years, a dog before the mast, and now he had thrown it up for ever.

And for the most part, it is just this sort of men--so many of whom are found among sailors--uncared for by a single soul, without ties, reckless, and impatient of the restraints of civilization, who are occasionally found quite at home upon the savage islands of the Pacific. And, glancing at their hard lot in their own country, what marvel at their choice?

According to the renegado, there was no other white man on the island;

and as the captain could have no reason to suppose that Hardy intended to deceive us, he concluded that the Frenchmen were in some way or other mistaken in what they had told us. However, when our errand was made known to the rest of our visitors, one of them, a fine, stalwart fellow, his face all eyes and expression, volunteered for a cruise. All the wages he asked was a red shirt, a pair of trousers, and a hat, which were to be put on there and then; besides a plug of tobacco and a pipe. The bargain was struck directly; but Wymontoo afterward came in with a codicil, to the effect that a friend of his, who had come along with him, should be given ten whole sea-biscuits, without crack or flaw, twenty perfectly new and symmetrically straight nails, and one jack-knife. This being agreed to, the articles were at once handed over; the native receiving them with great avidity, and in the absence of clothing, using his mouth as a pocket to put the nails in. Two of them, however, were first made to take the place of a pair of ear-ornaments, curiously fashioned out of bits of whitened wood.

It now began breezing strongly from seaward, and no time was to be lost in getting away from the land; so after an affecting rubbing of noses between our new shipmate and his countrymen, we sailed away with him.

To our surprise, the farewell shouts from the canoe, as we dashed along under bellied royals, were heard unmoved by our islander; but it was not long thus. That very evening, when the dark blue of his native hills sunk in the horizon, the poor savage leaned over the bulwarks, dropped his head upon his chest, and gave way to irrepressible emotions. The ship was plunging hard, and Wymontoo, sad to tell, in addition to his other pangs, was terribly sea-sick.

CHAPTER VIII.

THE TATTOOERS OF LA DOMINICA

FOR a while leaving Little Jule to sail away by herself, I will here put down some curious information obtained from Hardy.

The renegado had lived so long on the island that its customs were quite familiar; and I much lamented that, from the shortness of our stay, he could not tell us more than he did.

From the little intelligence gathered, however, I learned to my surprise that, in some things, the people of Hivarhoo, though of the same group of islands, differed considerably from my tropical friends in the valley of Typee.

As his tattooing attracted so much remark, Hardy had a good deal to say concerning the manner in which that art was practised upon the island.

Throughout the entire cluster the tattooers of Hivarhoo enjoyed no small reputation. They had carried their art to the highest perfection, and the profession was esteemed most honourable. No wonder, then, that like genteel tailors, they rated their services very high; so much so that none but those belonging to the higher classes could afford to employ them. So true was this, that the elegance of one's tattooing was in most cases a sure indication of birth and riches.

Professors in large practice lived in spacious houses, divided by screens of tappa into numerous little apartments, where subjects were waited upon in private. The arrangement chiefly grew out of a singular ordinance of the Taboo, which enjoined the strictest privacy upon all men, high and low, while under the hands of a tattooer. For the time, the slightest intercourse with others is prohibited, and the small portion of food allowed is pushed under the curtain by an unseen hand. The restriction with regard to food, is intended to reduce the blood, so as to diminish the inflammation consequent upon puncturing the skin. As it is, this comes on very soon, and takes some time to heal; so that the period of seclusion generally embraces many days, sometimes several weeks.

All traces of soreness vanished, the subject goes abroad; but only again to return; for, on account of the pain, only a small surface can be operated upon at once; and as the whole body is to be more or less embellished by a process so slow, the studios alluded to are constantly filled. Indeed, with a vanity elsewhere unheard of, many spend no small portion of their days thus sitting to an artist.

To begin the work, the period of adolescence is esteemed the most suitable. After casting about for some eminent tattooer, the friends of the youth take him to his house to have the outlines of the general plan laid out. It behoves the professor to have a nice eye, for a suit to be worn for life should be well cut.

Some tattooers, yearning after perfection, employ, at large wages, one or two men of the commonest order--vile fellows, utterly regardless of appearances, upon whom they first try their patterns and practise generally. Their backs remorselessly scrawled over, and no more canvas remaining, they are dismissed and ever after go about, the scorn of their countrymen.

Hapless wights! thus martyred in the cause of the Fine Arts.

Beside the regular practitioners, there are a parcel of shabby, itinerant tattooers, who, by virtue of their calling, stroll unmolested from one hostile bay to another, doing their work dog-cheap for the multitude. They always repair to the various religious festivals, which gather great crowds. When these are concluded, and the places where they are held vacated even by the tattooers, scores of little tents of coarse tappa are left standing, each with a solitary inmate, who, forbidden to talk to his unseen neighbours, is obliged to stay there till completely healed. The itinerants are a reproach to their profession, mere cobblers, dealing in nothing but jagged lines and clumsy patches, and utterly incapable of soaring to those heights of fancy attained by the gentlemen of the faculty.

All professors of the arts love to fraternize; and so, in Hannamanoo, the tattooers came together in the chapters of their worshipful order. In this society, duly organized, and conferring degrees, Hardy, from his influence as a white, was a sort of honorary Grand Master. The blue shark, and a sort of Urim and Thummim engraven upon his chest, were the seal of his initiation. All over Hivarhoo are established these orders of tattooers. The way in which the renegado's came to be founded is this. A year or two after his landing there happened to be a season of scarcity, owing to the partial failure of the breadfruit harvest for several consecutive seasons. This brought about such a falling off in the number of subjects for tattooing that the profession became quite needy. The royal ally of Hardy, however, hit upon a benevolent expedient to provide for their wants, at the same time conferring a boon upon many of his subjects.

By sound of conch-shell it was proclaimed before the palace, on the beach, and at the head of the valley, that Noomai, King of Hannamanoo, and friend of Hardee-Hardee, the white, kept open heart and table for all tattooers whatsoever; but to entitle themselves to this hospitality, they were commanded to practise without fee upon the meanest native soliciting their services.

Numbers at once flocked to the royal abode, both artists and sitters. It was a famous time; and the buildings of the palace being "taboo" to all but the tattooers and chiefs, the sitters bivouacked on the common, and formed an extensive encampment.

The "Lora Tattoo," or the Time of Tattooing, will be long remembered. An enthusiastic sitter celebrated the event in verse. Several lines were repeated to us by Hardy, some of which, in a sort of colloquial chant he translated nearly thus:

"Where is that sound?
In Hannamanoo.
And wherefore that sound?
The sound of a hundred hammers,
Tapping, tapping, tapping
The shark teeth."

"Where is that light?
Round about the king's house,
And the small laughter?
The small, merry laughter it is
Of the sons and daughters of the tattooed."

CHAPTER IX.

WE STEER TO THE WESTWARD--STATE OF AFFAIRS

THE night we left Hannamanoo was bright and starry, and so warm that, when the watches were relieved, most of the men, instead of going below, flung themselves around the foremast.

Toward morning, finding the heat of the forecastle unpleasant, I ascended to the deck where everything was noiseless. The Trades were blowing with a mild, steady strain upon the canvas, and the ship heading right out into the immense blank of the Western Pacific. The watch were asleep. With one foot resting on the rudder, even the man at the helm nodded, and the mate himself, with arms folded, was leaning against the capstan.

On such a night, and all alone, reverie was inevitable. I leaned over the side, and could not help thinking of the strange objects we might be sailing over.

But my meditations were soon interrupted by a gray, spectral shadow cast over the heaving billows. It was the dawn, soon followed by the first rays of the morning. They flashed into view at one end of the arched night, like--to compare great things with small--the gleamings of Guy Fawkes's lantern in the vaults of the Parliament House. Before long, what seemed a live ember rested for a moment on the rim of the ocean, and at last the blood-red sun stood full and round in the level East, and the long sea-day began.

Breakfast over, the first thing attended to was the formal baptism of Wymontoo, who, after thinking over his affairs during the night, looked dismal enough.

There were various opinions as to a suitable appellation. Some maintained that we ought to call him "Sunday," that being the day we caught him; others, "Eighteen Forty-two," the then year of our Lord; while Doctor Long Ghost remarked that he ought, by all means, to retain his original name,--Wymontoo-Hee, meaning (as he maintained), in the figurative language of the island, something analogous to one who had got himself into a scrape. The mate put an end to the discussion by sousing the poor fellow with a bucket of salt water, and bestowing upon him the nautical appellation of "Luff."

Though a certain mirthfulness succeeded his first pangs at leaving home, Wymontoo--we will call him thus--gradually relapsed into his former mood, and became very melancholy. Often I noticed him crouching apart in the forecastle, his strange eyes gleaming restlessly, and watching the slightest movement of the men. Many a time he must have been thinking of his bamboo hut, when they were talking of Sydney and its dance-houses.

We were now fairly at sea, though to what particular cruising-ground we were going, no one knew; and, to all appearances, few cared. The men, after a fashion of their own, began to settle down into the routine of sea-life, as if everything was going on prosperously. Blown along over a smooth sea, there was nothing to do but steer the ship, and relieve the "look-outs" at the mast-heads. As for the sick, they had two or three more added to their number--the air of the island having disagreed with the constitutions of several of the runaways. To crown all, the captain again relapsed, and became quite ill.

The men fit for duty were divided into two small watches, headed respectively by the mate and the Mowree; the latter by virtue of his being a harpooner, succeeding to the place of the second mate, who had absconded.

In this state of things whaling was out of the question; but in the face of everything, Jermin maintained that the invalids would soon be well. However that might be, with the same pale Hue sky overhead, we kept running steadily to the westward. Forever advancing, we seemed always in the same place, and every day was the former lived over again. We saw no ships, expected to see none. No sign of life was perceptible but the porpoises and other fish sporting under the bows like pups ashore. But, at intervals, the gray albatross, peculiar to these seas, came flapping his immense wings over us, and then skimmed away silently as if from a plague-ship. Or flights of the tropic bird, known among seamen as the "boatswain," wheeled round and round us, whistling shrilly as they flew.

The uncertainty hanging over our destination at this time, and the fact that we were abroad upon waters comparatively little traversed, lent an interest to this portion of the cruise which I shall never forget.

From obvious prudential considerations the Pacific has been principally sailed over in known tracts, and this is the reason why new islands are still occasionally discovered by exploring ships and adventurous whalers notwithstanding the great number of vessels of all kinds of late navigating this vast ocean. Indeed, considerable portions still remain wholly unexplored; and there is doubt as to the actual existence of certain shoals, and reefs, and small clusters of islands vaguely laid down in the charts. The mere circumstance, therefore, of a ship like ours penetrating into these regions, was sufficient to cause any reflecting mind to feel at least a little uneasy. For my own part, the many stories I had heard of ships striking at midnight upon unknown rocks, with all sail set, and a slumbering crew, often recurred to me, especially, as from the absence of discipline, and our being so shorthanded, the watches at night were careless in the extreme.

But no thoughts like these were entertained by my reckless shipmates; and along we went, the sun every evening setting right ahead of our jib boom.

For what reason the mate was so reserved with regard to our precise destination was never made known. The stories he told us, I, for one, did not believe; deeming them all a mere device to lull the crew.

He said we were bound to a fine cruising ground, scarcely known to other whalemen, which he had himself discovered when commanding a small brig upon a former voyage. Here, the sea was alive with large whales, so tame that all you had to do was to go up and kill them: they were too frightened to resist. A little to leeward of this was a small cluster of islands, where we were going to refit, abounding with delicious fruits, and peopled by a race almost wholly unsophisticated by intercourse with strangers.

In order, perhaps, to guard against the possibility of anyone finding out the precise latitude and longitude of the spot we were going to, Jermin never revealed to us the ship's place at noon, though such is the custom aboard of most vessels.

Meanwhile, he was very assiduous in his attention to the invalids. Doctor Long Ghost having given up the keys of the medicine-chest, they were handed over to him; and, as physician, he discharged his duties to the satisfaction of all. Pills and powders, in most cases, were thrown to the fish, and in place thereof, the contents of a mysterious little quarter cask were produced, diluted with water from the "butt." His draughts were mixed on the capstan, in cocoa-nut shells marked with the patients' names. Like shore doctors, he did not eschew his own medicines, for his professional calls in the forecastle were sometimes made when he was comfortably tipsy: nor did he omit keeping his invalids in good-humour, spinning his yarns to them, by the hour, whenever he went to see them.

Owing to my lameness, from which I soon began to recover, I did no active duty, except standing an occasional "trick" at the helm. It was in the forecastle chiefly, that I spent my time, in company with the Long Doctor, who was at great pains to make himself agreeable. His books, though sadly torn and tattered, were an invaluable resource. I read them through again and again, including a learned treatise on the yellow fever. In addition to these, he had an old file of Sydney papers, and I soon became intimately acquainted with the localities of all the advertising tradesmen there. In particular, the rhetorical flourishes of Stubbs, the real-estate auctioneer, diverted me exceedingly, and I set him down as no other than a pupil of Robins the Londoner.

Aside from the pleasure of his society, my intimacy with Long Ghost was of great service to me in other respects. His disgrace in the cabin only confirmed the good-will of the democracy in the forecastle; and they not only treated him in the most friendly manner, but looked up to him with the utmost deference, besides laughing heartily at all his jokes. As his chosen associate, this feeling for him extended to me, and gradually we came to be regarded in the light of distinguished guests. At meal-times we were always first served, and otherwise were treated with much respect.

Among other devices to kill time, during the frequent calms, Long Ghost hit upon the game of chess. With a jack-knife, we carved the pieces quite tastefully out of bits of wood, and our board was the middle of a chest-lid, chalked into squares, which, in playing, we straddled at either end. Having no other suitable way of distinguishing the sets, I marked mine by tying round them little scarfs of black silk, torn from an old neck-handkerchief. Putting them in mourning this way, the doctor said, was quite appropriate, seeing that they had reason to feel sad three games out of four. Of chess, the men never could make head nor tail; indeed, their wonder rose to such a pitch that they at last regarded the mysterious movements of the game with something more than perplexity; and after puzzling over them through several long engagements, they came to the conclusion that we must be a couple of necromancers.

CHAPTER X.

A SEA-PARLOUR DESCRIBED, WITH SOME OF ITS TENANTS

I MIGHT as well give some idea of the place in which the doctor and I lived together so sociably.

Most persons know that a ship's forecastle embraces the forward part of the deck about the bowsprit: the same term, however, is generally bestowed upon the sailors' sleeping-quarters, which occupy a space immediately beneath, and are partitioned off by a bulkhead.

Planted right in the bows, or, as sailors say, in the very eyes of the ship, this delightful apartment is of a triangular shape, and is generally fitted with two tiers of rude bunks. Those of the Julia were in a most deplorable condition, mere wrecks, some having been torn down altogether to patch up others; and on one side there were but two standing. But with most of the men it made little difference whether they had a bunk or not, since, having no bedding, they had nothing to put in it but themselves.

Upon the boards of my own crib I spread all the old canvas and old clothes I could pick up. For a pillow, I wrapped an old jacket round a log. This helped a little the wear and tear of one's bones when the ship rolled.

Rude hammocks made out of old sails were in many cases used as substitutes for the demolished bunks; but the space they swung in was so confined that they were far from being agreeable.

The general aspect of the forecastle was dungeon-like and dingy in the extreme. In the first place, it was not five feet from deck to deck and even this space was encroached upon by two outlandish cross-timbers bracing the vessel, and by the sailors' chests, over which you must needs crawl in getting about. At meal-times, and especially when we indulged in after-dinner chat, we sat about the chests like a parcel of tailors.

In the middle of all were two square, wooden columns, denominated in marine architecture "Bowsprit Bitts." They were about a foot apart, and between them, by a rusty chain, swung the forecastle lamp, burning day and night, and forever casting two long black shadows. Lower down, between the bitts, was a locker, or sailors' pantry, kept in abominable disorder, and sometimes requiring a vigorous cleaning and fumigation.

All over, the ship was in a most dilapidated condition; but in the forecastle it looked like the hollow of an old tree going to decay. In every direction the wood was damp and discoloured, and here and there soft and porous. Moreover, it was hacked and hewed without mercy, the cook frequently helping himself to splinters for kindling-wood from the bitts and beams. Overhead, every carline was sooty, and here and there deep holes were burned in them, a freak of some drunken sailors on a voyage long previous.

From above, you entered by a plank, with two elects, slanting down from the scuttle, which was a mere hole in the deck. There being no slide to draw over in case of emergency, the tarpaulin temporarily placed there was little protection from the spray heaved over the bows; so that in anything of a breeze the place was miserably wet. In a squall, the water fairly poured down in sheets like a cascade, swashing about, and afterward spirting up between the chests like the jets of a fountain.

Such were our accommodations aboard of the Julia; but bad as they were, we had not the undisputed possession of them. Myriads of cockroaches, and regiments of rats disputed the place with us. A greater calamity than this can scarcely befall a vessel in the South Seas.

So warm is the climate that it is almost impossible to get rid of them. You may seal up every hatchway, and fumigate the hull till the smoke forces itself out at the seams, and enough will survive to repeople the ship in an incredibly short period. In some vessels, the crews of which after a hard fight have given themselves up, as it were, for lost, the vermin seem to take actual possession, the sailors being mere tenants by sufferance. With Sperm Whalemen, hanging about the Line, as many of them do for a couple of years on a stretch, it is infinitely worse than with other vessels.

As for the Julia, these creatures never had such free and easy times as they did in her crazy old hull; every chink and cranny swarmed with them; they did not live among you, but you among them. So true was this, that the business of eating and drinking was better done in the dark than in the light of day.

Concerning the cockroaches, there was an extraordinary phenomenon, for which none of us could ever account.

Every night they had a jubilee. The first symptom was an unusual clustering and humming among the swarms lining the beams overhead, and the inside of the sleeping-places. This was succeeded by a prodigious coming and going on the part of those living out of sight Presently they all came forth; the larger sort racing over the chests and planks; winged monsters darting to and fro in the air; and the small fry buzzing in heaps almost in a state of fusion.

On the first alarm, all who were able darted on deck; while some of the sick who were too feeble, lay perfectly quiet--the distracted vermin running over them at pleasure. The performance lasted some ten minutes, during which no hive ever hummed louder. Often it was lamented by us that the time of the visitation could never be predicted; it was liable to come upon us at any hour of the night, and what a relief it was, when it happened to fall in the early part of the evening.

Nor must I forget the rats: they did not forget me. Tame as Trenck's mouse, they stood in their holes peering at you like old grandfathers in a doorway. Often they darted in upon us at meal-times, and nibbled our food. The first time they approached Wymontoo, he was actually frightened; but becoming accustomed to it, he soon got along with them much better than the rest. With curious dexterity he seized the animals by their legs, and flung them up the scuttle to find a watery grave.

But I have a story of my own to tell about these rats. One day the cabin steward made me a present of some molasses, which I was so choice of that I kept it hid away in a tin can in the farthest corner of my bunk.. Faring as we did, this molasses dropped upon a biscuit was a positive luxury, which I shared with none but the doctor, and then only in private. And sweet as the treacle was, how could bread thus prepared and eaten in secret be otherwise than pleasant?

One night our precious can ran low, and in canting it over in the dark, something beside the molasses slipped out. How long it had been there, kind Providence never revealed; nor were we over anxious to know; for we hushed up the bare thought as quickly as possible. The creature certainly died a luscious death, quite equal to Clarence's in the butt of Malmsey.

CHAPTER XI.

DOCTOR LONG GHOST A WAG--ONE OF HIS CAPERS

GRAVE though he was at times, Doctor Long Ghost was a decided wag.

Everyone knows what lovers of fun sailors are ashore--afloat, they are absolutely mad after it. So his pranks were duly appreciated.

The poor old black cook! Unlashing his hammock for the night, and finding a wet log fast asleep in it; and then waking in the morning with his woolly head tarred. Opening his coppers, and finding an old boot boiling away as saucy as could be, and sometimes cakes of pitch candying in his oven.

Baltimore's tribulations were indeed sore; there was no peace for him day nor night. Poor fellow! he was altogether too good-natured. Say what they will about easy-tempered people, it is far better, on some accounts, to have the temper of a wolf. Whoever thought of taking liberties with gruff Black Dan?

The most curious of the doctor's jokes, was hoisting the men aloft by the foot or shoulder, when they fell asleep on deck during the night-watches.

Ascending from the forecastle on one occasion, he found every soul napping, and forthwith went about his capers. Fastening a rope's end to each sleeper, he rove the lines through a number of blocks, and conducted them all to the windlass; then, by heaving round cheerily, in spite of cries and struggles, he soon had them dangling aloft in all directions by arms and legs. Waked by the uproar, we rushed up from below, and found the poor fellows swinging in the moonlight from the tops and lower yard-arms, like a parcel of pirates gibbeted at sea by a cruiser.

Connected with this sort of diversion was another prank of his. During the night some of those on deck would come below to light a pipe, or take a mouthful of beef and biscuit. Sometimes they fell asleep; and being missed directly that anything was to be done, their shipmates often amused themselves by running them aloft with a pulley dropped down the scuttle from the fore-top.

One night, when all was perfectly still, I lay awake in the forecastle; the lamp was burning low and thick, and swinging from its blackened beam; and with the uniform motion of the ship, the men in the bunks rolled slowly from side to side; the hammocks swaying in unison.

Presently I heard a foot upon the ladder, and looking up, saw a wide trousers' leg. Immediately, Navy Bob, a stout old Triton, stealthily descended, and at once went to groping in the locker after something to eat.

Supper ended, he proceeded to load his pipe. Now, for a good comfortable smoke at sea, there never was a better place than the Julia's forecastle at midnight. To enjoy the luxury, one wants to fall into a kind of dreamy reverie, only known to the children of the weed. And the very atmosphere of the place, laden as it was with the snores of the sleepers, was inducive of this. No wonder, then, that after a while Bob's head sunk upon his breast; presently his hat fell off, the extinguished pipe dropped from his mouth, and the next moment he lay out on the chest as tranquil as an infant.

Suddenly an order was heard on deck, followed by the trampling of feet and the hauling of rigging. The yards were being braced, and soon after the sleeper was missed: for there was a whispered conference over the scuttle.

Directly a shadow glided across the forecastle and noiselessly approached the unsuspecting Bob. It was one of the watch with the end of a rope leading out of sight up the scuttle. Pausing an instant, the sailor pressed softly the chest of his victim, sounding his slumbers; and then hitching the cord to his ankle, returned to the deck.

Hardly was his back turned, when a long limb was thrust from a hammock opposite, and Doctor Long Ghost, leaping forth warily, whipped the rope from Bob's ankle, and fastened it like lightning to a great lumbering chest, the property of the man who had just disappeared.

Scarcely was the thing done, when lo! with a thundering bound, the clumsy box was torn from its fastenings, and banging from side to side, flew toward the scuttle. Here it jammed; and thinking that Bob, who was as strong as a windlass, was grappling a beam and trying to cut the line, the jokers on deck strained away furiously. On a sudden, the chest went aloft, and striking against the mast, flew open, raining down on the heads of a party the merciless shower of things too numerous to mention.

Of course the uproar roused all hands, and when we hurried on deck, there was the owner of the box, looking aghast at its scattered contents, and with one wandering hand taking the altitude of a bump on his head.

CHAPTER XII.

DEATH AND BURIAL OF TWO OF THE CREW

THE mirthfulness which at times reigned among us was in strange and shocking contrast with the situation of some of the invalids. Thus at least did it seem to me, though not to others.

But an event occurred about this period, which, in removing by far the most pitiable cases of suffering, tended to make less grating to my feelings the subsequent conduct of the crew.

We had been at sea about twenty days, when two of the sick who had rapidly grown worse, died one night within an hour of each other.

One occupied a bunk right next to mine, and for several days had not risen from it. During this period he was often delirious, starting up and glaring around him, and sometimes wildly tossing his arms.

On the night of his decease, I retired shortly after the middle watch began, and waking from a vague dream of horrors, felt something clammy resting on me. It was the sick man's hand. Two or three times during the evening previous, he had thrust it into my bunk, and I had quietly removed it; but now I started and flung it from me. The arm fell stark and stiff, and I knew that he was dead.

Waking the men, the corpse was immediately rolled up in the strips of blanketing upon which it lay, and carried on deck. The mate was then called, and preparations made for an instantaneous' burial. Laying the body out on the forehatch, it was stitched up in one of the hammocks, some "kentledge" being placed at the feet instead of shot. This done, it was borne to the gangway, and placed on a plank laid across the bulwarks. Two men supported the inside end. By way of solemnity, the ship's headway was then stopped by hauling aback the main-top-sail.

The mate, who was far from being sober, then staggered up, and holding on to a shroud, gave the word. As the plank tipped, the body slid off slowly, and fell with a splash into the sea. A bubble or two, and nothing more was seen.

"Brace forward!" The main-yard swung round to its place, and the ship glided on, whilst the corpse, perhaps, was still sinking.

We had tossed a shipmate to the sharks, but no one would have thought it, to have gone among the crew immediately after. The dead man had been a churlish, unsocial fellow, while alive, and no favourite; and now that he was no more, little thought was bestowed upon him. All that was said was concerning the disposal of his chest, which, having been always kept locked, was supposed to contain money. Someone volunteered to break it open, and distribute its contents, clothing and all, before the captain should demand it.

While myself and others were endeavouring to dissuade them from this, all started at a cry from the forecastle. There could be no one there but two of the sick, unable to crawl on deck. We went below, and found one of them dying on a chest. He had fallen out of his hammock in a fit, and was insensible. The eyes were open and fixed, and his breath coming and going convulsively. The men shrunk from him; but the doctor, taking his hand, held it a few moments in his, and suddenly letting it fall, exclaimed, "He's gone!" The body was instantly borne up the ladder.

Another hammock was soon prepared, and the dead sailor stitched up as before. Some additional ceremony, however, was now insisted upon, and a Bible was called for. But none was to be had, not even a Prayer Book. When this was made known, Antone, a Portuguese, from the Cape-de-Verd Islands, stepped up, muttering something over the corpse of his countryman, and, with his finger, described upon the back of the hammock the figure of a large cross; whereupon it received the death-launch.

These two men both perished from the proverbial indiscretions of seamen, heightened by circumstances apparent; but had either of them been ashore under proper treatment, he would, in all human probability, have recovered.

Behold here the fate of a sailor! They give him the last toss, and no one asks whose child he was.

For the rest of that night there was no more sleep. Many stayed on deck until broad morning, relating to each other those marvellous tales of the sea which the occasion was calculated to call forth. Little as I believed in such things, I could not listen to some of these stories unaffected. Above all was I struck by one of the carpenter's.

On a voyage to India, they had a fever aboard, which carried off nearly half the crew in the space of a few days. After this the men never went aloft in the night-time, except in couples. When topsails were to be reefed, phantoms were seen at the yard-arm ends; and in tacking ship, voices called aloud from the tops. The carpenter himself, going with another man to furl the main-top-gallant-sail in a squall, was nearly pushed from the rigging by an unseen hand; and his shipmate swore that a wet hammock was flirted in his face.

Stories like these were related as gospel truths, by those who declared themselves eye-witnesses.

It is a circumstance not generally known, perhaps, that among ignorant seamen, Philanders, or Finns, as they are more commonly called, are regarded with peculiar superstition. For some reason or other, which I never could get at, they are supposed to possess the gift of second sight, and the power to wreak supernatural vengeance upon those who offend them. On this account they have great influence among sailors, and two or three with whom I have sailed at different times were persons well calculated to produce this sort of impression, at least upon minds disposed to believe in such things.

Now, we had one of these sea-prophets aboard; an old, yellow-haired fellow, who always wore a rude seal-skin cap of his own make, and carried his tobacco in a large pouch made of the same stuff. Van, as we called him, was a quiet, inoffensive man, to look at, and, among such a set, his occasional peculiarities had hitherto passed for nothing. At this time, however, he came out with a prediction, which was none the less remarkable from its absolute fulfilment, though not exactly in the spirit in which it was given out.

The night of the burial he laid his hand on the old horseshoe nailed as a charm to the foremast, and solemnly told us that, in less than three weeks, not one quarter of our number would remain aboard the ship--by that time they would have left her for ever.

Some laughed; Flash Jack called him an old fool; but among the men generally it produced a marked effect. For several days a degree of quiet reigned among us, and allusions of such a kind were made to recent events, as could be attributed to no other cause than the Finn's omen.

For my own part, what had lately come to pass was not without its influence. It forcibly brought to mind our really critical condition. Doctor Long Ghost, too, frequently revealed his apprehensions, and once assured me that he would give much to be safely landed upon any island around us.

Where we were, exactly, no one but the mate seemed to know, nor whither we were going. The captain--a mere cipher--was an invalid in his cabin; to say nothing more of so many of his men languishing in the forecastle.

Our keeping the sea under these circumstances, a matter strange enough at first, now seemed wholly unwarranted; and added to all was the thought that our fate was absolutely in the hand of the reckless Jermin. Were anything to happen to him, we would be left without a navigator, for, according to Jermin himself, he had, from the commencement of the voyage, always kept the ship's reckoning, the captain's nautical knowledge being insufficient.

But considerations like these, strange as it may seem, seldom or never occurred to the crew. They were alive only to superstitious fears; and when, in apparent contradiction to the Finn's prophecy, the sick men rallied a little, they began to recover their former spirits, and the recollection of what had occurred insensibly faded from their minds. In a week's time, the unworthiness of Little Jule as a sea vessel, always a subject of jest, now became more so than ever. In the forecastle, Flash Jack, with his knife, often dug into the dank, rotten planks ribbed between us and death, and flung away the splinters with some sea joke.

As to the remaining invalids, they were hardly ill enough to occasion any serious apprehension, at least for the present, in the breasts of such thoughtless beings as themselves. And even those who suffered the most, studiously refrained from any expression of pain.

The truth is, that among sailors as a class, sickness at sea is so heartily detested, and the sick so little cared for, that the greatest invalid generally strives to mask his sufferings. He has given no sympathy to others, and he expects none in return. Their conduct, in this respect, so opposed to their generous-hearted behaviour ashore, painfully affects the landsman on his first intercourse with them as a sailor.

Sometimes, but seldom, our invalids inveighed against their being kept at sea, where they could be of no service, when they ought to be ashore and in the way of recovery. But--"Oh! cheer up--cheer up, my hearties!"--the mate would say. And after this fashion he put a stop to their murmurings.

But there was one circumstance, to which heretofore I have but barely alluded, that tended more than anything else to reconcile many to their situation. This was the receiving regularly, twice every day, a certain portion of Pisco, which was served out at the capstan, by the steward, in little tin measures called "tots."

The lively affection seamen have for strong drink is well known; but in the South Seas, where it is so seldom to be had, a thoroughbred sailor deems scarcely any price too dear which will purchase his darling "tot." Nowadays, American whalemen in the Pacific never think of carrying spirits as a ration; and aboard of most of them, it is never served out even in times of the greatest hardships. All Sydney whalemen, however, still cling to the old custom, and carry it as a part of the regular supplies for the voyage.

In port, the allowance of Pisco was suspended; with a view, undoubtedly, of heightening the attractions of being out of sight of land.

Now, owing to the absence of proper discipline, our sick, in addition to what they took medicinally, often came in for their respective "tots" convivially; and, added to all this, the evening of the last day of the week was always celebrated by what is styled on board of English vessels "The Saturday-night bottles." Two of these were sent down into the forecastle, just after dark; one for the starboard watch, and the other for the larboard.

By prescription, the oldest seaman in each claims the treat as his, and, accordingly, pours out the good cheer and passes it round like a lord doing the honours of his table. But the Saturday-night bottles were not all. The carpenter and cooper, in sea parlance, Chips and Bungs, who were the "Cods," or leaders of the forecastle, in some way or other, managed to obtain an extra supply, which perpetually kept them in fine after-dinner spirits, and, moreover, disposed them to look favourably upon a state of affairs like the present.

But where were the sperm whales all this time? In good sooth, it made little matter where they were, since we were in no condition to capture them. About this time, indeed, the men came down from the mast-heads, where, until now, they had kept up the form of relieving each other every two hours. They swore they would go there no more. Upon this, the mate carelessly observed that they would soon be where look-outs were entirely unnecessary, the whales he had in his eye (though Flash Jack said they were all in his) being so tame that they made a practice of coming round ships, and scratching their backs against them.

Thus went the world of waters with us, some four weeks or more after leaving Hannamanoo.

CHAPTER XIII.

OUR DESTINATION CHANGED

IT was not long after the death of the two men, that Captain Guy was reported as fast declining, and in a day or two more, as dying. The doctor, who previously had refused to enter the cabin upon any consideration, now relented, and paid his old enemy a professional visit.

He prescribed a warm bath, which was thus prepared. The skylight being removed, a cask was lowered down into the cabin, and then filled with buckets of water from the ship's coppers. The cries of the patient, when dipped into his rude bath, were most painful to hear. They at last laid him on the transom, more dead than alive.

That evening, the mate was perfectly sober, and coming forward to the windlass, where we were lounging, summoned aft the doctor, myself, and two or three others of his favourites; when, in the presence of Bembo the Mowree, he spoke to us thus:

"I have something to say to ye, men. There's none but Bembo here as belongs aft, so I've picked ye out as the best men for'ard to take counsel with, d'ye see, consarning the ship. The captain's anchor is pretty nigh atrip; I shouldn't wonder if he croaked afore morning. So what's to be done? If we have to sew him up, some of those pirates there for'ard may take it into their heads to run off with the ship, because there's no one at the tiller. Now, I've detarmined what's best to be done; but I don't want to do it unless I've good men to back me, and make things all fair and square if ever we get home again."

We all asked what his plan was.

"I'll tell ye what it is, men. If the skipper dies, all agree to obey my orders, and in less than three weeks I'll engage to have five hundred barrels of sperm oil under hatches: enough to give every mother's son of ye a handful of dollars when we get to Sydney. If ye don't agree to this, ye won't have a farthing coming to ye."

Doctor Long Ghost at once broke in. He said that such a thing was not to be dreamt of; that if the captain died, the mate was in duty bound to navigate the ship to the nearest civilized port, and deliver her up into an English consul's hands; when, in all probability, after a run ashore, the crew would be sent home. Everything forbade the mate's plan. "Still," said he, assuming an air of indifference, "if the men say stick it out, stick it out say I; but in that case, the sooner we get to those islands of yours the better."

Something more he went on to say; and from the manner in which the rest regarded him, it was plain that our fate was in his hands. It was finally resolved upon, that if Captain Guy was no better in twenty-four hours, the ship's head should be pointed for the island of Tahiti.

This announcement produced a strong sensation--the sick rallied--and the rest speculated as to what was next to befall us; while the doctor, without alluding to Guy, congratulated me upon the prospect of soon beholding a place so famous as the island in question.

The night after the holding of the council, I happened to go on deck in the middle watch, and found the yards braced sharp up on the larboard tack, with the South East Trades strong on our bow. The captain was no better; and we were off for Tahiti.

CHAPTER XIV.

ROPE YARN

WHILE gliding along on our way, I cannot well omit some account of a poor devil we had among us, who went by the name of Rope Yarn, or Ropey.

He was a nondescript who had joined the ship as a landsman. Being so excessively timid and awkward, it was thought useless to try and make a sailor of him; so he was translated into the cabin as steward; the man previously filling that post, a good seaman, going among the crew and taking his place. But poor Ropey proved quite as clumsy among the crockery as in the rigging; and one day when the ship was pitching, having stumbled into the cabin with a wooden tureen of soup, he scalded the officers so that they didn't get over it in a week. Upon which, he was dismissed, and returned to the forecastle.

Now, nobody is so heartily despised as a pusillanimous, lazy, good-for-nothing land-lubber; a sailor has no bowels of compassion for him. Yet, useless as such a character may be in many respects, a ship's company is by no means disposed to let him reap any benefit from his deficiencies. Regarded in the light of a mechanical power, whenever there is any plain, hard work to be done, he is put to it like a lever; everyone giving him a pry.

Then, again, he is set about all the vilest work. Is there a heavy job at tarring to be done, he is pitched neck and shoulders into a tar-barrel, and set to work at it. Moreover, he is made to fetch and carry like a dog. Like as not, if the mate sends him after his quadrant, on the way he is met by the captain, who orders him to pick some oakum; and while he is hunting up a bit of rope, a sailor comes along and wants to know what the deuce he's after, and bids him be off to the forecastle.

"Obey the last order," is a precept inviolable at sea. So the land-lubber, afraid to refuse to do anything, rushes about distracted, and does nothing: in the end receiving a shower of kicks and cuffs from all quarters.

Added to his other hardships, he is seldom permitted to open his mouth unless spoken to; and then, he might better keep silent. Alas for him! if he should happen to be anything of a droll; for in an evil hour should he perpetrate a joke, he would never know the last of it.

The witticisms of others, however, upon himself, must be received in the greatest good-humour.

Woe be unto him, if at meal-times he so much as look sideways at the beef-kid before the rest are helped.

Then he is obliged to plead guilty to every piece of mischief which the real perpetrator refuses to acknowledge; thus taking the place of that sneaking rascal nobody, ashore. In short, there is no end to his tribulations.

The land-lubber's spirits often sink, and the first result of his being moody and miserable is naturally enough an utter neglect of his toilet.

The sailors perhaps ought to make allowances; but heartless as they are, they do not. No sooner is his cleanliness questioned than they rise upon him like a mob of the Middle Ages upon a Jew; drag him into the lee-scuppers, and strip him to the buff. In vain he bawls for mercy; in vain calls upon the captain to save him.

Alas! I say again, for the land-lubber at sea. He is the veriest wretch the watery world over. And such was Bope Tarn; of all landlubbers, the most lubberly and most miserable. A forlorn, stunted, hook-visaged mortal he was too; one of those whom you know at a glance to have been tried hard and long in the furnace of affliction. His face was an absolute puzzle; though sharp and sallow, it had neither the wrinkles of age nor the smoothness of youth; so that for the soul of me, I could hardly tell whether he was twenty-five or fifty.

But to his history. In his better days, it seems he had been a journeyman baker in London, somewhere about Holborn; and on Sundays wore a Hue coat and metal buttons, and spent his afternoons in a tavern, smoking his pipe and drinking his ale like a free and easy journeyman baker that he was. But this did not last long; for an intermeddling old fool was the ruin of him. He was told that London might do very well for elderly gentlemen and invalids; but for a lad of spirit, Australia was the Land of Promise. In a dark day Ropey wound up his affairs and embarked.

Arriving in Sydney with a small capital, and after a while waxing snug and comfortable by dint of hard kneading, he took unto himself a wife; and so far as she was concerned, might then have gone into the country and retired; for she effectually did his business. In short, the lady worked him woe in heart and pocket; and in the end, ran off with his till and his foreman. Ropey went to the sign of the Pipe and Tankard; got fuddled; and over his fifth pot meditated suicide--an intention carried out; for the next day he shipped as landsman aboard the Julia, South Seaman.

The ex-baker would have fared far better, had it not been for his heart, which was soft and underdone. A kind word made a fool of him; and hence most of the scrapes he got into. Two or three wags, aware of his infirmity, used to "draw him out" in conversation whenever the most crabbed and choleric old seamen were present.

To give an instance. The watch below, just waked from their sleep, are all at breakfast; and Ropey, in one corner, is disconsolately partaking of its delicacies. "Now, sailors newly waked are no cherubs; and therefore not a word is spoken, everybody munching his biscuit, grim and unshaven. At this juncture an affable-looking scamp--Flash Jack--crosses the forecastle, tin can in hand, and seats himself beside the land-lubber.

"Hard fare this, Ropey," he begins; "hard enough, too, for them that's known better and lived in Lun'nun. I say now, Ropey, s'posing you were back to Holborn this morning, what would you have for breakfast, eh?"

"Have for breakfast!" cried Ropey in a rapture. "Don't speak of it!"

"What ails that fellow?" here growled an old sea-bear, turning round savagely.

"Oh, nothing, nothing," said Jack; and then, leaning over to Rope Yarn, he bade him go on, but speak lower.

"Well, then," said he, in a smuggled tone, his eyes lighting up like two lanterns, "well, then, I'd go to Mother Moll's that makes the great muffins: I'd go there, you know, and cock my foot on the 'ob, and call for a noggin o' somethink to begin with."

"What then, Ropey?"

"Why then, Flashy," continued the poor victim, unconsciously warming with his theme: "why then, I'd draw my chair up and call for Betty, the gal wot tends to customers. Betty, my dear, says I, you looks charmin' this mornin'; give me a nice rasher of bacon and h'eggs, Betty my love; and I wants a pint of h'ale, and three nice h'ot muffins and butter--and a slice of Cheshire; and Betty, I wants--"

"A shark-steak, and be hanged to you!" roared Black Dan, with an oath. Whereupon, dragged over the chests, the ill-starred fellow is pummelled on deck.

I always made a point of befriending poor Ropey when I could; and, for this reason, was a great favourite of his.

CHAPTER XV.

CHIPS AND BUNGS

BOUND into port, Chips and Bungs increased their devotion to the bottle; and, to the unspeakable envy of the rest, these jolly companions--or "the Partners," as the men called them--rolled about deck, day after day, in the merriest mood imaginable.

But jolly as they were in the main, two more discreet tipplers it would be hard to find. No one ever saw them take anything, except when the regular allowance was served out by the steward; and to make them quite sober and sensible, you had only to ask them how they contrived to keep otherwise. Some time after, however, their secret leaked out.

The casks of Pisco were kept down the after-hatchway, which, for this reason, was secured with bar and padlock. The cooper, nevertheless, from time to time, effected a burglarious entry, by descending into the fore-hold; and then, at the risk of being jammed to death, crawling along over a thousand obstructions, to where the casks were stowed.

On the first expedition, the only one to be got at lay among others, upon its bilge with the bung-hole well over. With a bit of iron hoop, suitably bent, and a good deal of prying and punching, the bung was forced in; and then the cooper's neck-handkerchief, attached to the end of the hoop, was drawn in and out--the absorbed liquor being deliberately squeezed into a small bucket.

Bungs was a man after a barkeeper's own heart. Drinking steadily, until just manageably tipsy, he contrived to continue so; getting neither more nor less inebriated, but, to use his own phrase, remaining "just about right." When in this interesting state, he had a free lurch in his gait, a queer way of hitching up his waistbands, looked unnecessarily steady at you when speaking, and for the rest, was in very tolerable spirits. At these times, moreover, he was exceedingly patriotic; and in a most amusing way, frequently showed his patriotism whenever he happened to encounter Dunk, a good-natured, square-faced Dane, aboard.

It must be known here, by the bye, that the cooper had a true sailor admiration for Lord Nelson. But he entertained a very erroneous idea of the personal appearance of the hero. Not content with depriving him of an eye and an arm, he stoutly maintained that he had also lost a leg in one of his battles. Under this impression, he sometimes hopped up to Dunk with one leg curiously locked behind him into his right arm, at the same time closing an eye.

In this attitude he would call upon him to look up, and behold the man who gave his countrymen such a thrashing at Copenhagen. "Look you, Dunk," says he, staggering about, and winking hard with one eye to keep the other shut, "Look you; one man--hang me, half a man--with one leg, one arm, one eye--hang me, with only a piece of a carcase, flogged your whole shabby nation. Do you deny it you lubber?"

The Dane was a mule of a man, and understanding but little English, seldom made anything of a reply; so the cooper generally dropped his leg, and marched off, with the air of a man who despised saying anything further.

CHAPTER XVI.

WE ENCOUNTER A GALE

THE mild blue weather we enjoyed after leaving the Marquesas gradually changed as we ran farther south and approached Tahiti. In these generally tranquil seas, the wind sometimes blows with great violence; though, as every sailor knows, a spicy gale in the tropic latitudes of the Pacific is far different from a tempest in the howling North Atlantic. We soon found ourselves battling with the waves, while the before mild Trades, like a woman roused, blew fiercely, but still warmly, in our face.

For all this, the mate carried sail without stint; and as for brave little Jule, she stood up to it well; and though once in a while floored in the trough of a sea, sprang to her keel again and showed play. Every old timber groaned--every spar buckled--every chafed cord strained; and yet, spite of all, she plunged on her way like a racer. Jermin, sea-jockey that he was, sometimes stood in the fore-chains, with the spray every now and then dashing over him, and shouting out, "Well done, Jule--dive into it, sweetheart. Hurrah!"

One afternoon there was a mighty queer noise aloft, which set the men running in every direction. It was the main-t'-gallant-mast. Crash! it broke off just above the cap, and held there by the rigging, dashed with every roll from side to side, with all the hamper that belonged to it. The yard hung by a hair, and at every pitch, thumped against the cross-trees; while the sail streamed in ribbons, and the loose ropes coiled, and thrashed the air, like whip-lashes. "Stand from under!" and down came the rattling blocks, like so many shot. The yard, with a snap and a plunge, went hissing into the sea, disappeared, and shot its full length out again. The crest of a great wave then broke over it--the ship rushed by--and we saw the stick no more.

While this lively breeze continued, Baltimore, our old black cook, was in great tribulation.

Like most South Seamen, the Julia's "caboose," or cook-house, was planted on the larboard side of the forecastle. Under such a press of canvas, and with the heavy sea running the barque, diving her bows under, now and then shipped green glassy waves, which, breaking over the head-rails, fairly deluged that part of the ship, and washed clean aft. The caboose-house--thought to be fairly lashed down to its place--served as a sort of breakwater to the inundation.

About these times, Baltimore always wore what he called his "gale suit," among other things comprising a Sou'-wester and a huge pair of well-anointed sea-boots, reaching almost to his knees. Thus equipped for a ducking or a drowning, as the case might be, our culinary high-priest drew to the slides of his temple, and performed his sooty rites in secret.

So afraid was the old man of being washed overboard that he actually fastened one end of a small line to his waistbands, and coiling the rest about him, made use of it as occasion required. When engaged outside, he unwound the cord, and secured one end to a ringbolt in the deck; so that if a chance sea washed him off his feet, it could do nothing more.

One evening just as he was getting supper, the Julia reared up on her stern like a vicious colt, and when she settled again forward, fairly dished a tremendous sea. Nothing could withstand it. One side of the rotten head-bulwarks came in with a crash; it smote the caboose, tore it from its moorings, and after boxing it about, dashed it against the windlass, where it stranded. The water then poured along the deck like a flood rolling over and over, pots, pans, and kettles, and even old Baltimore himself, who went breaching along like a porpoise.

Striking the taffrail, the wave subsided, and washing from side to side, left the drowning cook high and dry on the after-hatch: his extinguished pipe still between his teeth, and almost bitten in two.

The few men on deck having sprung into the main-rigging, sailor-like, did nothing but roar at his calamity.

The same night, our flying-jib-boom snapped off like a pipe-stem, and our spanker-gaff came down by the run.

By the following morning, the wind in a great measure had gone down; the sea with it; and by noon we had repaired our damages as well as we could, and were sailing along as pleasantly as ever.

But there was no help for the demolished bulwarks; we had nothing to replace them; and so, whenever it breezed again, our dauntless craft went along with her splintered prow dripping, but kicking up her fleet heels just as high as before.

CHAPTER XVII.

THE CORAL ISLANDS

HOW far we sailed to the westward after leaving the Marquesas, or what might have been our latitude and longitude at any particular time, or how many leagues we voyaged on our passage to Tahiti, are matters about which, I am sorry to say, I cannot with any accuracy enlighten the reader. Jermin, as navigator, kept our reckoning; and, as hinted before, kept it all to himself. At noon, he brought out his quadrant, a rusty old thing, so odd-looking that it might have belonged to an astrologer.

Sometimes, when rather flustered from his potations, he went staggering about deck, instrument to eye, looking all over for the sun--a phenomenon which any sober observer might have seen right overhead. How upon earth he contrived, on some occasions, to settle his latitude, is more than I can tell. The longitude he must either have obtained by the Rule of Three, or else by special revelation. Not that the chronometer in the cabin was seldom to be relied on, or was any ways fidgety; quite the contrary; it stood stock-still; and by that means, no doubt, the true Greenwich time--at the period of stopping, at least--was preserved to a second.

The mate, however, in addition to his "Dead Reckoning," pretended to ascertain his meridian distance from Bow Bells by an occasional lunar observation. This, I believe, consists in obtaining with the proper instruments the angular distance between the moon and some one of the stars. The operation generally requires two observers to take sights, and at one and the same time.

Now, though the mate alone might have been thought well calculated for this, inasmuch as he generally saw things double, the doctor was usually called upon to play a sort of second quadrant to Jermin's first; and what with the capers of both, they used to furnish a good deal of diversion. The mate's tremulous attempts to level his instrument at the star he was after, were comical enough. For my own part, when he did catch sight of it, I hardly knew how he managed to separate it from the astral host revolving in his own brain.

However, by hook or by crook, he piloted us along; and before many days, a fellow sent aloft to darn a rent in the fore-top-sail, threw his hat into the air, and bawled out "Land, ho!"

Land it was; but in what part of the South Seas, Jermin alone knew, and some doubted whether even he did. But no sooner was the announcement made, than he came running on deck, spy-glass in hand, and clapping it to his eye, turned round with the air of a man receiving indubitable assurance of something he was quite certain of before. The land was precisely that for which he had been steering; and, with a wind, in less than twenty-four hours we would sight Tahiti. What he said was verified.

The island turned out to be one of the Pomotu or Low Group--sometimes called the Coral Islands--perhaps the most remarkable and interesting in the Pacific. Lying to the east of Tahiti, the nearest are within a day's sail of that place.

They are very numerous; mostly small, low, and level; sometimes wooded, but always covered with verdure. Many are crescent-shaped; others resemble a horse-shoe in figure. These last are nothing more than narrow circles of land surrounding a smooth lagoon, connected by a single opening with the sea. Some of the lagoons, said to have subterranean outlets, have no visible ones; the inclosing island, in such cases, being a complete zone of emerald. Other lagoons still, are girdled by numbers of small, green islets, very near to each other.

The origin of the entire group is generally ascribed to the coral insect.

According to some naturalists, this wonderful little creature, commencing its erections at the bottom of the sea, after the lapse of centuries, carries them up to the surface, where its labours cease. Here, the inequalities of the coral collect all floating bodies; forming, after a time, a soil, in which the seeds carried thither by birds germinate, and cover the whole with vegetation. Here and there, all over this archipelago, numberless naked, detached coral formations are seen, just emerging, as it were from the ocean. These would appear to be islands in the very process of creation--at any rate, one involuntarily concludes so, on beholding them.

As far as I know, there are but few bread-fruit trees in any part of the Pomotu group. In many places the cocoa-nut even does not grow; though, in others, it largely flourishes. Consequently, some of the islands are altogether uninhabited; others support but a single family; and in no place is the population very large. In some respects the natives resemble the Tahitians: their language, too, is very similar. The people of the southeasterly clusters--concerning whom, however, but little is known--have a bad name as cannibals; and for that reason their hospitality is seldom taxed by the mariner.

Within a few years past, missionaries from the Society group have settled among the Leeward Islands, where the natives have treated them kindly. Indeed, nominally, many of these people are now Christians; and, through the political influence of their instructors, no doubt, a short time since came tinder the allegiance of Pomaree, the Queen of Tahiti; with which island they always carried on considerable intercourse.

The Coral Islands are principally visited by the pearl-shell fishermen, who arrive in small schooners, carrying not more than five or six men.

For a long while the business was engrossed by Merenhout, the French Consul at Tahiti, but a Dutchman by birth, who, in one year, is said to have sent to France fifty thousand dollars' worth of shells. The oysters are found in the lagoons, and about the reefs; and, for half-a-dozen nails a day, or a compensation still less, the natives are hired to dive after them.

A great deal of cocoa-nut oil is also obtained in various places. Some of the uninhabited islands are covered with dense groves; and the ungathered nuts which have fallen year after year, lie upon the ground in incredible quantities. Two or three men, provided with the necessary apparatus for trying out the oil, will, in the course of a week or two, obtain enough to load one of the large sea-canoes.

Cocoa-nut oil is now manufactured in different parts of the South Seas, and forms no small part of the traffic carried on with trading vessels. A considerable quantity is annually exported from the Society Islands to Sydney. It is used in lamps and for machinery, being much cheaper than the sperm, and, for both purposes, better than the right-whale oil. They bottle it up in large bamboos, six or eight feet long; and these form part of the circulating medium of Tahiti.

To return to the ship. The wind dying away, evening came on before we drew near the island. But we had it in view during the whole afternoon.

It was small and round, presenting one enamelled level, free from trees, and did not seem four feet above the water. Beyond it was another and larger island, about which a tropical sunset was throwing its glories; flushing all that part of the heavens, and making it flame like a vast dyed oriel illuminated.

The Trades scarce filled our swooning sails; the air was languid with the aroma of a thousand strange, flowering shrubs. Upon inhaling it, one of the sick, who had recently shown symptoms of scurvy, cried out in pain, and was carried below. This is no unusual effect in such instances.

On we glided, within less than a cable's length of the shore which was margined with foam that sparkled all round. Within, nestled the still, blue lagoon. No living thing was seen, and, for aught we knew, we might have been the first mortals who had ever beheld the spot. The thought was quickening to the fancy; nor could I help dreaming of the endless grottoes and galleries, far below the reach of the mariner's lead.

And what strange shapes were lurking there! Think of those arch creatures, the mermaids, chasing each other in and out of the coral cells, and catching their long hair in the coral twigs!

CHAPTER XVIII.

TAHITI

AT early dawn of the following morning we saw the Peaks of Tahiti. In clear weather they may be seen at the distance of ninety miles.

"Hivarhoo!" shouted Wymontoo, overjoyed, and running out upon the bowsprit when the land was first faintly descried in the distance. But when the clouds floated away, and showed the three peaks standing like obelisks against the sky; and the bold shore undulating along the horizon, the tears gushed from his eyes. Poor fellow! It was not Hivarhoo. Green Hivarhoo was many a long league off.

Tahiti is by far the most famous island in the South Seas; indeed, a variety of causes has made it almost classic. Its natural features alone distinguish it from the surrounding groups. Two round and lofty promontories, whose mountains rise nine thousand feet above the level of the ocean, are connected by a low, narrow isthmus; the whole being some one hundred miles in circuit. From the great central peaks of the larger peninsula--Orohena, Aorai, and Pirohitee--the land radiates on all sides to the sea in sloping green ridges. Between these are broad and shadowy valleys--in aspect, each a Tempe--watered with fine streams, and thickly wooded. Unlike many of the other islands, there extends nearly all round Tahiti a belt of low, alluvial soil, teeming with the richest vegetation. Here, chiefly, the natives dwell.

Seen from the sea, the prospect is magnificent. It is one mass of shaded tints of green, from beach to mountain top; endlessly diversified with valleys, ridges, glens, and cascades. Over the ridges, here and there, the loftier peaks fling their shadows, and far down the valleys. At the head of these, the waterfalls flash out into the sunlight, as if pouring through vertical bowers of verdure. Such enchantment, too, breathes over the whole, that it seems a fairy world, all fresh and blooming from the hand of the Creator.

Upon a near approach, the picture loses not its attractions. It is no exaggeration to say that, to a European of any sensibility, who, for the first time, wanders back into these valleys--away from the haunts of the natives--the ineffable repose and beauty of the landscape is such, that every object strikes him like something seen in a dream; and for a time he almost refuses to believe that scenes like these should have a commonplace existence. No wonder that the French bestowed upon the island the appellation of the New Cytherea. "Often," says De Bourgainville, "I thought I was walking in the Garden of Eden."

Nor, when first discovered, did the inhabitants of this charming country at all diminish the wonder and admiration of the voyager. Their physical beauty and amiable dispositions harmonized completely with the softness of their clime. In truth, everything about them was calculated to awaken the liveliest interest. Glance at their civil and religious institutions. To their king, divine rights were paid; while for poetry, their mythology rivalled that of ancient Greece.

Of Tahiti, earlier and more full accounts were given, than of any other island in Polynesia; and this is the reason why it still retains so strong a hold on the sympathies of all readers of South Sea voyages. The journals of its first visitors, containing, as they did, such romantic descriptions of a country and people before unheard of, produced a marked sensation throughout Europe; and when the first Tahitiana were carried thither, Omai in London, and Aotooroo in Paris, were caressed by nobles, scholars, and ladies.

In addition to all this, several eventful occurrences, more or less connected with Tahiti, have tended to increase its celebrity. Over two centuries ago, Quiros, the Spaniard, is supposed to have touched at the island; and at intervals, Wallis, Byron, Cook, De Bourgainville, Vancouver, Le Perouse, and other illustrious navigators refitted their vessels in its harbours. Here the famous Transit of Venus was observed, in 1769. Here the memorable mutiny of the Bounty afterwards had its origin. It was to the pagans of Tahiti that the first regularly constituted Protestant missionaries were sent; and from their shores also, have sailed successive missions to the neighbouring islands.

These, with other events which might be mentioned, have united in keeping up the first interest which the place awakened; and the recent proceedings of the French have more than ever called forth the sympathies of the public.

CHAPTER XIX.

A SURPRISE--MORE ABOUT BEMBO

THE sight of the island was right welcome. Going into harbour after a cruise is always joyous enough, and the sailor is apt to indulge in all sorts of pleasant anticipations. But to us, the occasion was heightened by many things peculiar to our situation.

Since steering for the land, our prospects had been much talked over. By many it was supposed that, should the captain leave the ship, the crew were no longer bound by her articles. This was the opinion of our forecastle Cokes; though, probably, it would not have been sanctioned by the Marine Courts of Law. At any rate, such was the state of both vessel and crew that, whatever might be the event, a long stay, and many holidays in Tahiti, were confidently predicted.

Everybody was in high spirits. The sick, who had been improving day by day since the change in our destination, were on deck, and leaning over the bulwarks; some all animation, and others silently admiring an object unrivalled for its stately beauty--Tahiti from the sea.

The quarter-deck, however, furnished a marked contrast to what was going on at the other end of the ship. The Mowree was there, as usual, scowling by himself; and Jermin walked to and fro in deep thought, every now and then looking to windward, or darting into the cabin and quickly returning.

With all our light sails wooingly spread, we held on our way, until, with the doctor's glass, Papeetee, the village metropolis of Tahiti, came into view. Several ships were descried lying in the harbour, and among them, one which loomed up black and large; her two rows of teeth proclaiming a frigate. This was the Reine Blanche, last from the Marquesas, and carrying at the fore the flag of Rear-Admiral Du Petit Thouars. Hardly had we made her out, when the booming of her guns came over the water. She was firing a salute, which afterwards turned out to be in honour of a treaty; or rather--as far as the natives were concerned--a forced cession of Tahiti to the French, that morning concluded.

The cannonading had hardly died away, when Jermin's voice was heard giving an order so unexpected that everyone started. "Stand by to haul back the main-yard!"

"What's that mean?" shouted the men, "are we not going into port?"

"Tumble after here, and no words!" cried the mate; and in a moment the main-yard swung round, when, with her jib-boom pointing out to sea, the Julia lay as quiet as a duck. We all looked blank--what was to come next?

Presently the steward made his appearance, carrying a mattress, which he spread out in the stern-sheets of the captain's boat; two or three chests, and other things belonging to his master, were similarly disposed of.

This was enough. A slight hint suffices for a sailor.

Still adhering to his resolution to keep the ship at sea in spite of everything, the captain, doubtless, intended to set himself ashore, leaving the vessel, under the mate, to resume her voyage at once; but after a certain period agreed upon, to touch at the island, and take him off. All this, of course, could easily be done without approaching any nearer the land with the Julia than we now were. Invalid whaling captains often adopt a plan like this; but, in the present instance, it was wholly unwarranted; and, everything considered, at war with the commonest principles of prudence and humanity. And, although, on Guy's part, this resolution showed more hardihood than he had ever been given credit for, it, at the same time, argued an unaccountable simplicity, in supposing that such a crew would, in any way, submit to the outrage.

It was soon made plain that we were right in our suspicions; and the men became furious. The cooper and carpenter volunteered to head a mutiny forthwith; and while Jermin was below, four or five rushed aft to fasten down the cabin scuttle; others, throwing down the main-braces, called out to the rest to lend a hand, and fill away for the land. All this was done in an instant; and things were looking critical, when Doctor Long Ghost and myself prevailed upon them to wait a while, and do nothing hastily; there was plenty of time, and the ship was completely in our power.

While the preparations were still going on in the cabin, we mustered the men together, and went into counsel upon the forecastle.

It was with much difficulty that we could bring these rash spirits to a calm consideration of the case. But the doctor's influence at last began to tell; and, with a few exceptions, they agreed to be guided by him; assured that, if they did so, the ship would eventually be brought to her anchors without anyone getting into trouble. Still they told us, up and down, that if peaceable means failed, they would seize Little Jule, and carry her into Papeetee, if they all swung for it; but, for the present, the captain should have his own way.

By this time everything was ready; the boat was lowered and brought to the gangway; and the captain was helped on deck by the mate and steward. It was the first time we had seen him in more than two weeks, and he was greatly altered. As if anxious to elude every eye, a broad-brimmed Payata hat was pulled down over his brow; so that his face was only visible when the brim flapped aside. By a sling, rigged from the main-yard, the cook and Bembo now assisted in lowering him into the boat. As he went moaning over the side, he must have heard the whispered maledictions of his crew.

While the steward was busy adjusting matters in the boat, the mate, after a private interview with the Mowree, turned round abruptly, and told us that he was going ashore with the captain, to return as soon as possible. In his absence, Bembo, as next in rank, would command; there being nothing to do but keep the ship at a safe distance from the land. He then sprang into the boat, and, with only the cook and steward as oarsmen, steered for the shore.

Guy's thus leaving the ship in the men's hands, contrary to the mate's advice, was another evidence of his simplicity; for at this particular juncture, had neither the doctor nor myself been aboard, there is no telling what they might have done.

For the nonce, Bembo was captain; and, so far as mere seamanship was concerned, he was as competent to command as anyone. In truth, a better seaman never swore. This accomplishment, by the bye, together with a surprising familiarity with most nautical names and phrases, comprised about all the English he knew.

Being a harpooner, and, as such, having access to the cabin, this man, though not yet civilized, was, according to sea usages, which know no exceptions, held superior to the sailors; and therefore nothing was said against his being left in charge of the ship; nor did it occasion any surprise.

Some additional account must be given of Bembo. In the first place, he was far from being liked. A dark, moody savage, everybody but the mate more or less distrusted or feared him. Nor were these feelings unreciprocated. Unless duty called, he seldom went among the crew. Hard stories too were told about him; something, in particular, concerning an hereditary propensity to kill men and eat them. True, he came from a race of cannibals; but that was all that was known to a certainty.

Whatever unpleasant ideas were connected with the Mowree, his personal appearance no way lessened them. Unlike most of his countrymen, he was, if anything, below the ordinary height; but then, he was all compact, and under his swart, tattooed skin, the muscles worked like steel rods. Hair, crisp and coal-black, curled over shaggy brows, and ambushed small, intense eyes, always on the glare. In short, he was none of your effeminate barbarians.

Previous to this, he had been two or three voyages in Sydney whalemen; always, however, as in the present instance, shipping at the Bay of Islands, and receiving his discharge there on the homeward-bound passage. In this way, his countrymen frequently enter on board the colonial whaling vessels.

There was a man among us who had sailed with the Mowree on his first voyage, and he told me that he had not changed a particle since then.

Some queer things this fellow told me. The following is one of his stories. I give it for what it is worth; premising, however, that from what I know of Bembo, and the foolhardy, dare-devil feats sometimes performed in the sperm-whale fishery, I believe in its substantial truth.

As may be believed, Bembo was a wild one after a fish; indeed, all New Zealanders engaged in this business are; it seems to harmonize sweetly with their blood-thirsty propensities. At sea, the best English they speak is the South Seaman's slogan in lowering away, "A dead whale, or a stove boat!" Game to the marrow, these fellows are generally selected for harpooners; a post in which a nervous, timid man would be rather out of his element.

In darting, the harpooner, of course, stands erect in the head of the boat, one knee braced against a support. But Bembo disdained this; and was always pulled up to his fish, balancing himself right on the gunwale.

But to my story. One morning, at daybreak, they brought him up to a large, long whale. He darted his harpoon, and missed; and the fish sounded. After a while, the monster rose again, about a mile off, and they made after him. But he was frightened, or "gallied," as they call it; and noon came, and the boat was still chasing him. In whaling, as long as the fish is in sight, and no matter what may have been previously undergone, there is no giving up, except when night comes; and nowadays, when whales are so hard to be got, frequently not even then. At last, Bembo's whale was alongside for the second time. He darted both harpoons; but, as sometimes happens to the best men, by some unaccountable chance, once more missed. Though it is well known that such failures will happen at times, they, nevertheless, occasion the bitterest disappointment to a boat's crew, generally expressed in curses both loud and deep. And no wonder. Let any man pull with might and main for hours and hours together, under a burning sun; and if it do not make him a little peevish, he is no sailor.

The taunts of the seamen may have maddened the Mowree; however it was, no sooner was he brought up again, than, harpoon in hand, he bounded upon the whale's back, and for one dizzy second was seen there. The next, all was foam and fury, and both were out of sight. The men sheered off, flinging overboard the line as fast as they could; while ahead, nothing was seen but a red whirlpool of blood and brine.

Presently, a dark object swam out; the line began to straighten; then smoked round the loggerhead, and, quick as thought, the boat sped like an arrow through the water. They were "fast," and the whale was running.

Where was the Mowree? His brown hand was on the boat's gunwale; and he was hauled aboard in the very midst of the mad bubbles that burst under the bows.

Such a man, or devil, if you will, was Bembo.

CHAPTER XX.

THE ROUND ROBIN--VISITORS FROM SHORE

AFTER the captain left, the land-breeze died away; and, as is usual about these islands, toward noon it fell a dead calm. There was nothing to do but haul up the courses, run down the jib, and lay and roll upon the swells. The repose of the elements seemed to communicate itself to the men; and for a time there was a lull.

Early in the afternoon, the mate, having left the captain at Papeetee, returned to the ship. According to the steward, they were to go ashore again right after dinner with the remainder of Guy's effects.

On gaining the deck, Jermin purposely avoided us and went below without saying a word. Meanwhile, Long Ghost and I laboured hard to diffuse the right spirit among the crew; impressing upon them that a little patience and management would, in the end, accomplish all that their violence could; and that, too, without making a serious matter of it.

For my own part, I felt that I was under a foreign flag; that an English consul was close at hand, and that sailors seldom obtain justice. It was best to be prudent. Still, so much did I sympathize with the men, so far, at least, as their real grievances were concerned; and so convinced was I of the cruelty and injustice of what

Captain Guy seemed bent upon, that if need were, I stood ready to raise a hand.

In spite of all we could do, some of them again became most refractory, breathing nothing but downright mutiny. When we went below to dinner these fellows stirred up such a prodigious tumult that the old hull fairly echoed. Many, and fierce too, were the speeches delivered, and uproarious the comments of the sailors. Among others Long Jim, or--as the doctor afterwards called him--Lacedaemonian Jim, rose in his place, and addressed the forecastle parliament in the following strain:

"Look ye, Britons! if after what's happened, this here craft goes to sea with us, we are no men; and that's the way to say it. Speak the word, my livelies, and I'll pilot her in. I've been to Tahiti before and I can do it." Whereupon, he sat down amid a universal pounding of chest-lids, and cymbaling of tin pans; the few invalids, who, as yet, had not been actively engaged with the rest, now taking part in the applause, creaking their bunk-boards and swinging their hammocks. Cries also were heard, of "Handspikes and a shindy!" "Out stun-sails!" "Hurrah!"

Several now ran on deck, and, for the moment, I thought it was all over with us; but we finally succeeded in restoring some degree of quiet.

At last, by way of diverting their thoughts, I proposed that a "Round Robin" should be prepared and sent ashore to the consul by Baltimore, the cook. The idea took mightily, and I was told to set about it at once. On turning to the doctor for the requisite materials, he told me he had none; there was not a fly-leaf, even in any of his books. So, after great search, a damp, musty volume, entitled "A History of the most Atrocious and Bloody Piracies," was produced, and its two remaining blank leaves being torn out, were by help of a little pitch lengthened into one sheet. For ink, some of the soot over the lamp was then mixed with water, by a fellow of a literary turn; and an immense quill, plucked from a distended albatross' wing, which, nailed against the bowsprit bitts, had long formed an ornament of the forecastle, supplied a pen.

Making use of the stationery thus provided, I indited, upon a chest-lid, a concise statement of our grievances; concluding with the earnest hope that the consul would at once come off, and see how matters stood for himself. Right beneath the note was described the circle about which the names were to be written; the great object of a Round Robin being to arrange the signatures in such a way that, although they are all found in a ring, no man can be picked out as the leader of it.

Few among them had any regular names; many answering to some familiar title, expressive of a personal trait; or oftener still, to the name of the place from which they hailed; and in one or two cases were known by a handy syllable or two, significant of nothing in particular but the men who bore them. Some, to be sure, had, for the sake of formality, shipped under a feigned cognomen, or "Purser's name"; these, however, were almost forgotten by themselves; and so, to give the document an air of genuineness, it was decided that every man's name should be put down as it went among the crew.

It is due to the doctor to say that the circumscribed device was his.

Folded, and sealed with a drop of tar, the Round Robin was directed to "The English Consul, Tahiti"; and, handed to the cook, was by him delivered into that gentleman's hands as soon as the mate went ashore.

On the return of the boat, sometime after dark, we learned a good deal from old Baltimore, who, having been allowed to run about as much as he pleased, had spent his time gossiping.

Owing to the proceedings of the French, everything in Tahiti was in an uproar. Pritchard, the missionary consul, was absent in England; but his place was temporarily filled by one Wilson, an educated white man, born on the island, and the son of an old missionary of that name still living.

With natives and foreigners alike, Wilson the younger was exceedingly unpopular, being held an unprincipled and dissipated man, a character verified by his subsequent conduct. Pritchard's selecting a man like this to attend to the duties of his office, had occasioned general dissatisfaction ashore.

Though never in Europe or America, the acting consul had been several voyages to Sydney in a schooner belonging to the mission; and therefore our surprise was lessened, when Baltimore told us, that he and Captain Guy were as sociable as could be--old acquaintances, in fact; and that the latter had taken up his quarters at Wilson's house. For us this boded ill.

The mate was now assailed by a hundred questions as to what was going to be done with us. His only reply was, that in the morning the consul would pay us a visit, and settle everything.

After holding our ground off the harbour during the night, in the morning a shore boat, manned by natives, was seen coming off. In it were Wilson and another white man, who proved to be a Doctor Johnson, an Englishman, and a resident physician of Papeetee.

Stopping our headway as they approached, Jermin advanced to the gangway to receive them. No sooner did the consul touch the deck, than he gave us a specimen of what he was.

"Mr. Jermin," he cried loftily, and not deigning to notice the respectful salutation of the person addressed, "Mr. Jermin, tack ship, and stand off from the land."

Upon this, the men looked hard at him, anxious to see what sort of a looking "cove" he was. Upon inspection, he turned out to be an exceedingly minute "cove," with a viciously pugged nose, and a decidedly thin pair of legs. There was nothing else noticeable about him. Jermin, with ill-assumed suavity, at once obeyed the order, and the ship's head soon pointed out to sea.

Now, contempt is as frequently produced at first sight as love; and thus was it with respect to Wilson. No one could look at him without conceiving a strong dislike, or a cordial desire to entertain such a feeling the first favourable opportunity. There was such an intolerable air of conceit about this man that it was almost as much as one could do to refrain from running up and affronting him.

"So the counsellor is come," exclaimed Navy Bob, who, like all the rest, invariably styled him thus, much to mine and the doctor's diversion. "Ay," said another, "and for no good, I'll be bound."

Such were some of the observations made, as Wilson and the mate went below conversing.

But no one exceeded the cooper in the violence with which he inveighed against the ship and everything connected with her. Swearing like a trooper, he called the main-mast to witness that, if he (Bungs) ever again went out of sight of land in the Julia, he prayed Heaven that a fate might be his--altogether too remarkable to be here related.

Much had he to say also concerning the vileness of what we had to eat--not fit for a dog; besides enlarging upon the imprudence of intrusting the vessel longer to a man of the mate's intemperate habits. With so many sick, too, what could we expect to do in the fishery? It was no use talking; come what come might, the ship must let go her anchor.

Now, as Bungs, besides being an able seaman, a "Cod" in the forecastle, and about the oldest man in it, was, moreover, thus deeply imbued with feelings so warmly responded to by the rest, he was all at once selected to officiate as spokesman, as soon as the consul should see fit to address us. The selection was made contrary to mine and the doctor's advice; however, all assured us they would keep quiet, and hear everything Wilson had to say, before doing anything decisive.

We were not kept long in suspense; for very soon he was seen standing in the cabin gangway, with the tarnished tin case containing the ship's papers; and Jennin at once sung out for the ship's company to muster on the quarter-deck.

CHAPTER XXI.

PROCEEDINGS OF THE CONSUL

THE order was instantly obeyed, and the sailors ranged themselves, facing the consul.

They were a wild company; men of many climes--not at all precise in their toilet arrangements, but picturesque in their very tatters. My friend, the Long Doctor, was there too; and with a view, perhaps, of enlisting the sympathies of the consul for a gentleman in distress, had taken more than ordinary pains with his appearance. But among the sailors, he looked like a land-crane blown off to sea, and consorting with petrels.

The forlorn Rope Yarn, however, was by far the most remarkable figure. Land-lubber that he was, his outfit of sea-clothing had long since been confiscated; and he was now fain to go about in whatever he could pick up. His upper garment--an unsailor-like article of dress which he persisted in wearing, though torn from his back twenty times in the day--was an old "claw-hammer jacket," or swallow-tail coat, formerly belonging to Captain Guy, and which had formed one of his perquisites when steward.

By the side of Wilson was the mate, bareheaded, his gray locks lying in rings upon his bronzed brow, and his keen eye scanning the crowd

as if he knew their every thought. His frock hung loosely, exposing
his round throat, mossy chest, and short and nervous arm embossed
with pugilistic bruises, and quaint with many a device in India ink.

In the midst of a portentous silence, the consul unrolled his papers,
evidently intending to produce an effect by the exceeding bigness of
his looks.

"Mr. Jermin, call off their names;" and he handed him a list of the
ship's company.

All answered but the deserters and the two mariners at the bottom of
the sea.

It was now supposed that the Round Robin would be produced, and
something said about it. But not so. Among the consul's papers that
unique document was thought to be perceived; but, if there, it was
too much despised to be made a subject of comment. Some present, very
justly regarding it as an uncommon literary production, had been
anticipating all sorts of miracles therefrom; and were, therefore,
much touched at this neglect.

"Well, men," began Wilson again after a short pause, "although you all
look hearty enough, I'm told there are some sick among you. Now then,
Mr. Jermin, call off the names on that sick-list of yours, and let
them go over to the other side of the deck--I should like to see who

they are."

"So, then," said he, after we had all passed over, "you are the sick fellows, are you? Very good: I shall have you seen to. You will go down into the cabin one by one, to Doctor Johnson, who will report your respective cases to me. Such as he pronounces in a dying state I shall have sent ashore; the rest will be provided with everything needful, and remain aboard."

At this announcement, we gazed strangely at each other, anxious to see who it was that looked like dying, and pretty nearly deciding to stay aboard and get well, rather than go ashore and be buried. There were some, nevertheless, who saw very plainly what Wilson was at, and they acted accordingly. For my own part, I resolved to assume as dying an expression as possible; hoping that, on the strength of it, I might be sent ashore, and so get rid of the ship without any further trouble.

With this intention, I determined to take no part in anything that might happen until my case was decided upon. As for the doctor, he had all along pretended to be more or less unwell; and by a significant look now given me, it was plain that he was becoming decidedly worse.

The invalids disposed of for the present, and one of them having gone below to be examined, the consul turned round to the rest, and addressed them as follows:--

"Men, I'm going to ask you two or three questions--let one of you answer yes or no, and the rest keep silent. Now then: Have you anything to say against your mate, Mr. Jermin?" And he looked sharply among the sailors, and, at last, right into the eye of the cooper, whom everybody was eyeing.

"Well, sir," faltered Bungs, "we can't say anything against Mr. Jermin's seamanship, but--"

"I want no buts," cried the consul, breaking in: "answer me yes or no--have you anything to say against Mr. Jermin?"

"I was going on to say, sir; Mr. Jermin's a very good man; but then--" Here the mate looked marlinespikes at Bungs; and Bungs, after stammering out something, looked straight down to a seam in the deck, and stopped short.

A rather assuming fellow heretofore, the cooper had sported many feathers in his cap; he was now showing the white one.

"So much then for that part of the business," exclaimed Wilson, smartly; "you have nothing to say against him, I see."

Upon this, several seemed to be on the point of saying a good deal;

but disconcerted by the cooper's conduct, checked themselves, and the consul proceeded.

"Have you enough to eat, aboard? answer me, you man who spoke before."

"Well, I don't know as to that," said the cooper, looking excessively uneasy, and trying to edge back, but pushed forward again. "Some of that salt horse ain't as sweet as it might be."

"That's not what I asked you," shouted the consul, growing brave quite fast; "answer my questions as I put them, or I'll find a way to make you."

This was going a little too far. The ferment, into which the cooper's poltroonery had thrown the sailors, now brooked no restraint; and one of them--a young American who went by the name of Salem--dashed out from among the rest, and fetching the cooper a blow that sent him humming over toward the consul, flourished a naked sheath-knife in the air, and burst forth with "I'm the little fellow that can answer your questions; just put them to me once, counsellor." But the "counsellor" had no more questions to ask just then; for at the alarming apparition of Salem's knife, and the extraordinary effect produced upon Bungs, he had popped his head down the companion-way, and was holding it there.

Upon the mate's assuring him, however, that it was all over, he looked up, quite flustered, if not frightened, but evidently determined to put as fierce a face on the matter as practicable. Speaking sharply, he warned all present to "look out"; and then repeated the question, whether there was enough to eat aboard. Everyone now turned spokesman; and he was assailed by a perfect hurricane of yells, in which the oaths fell like hailstones.

"How's this! what d'ye mean?" he cried, upon the first lull; "who told you all to speak at once? Here, you man with the knife, you'll be putting someone's eyes out yet; d'ye hear, you sir? You seem to have a good deal to say, who are you, pray; where did you ship?"

"I'm nothing more nor a bloody beach-comber," retorted Salem, stepping forward piratically and eyeing him; "and if you want to know, I shipped at the Islands about four months ago."

"Only four months ago? And here you have more to say than men who have been aboard the whole voyage;" and the consul made a dash at looking furious, but failed. "Let me hear no more from you, sir. Where's that respectable, gray-headed man, the cooper? he's the one to answer my questions."

"There's no 'spectable, gray-headed men aboard," returned Salem; "we're all a parcel of mutineers and pirates!"

All this time, the mate was holding his peace; and Wilson, now completely abashed, and at a loss what to do, took him by the arm, and walked across the deck. Returning to the cabin-scuttle, after a close conversation, he abruptly addressed the sailors, without taking any further notice of what had just happened.

"For reasons you all know, men, this ship has been placed in my hands. As Captain Guy will remain ashore for the present, your mate, Mr. Jermin, will command until his recovery. According to my judgment, there is no reason why the voyage should not be at once resumed; especially, as I shall see that you have two more harpooners, and enough good men to man three boats. As for the sick, neither you nor I have anything to do with them; they will be attended to by Doctor Johnson; but I've explained that matter before. As soon as things can be arranged--in a day or two, at farthest--you will go to sea for a three months' cruise, touching here, at the end of it, for your captain. Let me hear a good report of you, now, when you come back. At present, you will continue lying off and on the harbour. I will send you fresh provisions as soon as I can get them. There: I've nothing more to say; go forward to your stations."

And, without another word, he wheeled round to descend into the cabin. But hardly had he concluded before the incensed men were dancing about him on every side, and calling upon him to lend an ear. Each one for himself denied the legality of what he proposed to do; insisted upon the necessity for taking the ship in; and finally gave him to understand, roughly and roundly, that go to sea in her they would not.

In the midst of this mutinous uproar, the alarmed consul stood fast by the scuttle. His tactics had been decided upon beforehand; indeed, they must have been concerted ashore, between him and the captain; for all he said, as he now hurried below, was, "Go forward, men; I'm through with you: you should have mentioned these matters before: my arrangements are concluded: go forward, I say; I've nothing more to say to you." And, drawing over the slide of the scuttle, he disappeared. Upon the very point of following him down, the attention of the exasperated seamen was called off to a party who had just then taken the recreant Bungs in hand. Amid a shower of kicks and cuffs, the traitor was borne along to the forecastle, where--I forbear to relate what followed.

CHAPTER XXII.

THE CONSUL'S DEPARTURE

DURING THE scenes just described, Doctor Johnson was engaged in examining the sick, of whom, as it turned out, all but two were to remain in the ship. He had evidently received his cue from Wilson.

One of the last called below into the cabin, just as the quarter-deck gathering dispersed, I came on deck quite incensed. My lameness, which, to tell the truth, was now much better, was put down as, in a great measure, affected; and my name was on the list of those who would be fit for any duty in a day or two. This was enough. As for Doctor Long Ghost, the shore physician, instead of extending to him any professional sympathy, had treated him very cavalierly. To a certain extent, therefore, we were now both bent on making common cause with the sailors.

I must explain myself here. All we wanted was to have the ship snugly anchored in Papeetee Bay; entertaining no doubt that, could this be done, it would in some way or other peaceably lead to our emancipation. Without a downright mutiny, there was but one way to accomplish this: to induce the men to refuse all further duty, unless it were to work the vessel in. The only difficulty lay in restraining them within proper bounds. Nor was it without certain misgivings, that I found myself so situated, that I must necessarily link myself, however guardedly, with such a desperate company; and in an enterprise, too, of which it was hard to conjecture what might be the result. But anything like neutrality was out of the question; and unconditional submission was equally so.

On going forward, we found them ten times more tumultuous than ever. After again restoring some degree of tranquillity, we once more urged our plan of quietly refusing duty, and awaiting the result. At first, few would hear of it; but in the end, a good number were convinced by our representations. Others held out. Nor were those who thought with us in all things to be controlled.

Upon Wilson's coming on deck to enter his boat, he was beset on all sides; and, for a moment, I thought the ship would be seized before his very eyes.

"Nothing more to say to you, men: my arrangements are made. Go forward, where you belong. I'll take no insolence;" and, in a tremor, Wilson hurried over the side in the midst of a volley of execrations.

Shortly after his departure, the mate ordered the cook and steward into his boat; and saying that he was going to see how the captain did, left us, as before, under the charge of Bembo.

At this time we were lying becalmed, pretty close in with the land (having gone about again), our main-topsail flapping against the mast with every roll.

The departure of the consul and Jermin was followed by a scene absolutely indescribable. The sailors ran about deck like madmen; Bembo, all the while leaning against the taff-rail by himself, smoking his heathenish stone pipe, and never interfering.

The cooper, who that morning had got himself into a fluid of an exceedingly high temperature, now did his best to regain the favour of the crew. "Without distinction of party," he called upon all hands to step up, and partake of the contents of his bucket.

But it was quite plain that, before offering to intoxicate others, he had taken the wise precaution of getting well tipsy himself. He was now once more happy in the affection of his shipmates, who, one and all, pronounced him sound to the kelson.

The Pisco soon told; and, with great difficulty, we restrained a party in the very act of breaking into the after-hold in pursuit of more. All manner of pranks were now played.

"Mast-head, there! what d'ye see?" bawled Beauty, hailing the main-truck through an enormous copper funnel. "Stand by for stays," roared Flash Jack, bawling off with the cook's axe, at the fastening of the main-stay. "Looky out for 'quails!" shrieked the Portuguese, Antone, darting a handspike through the cabin skylight. And "Heave round cheerly, men," sung out Navy Bob, dancing a hornpipe on the forecastle.

CHAPTER XXIII.

THE SECOND NIGHT OFF PAPEETEE

TOWARD sunset, the mate came off, singing merrily, in the stern of his boat; and in attempting to climb up the side, succeeded in going plump into the water. He was rescued by the steward, and carried across the deck with many moving expressions of love for his bearer. Tumbled into the quarter-boat, he soon fell asleep, and waking about midnight, somewhat sobered, went forward among the men. Here, to prepare for what follows, we must leave him for a moment.

It was now plain enough that Jermin was by no means unwilling to take the Julia to sea; indeed, there was nothing he so much desired; though what his reasons were, seeing our situation, we could only conjecture. Nevertheless, so it was; and having counted much upon his rough popularity with the men to reconcile them to a short cruise under him, he had consequently been disappointed in their behaviour. Still, thinking that they would take a different view of the matter, when they came to know what fine times he had in store for them, he resolved upon trying a little persuasion.

So on going forward, he put his head down the forecastle scuttle, and hailed us quite cordially, inviting us down into the cabin; where, he said, he had something to make merry withal. Nothing loth, we went; and throwing ourselves along the transom, waited for the steward to serve us.

As the can circulated, Jermin, leaning on the table and occupying the captain's arm-chair secured to the deck, opened his mind as bluntly and freely as ever. He was by no means yet sober.

He told us we were acting very foolishly; that if we only stuck to the ship, he would lead us all a jovial life of it; enumerating the casks still remaining untapped in the Julia's wooden cellar. It was even hinted vaguely that such a thing might happen as our not coming back for the captain; whom he spoke of but lightly; asserting, what he had often said before, that he was no sailor.

Moreover, and perhaps with special reference to Doctor Long Ghost and myself, he assured us generally that, if there were any among us studiously inclined, he would take great pleasure in teaching such the whole art and mystery of navigation, including the gratuitous use of his quadrant.

I should have mentioned that, previous to this, he had taken the doctor aside, and said something about reinstating him in the cabin with augmented dignity; beside throwing out a hint that I myself was in some way or other to be promoted. But it was all to no purpose; bent the men were upon going ashore, and there was no moving them.

At last he flew into a rage--much increased by the frequency of his potations--and with many imprecations, concluded by driving everybody out of the cabin. We tumbled up the gangway in high good-humour.

Upon deck everything looked so quiet that some of the most pugnacious spirits actually lamented that there was so little prospect of an exhilarating disturbance before morning. It was not five minutes, however, ere these fellows were gratified.

Sydney Ben--said to be a runaway Ticket-of-Leave-Man, and for reasons of his own, one of the few who still remained on duty--had, for the sake of the fun, gone down with the rest into the cabin; where Bembo, who meanwhile was left in charge of the deck, had frequently called out for him. At first, Ben pretended not to hear; but on being sung out for again and again, bluntly refused; at the same time, casting some illiberal reflections on the Mowree's maternal origin, which the latter had been long enough among the sailors to understand as in the highest degree offensive. So just after the men came up from below, Bembo singled him out, and gave him such a cursing in his broken lingo that it was enough to frighten one. The convict was the worse for liquor; indeed the Mowree had been tippling also, and before we knew it, a blow was struck by Ben, and the two men came together like magnets.

The Ticket-of-Leave-Man was a practised bruiser; but the savage knew nothing of the art pugilistic: and so they were even. It was clear hugging and wrenching till both came to the deck. Here they rolled over and over in the middle of a ring which seemed to form of itself. At last the white man's head fell back, and his face grew purple. Bembo's teeth were at his throat. Rushing in all round, they hauled the savage off, but not until repeatedly struck on the head would he let go.

His rage was now absolutely demoniac; he lay glaring and writhing on the deck, without attempting to rise. Cowed, as they supposed he was, from his attitude, the men, rejoiced at seeing him thus humbled, left him; after rating him, in sailor style, for a cannibal and a coward.

Ben was attended to, and led below.

Soon after this, the rest also, with but few exceptions, retired into the forecastle; and having been up nearly all the previous night, they quickly dropped about the chests and rolled into the hammocks. In an hour's time, not a sound could be heard in that part of the ship.

Before Bembo was dragged away, the mate had in vain endeavoured to separate the combatants, repeatedly striking the Mowree; but the seamen interposing, at last kept him off.

And intoxicated as he was, when they dispersed, he knew enough to charge the steward--a steady seaman be it remembered--with the present safety of the ship; and then went below, when he fell directly into another drunken sleep.

Having remained upon deck with the doctor some time after the rest had gone below, I was just on the point of following him down, when I saw the Mowree rise, draw a bucket of water, and holding it high above his head, pour its contents right over him. This he repeated several times. There was nothing very peculiar in the act, but something else about him struck me. However, I thought no more of it, but descended the scuttle.

After a restless nap, I found the atmosphere of the forecastle so close, from nearly all the men being down at the same time, that I hunted up an old pea-jacket and went on deck; intending to sleep it out there till morning. Here I found the cook and steward, Wymontoo, Hope Yarn, and the Dane; who, being all quiet, manageable fellows, and holding aloof from the rest since the captain's departure, had been ordered by the mate not to go below until sunrise. They were lying under the lee of the bulwarks; two or three fast asleep, and the others smoking their pipes, and conversing.

To my surprise, Bembo was at the helm; but there being so few to stand there now, they told me, he had offered to take his turn with the rest, at the same time heading the watch; and to this, of course, they made no objection.

It was a fine, bright night; all moon and stars, and white crests of waves. The breeze was light, but freshening; and close-hauled, poor little Jule, as if nothing had happened, was heading in for the land, which rose high and hazy in the distance.

After the day's uproar, the tranquillity of the scene was soothing, and I leaned over the side to enjoy it.

More than ever did I now lament my situation--but it was useless to repine, and I could not upbraid myself. So at last, becoming drowsy, I made a bed with my jacket under the windlass, and tried to forget myself.

How long I lay there, I cannot tell; but as I rose, the first object that met my eye was Bembo at the helm; his dark figure slowly rising and falling with the ship's motion against the spangled heavens behind. He seemed all impatience and expectation; standing at arm's length from the spokes, with one foot advanced, and his bare head thrust forward. Where I was, the watch were out of sight; and no one else was stirring; the deserted decks and broad white sails were gleaming in the moonlight.

Presently, a swelling, dashing sound came upon my ear, and I had a sort of vague consciousness that I had been hearing it before. The next instant I was broad awake and on my feet. Eight ahead, and so near that my heart stood still, was a long line of breakers, heaving and frothing. It was the coral reef girdling the island. Behind it, and almost casting their shadows upon the deck, were the sleeping mountains, about whose hazy peaks the gray dawn was just breaking. The breeze had freshened, and with a steady, gliding motion, we were running straight for the reef.

All was taken in at a glance; the fell purpose of Bembo was obvious, and with a frenzied shout to wake the watch, I rushed aft. They sprang to their feet bewildered; and after a short, but desperate scuffle, we tore him from the helm. In wrestling with him, the wheel--left for a moment unguarded--flew to leeward, thus, fortunately, bringing the ship's head to the wind, and so retarding her progress. Previous to this, she had been kept three or four points free, so as to close with the breakers. Her headway now shortened, I steadied the helm, keeping the sails just lifting, while we glided obliquely toward the land. To have run off before the wind--an easy thing--would have been almost instant destruction, owing to a curve of the reef in that direction. At this time, the Dane and the steward were still struggling with the furious Mowree, and the others were running about irresolute and shouting.

But darting forward the instant I had the helm, the old cook thundered on the forecastle with a handspike, "Breakers! breakers close aboard!--'bout ship! 'bout ship!"

Up came the sailors, staring about them in stupid horror.

"Haul back the head-yards!" "Let go the lee fore-brace!" "Beady about! about!" were now shouted on all sides; while distracted by a thousand orders, they ran hither and thither, fairly panic-stricken.

It seemed all over with us; and I was just upon the point of throwing the ship full into the wind (a step, which, saving us for the instant, would have sealed our fate in the end), when a sharp cry shot by my ear like the flight of an arrow.

It was Salem: "All ready for'ard; hard down!"

Round and round went the spokes--the Julia, with her short keel, spinning to windward like a top. Soon, the jib-sheets lashed the stays, and the men, more self-possessed, flew to the braces.

"Main-sail haul!" was now heard, as the fresh breeze streamed fore and aft the deck; and directly the after-yards were whirled round.

In a half-a-minute more, we were sailing away from the land on the other tack, with every sail distended.

Turning on her heel within little more than a biscuit's toss of the reef, no earthly power could have saved us, were it not that, up to the very brink of the coral rampart, there are no soundings.

CHAPTER XXIV.

OUTBREAK OF THE CREW

THE purpose of Bembo had been made known to the men generally by the watch; and now that our salvation was certain, by an instinctive impulse they raised a cry, and rushed toward him.

Just before liberated by Dunk and the steward, he was standing doggedly by the mizzen-mast; and, as the infuriated sailors came on, his bloodshot eye rolled, and his sheath-knife glittered over his head.

"Down with him!" "Strike him down!" "Hang him at the main-yard!" such were the shouts now raised. But he stood unmoved, and, for a single instant, they absolutely faltered.

"Cowards!" cried Salem, and he flung himself upon him. The steel descended like a ray of light; but did no harm; for the sailor's heart was beating against the Mowree's before he was aware.

They both fell to the deck, when the knife was instantly seized, and Bembo secured.

"For'ard! for'ard with him!" was again the cry; "give him a sea-toss!" "Overboard with him!" and he was dragged along the deck, struggling and fighting with tooth and nail.

All this uproar immediately over the mate's head at last roused him from his drunken nap, and he came staggering on deck.

"What's this?" he shouted, running right in among them.

"It's the Mowree, zur; they are going to murder him, zur," here sobbed poor Rope Yarn, crawling close up to him.

"Avast! avast!" roared Jermin, making a spring toward Bembo, and dashing two or three of the sailors aside. At this moment the wretch was partly flung over the bulwarks, which shook with his frantic struggles. In vain the doctor and others tried to save him: the men listened to nothing.

"Murder and mutiny, by the salt sea!" shouted the mate; and dashing his arms right and left, he planted his iron hand upon the Mowree's shoulder.

"There are two of us now; and as you serve him, you serve me," he cried, turning fiercely round.

"Over with them together, then," exclaimed the carpenter, springing forward; but the rest fell back before the courageous front of Jermin, and, with the speed of thought, Bembo, unharmed, stood upon deck.

"Aft with ye!" cried his deliverer; and he pushed him right among the men, taking care to follow him up close. Giving the sailors no time to recover, he pushed the Mowree before him, till they came to the cabin scuttle, when he drew the slide over him, and stood still. Throughout, Bembo never spoke one word.

"Now for'ard where ye belong!" cried the mate, addressing the seamen, who by this time, rallying again, had no idea of losing their victim.

"The Mowree! the Mowree!" they shouted.

Here the doctor, in answer to the mate's repeated questions, stepped forward, and related what Bembo had been doing; a matter which the mate but dimly understood from the violent threatenings he had been hearing.

For a moment he seemed to waver; but at last, turning the key of the padlock of the slide, he breathed through his set teeth--"Ye can't have him; I'll hand him over to the consul; so for'ard with ye, I say: when there's any drowning to be done, I'll pass the word; so away with ye, ye blood-thirsty pirates."

It was to no purpose that they begged or threatened: Jermin, although by no means sober, stood his ground manfully, and before long they dispersed, soon to forget everything that had happened.

Though we had no opportunity to hear him confess it, Bembo's intention to destroy us was beyond all question. His only motive could have been a desire to revenge the contumely heaped upon him the night previous, operating upon a heart irreclaimably savage, and at no time fraternally disposed toward the crew.

During the whole of this scene the doctor did his best to save him. But well knowing that all I could do would have been equally useless, I maintained my place at the wheel. Indeed, no one but Jermin could have prevented this murder.

CHAPTER XXV.

JERMIN ENCOUNTERS AN OLD SHIPMATE

DURING the morning of the day which dawned upon the events just recounted, we remained a little to leeward of the harbour, waiting the appearance of the consul, who had promised the mate to come off in a shore boat for the purpose of seeing him.

By this time the men had forced his secret from the cooper, and the consequence was that they kept him continually coming and going from the after-hold. The mate must have known this; but he said nothing, notwithstanding all the dancing and singing, and occasional fighting which announced the flow of the Pisco.

The peaceable influence which the doctor and myself had heretofore been exerting, was now very nearly at an end.

Confident, from the aspect of matters, that the ship, after all, would be obliged to go in; and learning, moreover, that the mate had said so, the sailors, for the present, seemed in no hurry about it; especially as the bucket of Bungs gave such generous cheer.

As for Bembo, we were told that, after putting him in double irons, the mate had locked him up in the captain's state-room, taking the additional precaution of keeping the cabin scuttle secured. From this time forward we never saw the Mowree again, a circumstance which will explain itself as the narrative proceeds.

Noon came, and no consul; and as the afternoon advanced without any word even from the shore, the mate was justly incensed; more especially as he had taken great pains to keep perfectly sober against Wilson's arrival.

Two or three hours before sundown, a small schooner came out of the harbour, and headed over for the adjoining island of Imeeo, or Moreea, in plain sight, about fifteen miles distant. The wind failing, the current swept her down under our bows, where we had a fair glimpse of the natives on her decks.

There were a score of them, perhaps, lounging upon spread mats, and smoking their pipes. On floating so near, and hearing the maudlin cries of our crew, and beholding their antics, they must have taken us for a pirate; at any rate, they got out their sweeps, and pulled away as fast as they could; the sight of our two six-pounders, which, by way of a joke, were now run out of the side-ports, giving a fresh impetus to their efforts. But they had not gone far, when a white man, with a red sash about his waist, made his appearance on deck, the natives immediately desisting.

Hailing us loudly, he said he was coming aboard; and after some confusion on the schooner's decks, a small canoe was launched over-hoard, and, in a minute or two, he was with us. He turned out to be an old shipmate of Jermin's, one Viner, long supposed dead, but now resident on the island.

The meeting of these men, under the circumstances, is one of a thousand occurrences appearing exaggerated in fiction; but, nevertheless, frequently realized in actual lives of adventure.

Some fifteen years previous, they had sailed together as officers of the barque Jane, of London, a South Seaman. Somewhere near the New Hebrides, they struck one night upon an unknown reef; and, in a few hours, the Jane went to pieces. The boats, however, were saved; some provisions also, a quadrant, and a few other articles. But several of the men were lost before they got clear of the wreck.

The three boats, commanded respectively by the captain, Jermin, and the third mate, then set sail for a small English settlement at the Bay of Islands in New Zealand. Of course they kept together as much as possible. After being at sea about a week, a Lascar in the captain's boat went crazy; and, it being dangerous to keep him, they tried to throw him overboard. In the confusion that ensued the boat capsized from the sail's "jibing"; and a considerable sea running at the time, and the other boats being separated more than usual, only one man was picked up. The very next night it blew a heavy gale; and the remaining boats taking in all sail, made bundles of their oars, flung them overboard, and rode to them with plenty of line. When morning broke, Jermin and his men were alone upon the ocean: the third mate's boat, in all probability, having gone down.

After great hardships, the survivors caught sight of a brig, which took them on board, and eventually landed them at Sydney.

Ever since then our mate had sailed from that port, never once hearing of his lost shipmates, whom, by this time, of course, he had long given up. Judge, then, his feelings when Viner, the lost third mate, the instant he touched the deck, rushed up and wrung him by the hand.

During the gale his line had parted; so that the boat, drifting fast to leeward, was out of sight by morning. Reduced, after this, to great extremities, the boat touched, for fruit, at an island of which they knew nothing. The natives, at first, received them kindly; but one of the men getting into a quarrel on account of a woman, and the rest taking his part, they were all massacred but Viner, who, at the time, was in an adjoining village. After staying on the island more than two years, he finally escaped in the boat of an American whaler, which landed him at Valparaiso. From this period he had continued to follow the seas, as a man before the mast, until about eighteen months previous, when he went ashore at Tahiti, where he now owned the schooner we saw, in which he traded among the neighbouring islands.

The breeze springing up again just after nightfall, Viner left us, promising his old shipmate to see him again, three days hence, in

Papeetee harbour.

CHAPTER XXVI.

WE ENTER THE HARBOUR--JIM THE PILOT

EXHAUSTED by the day's wassail, most of the men went below at an early hour, leaving the deck to the steward and two of the men remaining on duty; the mate, with Baltimore and the Dane, engaging to relieve them at midnight. At that hour, the ship--now standing off shore, under short sail--was to be tacked.

It was not long after midnight, when we were wakened in the forecastle by the lion roar of Jermin's voice, ordering a pull at the jib-halyards; and soon afterwards, a handspike struck the scuttle, and all hands were called to take the ship into port.

This was wholly unexpected; but we learned directly that the mate, no longer relying upon the consul, and renouncing all thought of inducing the men to change their minds, had suddenly made up his own. He was going to beat up to the entrance of the harbour, so as to show a signal for a pilot before sunrise.

Notwithstanding this, the sailors absolutely refused to assist in working the ship under any circumstances whatever: to all mine and the doctor's entreaties lending a deaf ear. Sink or strike, they swore they would have nothing more to do with her. This perverse-ness was to be attributed, in a great measure, to the effects of their late debauch.

With a strong breeze, all sail set, and the ship in the hands of four or five men, exhausted by two nights' watching, our situation was bad enough; especially as the mate seemed more reckless than ever, and we were now to tack ship several times close under the land.

Well knowing that if anything untoward happened to the vessel before morning, it would be imputed to the conduct of the crew, and so lead to serious results, should they ever be brought to trial; I called together those on deck to witness my declaration;--that now that the Julia was destined for the harbour (the only object for which I, at least, had been struggling), I was willing to do what I could toward carrying her in safely. In this step I was followed by the doctor.

The hours passed anxiously until morning; when, being well to windward of the mouth of the harbour, we bore up for it, with the union-jack at the fore. No sign, however, of boat or pilot was seen; and after running close in several times, the ensign was set at the mizzen-peak, union down in distress. But it was of no avail.

Attributing to Wilson this unaccountable remissness on the part of those ashore, Jermin, quite enraged, now determined to stand boldly in upon his own responsibility; trusting solely to what he remembered of the harbour on a visit there many years previous.

This resolution was characteristic. Even with a competent pilot, Papeetee Bay, is considered a ticklish, one to enter. Formed by a bold sweep of the shore, it is protected seaward by the coral reef, upon which the rollers break with great violence. After stretching across the bay, the barrier extends on toward Point Venus, in the district of Matavia, eight or nine miles distant. Here there is an opening, by which ships enter, and glide down the smooth, deep canal, between the reef and the shore, to the harbour. But, by seamen generally, the leeward entrance is preferred, as the wind is extremely variable inside the reef. This latter entrance is a break in the barrier directly facing the bay and village of Papeetee. It is very narrow; and from the baffling winds, currents, and sunken rocks, ships now and then grate their keels against the coral.

But the mate was not to be daunted; so, stationing what men he had at the braces, he sprang upon the bulwarks, and, bidding everybody keep wide awake, ordered the helm up. In a few moments, we were running in. Being toward noon, the wind was fast leaving us, and, by the time the breakers were roaring on either hand, little more than steerage-way was left. But on we glided--smoothly and deftly; avoiding the green, darkling objects here and there strewn in our path; Jermin occasionally looking down in the water, and then about him, with the utmost calmness, and not a word spoken. Just fanned along thus, it was not many minutes ere we were past all danger, and floated into the placid basin within. This was the cleverest specimen of his seamanship that he ever gave us.

As we held on toward the frigate and shipping, a canoe, coming out from among them, approached. In it were a boy and an old man--both islanders; the former nearly naked, and the latter dressed in an old naval frock-coat. Both were paddling with might and main; the old man, once in a while, tearing his paddle out of the water; and, after rapping his companion over the head, both fell to with fresh vigour. As they came within hail, the old fellow, springing to his feet and flourishing his paddle, cut some of the queerest capers; all the while jabbering something which at first we could not understand.

Presently we made out the following:--"Ah! you pemi, ah!--you come!--What for you come?--You be fine for come no pilot.--I say, you hear?--I say, you ita maitui (no good).--You hear?--You no pilot.--Yes, you d---- me, you no pilot 't all; I d---- you; you hear?"

This tirade, which showed plainly that, whatever the profane old rascal was at, he was in right good earnest, produced peals of laughter from the ship. Upon which, he seemed to get beside himself; and the boy, who, with suspended paddle, was staring about him, received a sound box over the head, which set him to work in a twinkling, and brought the canoe quite near. The orator now opening afresh, it turned out that his vehement rhetoric was all addressed to the mate, still standing conspicuously on the bulwarks.

But Jermin was in no humour for nonsense; so, with a sailor's blessing, he ordered him off. The old fellow then flew into a regular frenzy, cursing and swearing worse than any civilized being I ever heard.

"You sabbee me?" he shouted. "You know me, ah? Well; me Jim, me pilot--been pilot now long time."

"Ay," cried Jermin, quite surprised, as indeed we all were, "you are the pilot, then, you old pagan. Why didn't you come off before this?"

"Ah! me scibbee,--me know--you piratee (pirate)--see you long time, but no me come--I sabbee you--you ita maitai nuee (superlatively bad)."

"Paddle away with ye," roared Jermin, in a rage; "be off! or I'll dart a harpoon at ye!"

But, instead of obeying the order, Jim, seizing his paddle, darted the canoe right up to the gangway, and, in two bounds, stood on deck.

Pulling a greasy silk handkerchief still lower over his brow, and improving the sit of his frock-coat with a vigorous jerk, he then strode up to the mate; and, in a more flowery style than ever, gave him to understand that the redoubtable "Jim," himself, was before him; that the ship was his until the anchor was down; and he should like to hear what anyone had to say to it.

As there now seemed little doubt that he was all he claimed to be, the Julia was at last surrendered.

Our gentleman now proceeded to bring us to an anchor, jumping up between the knight-heads, and bawling out "Luff! luff! keepy off! leeepy off!" and insisting upon each time being respectfully responded to by the man at the helm. At this time our steerage-way was almost gone; and yet, in giving his orders, the passionate old man made as much fuss as a white squall aboard the Flying Dutchman.

Jim turned out to be the regular pilot of the harbour; a post, be it known, of no small profit; and, in his eyes, at least, invested with immense importance. Our unceremonious entrance, therefore, was regarded as highly insulting, and tending to depreciate both the dignity and lucrativeness of his office.

The old man is something of a wizard. Having an understanding with the elements, certain phenomena of theirs are exhibited for his particular benefit. Unusually clear weather, with a fine steady breeze, is a certain sign that a merchantman is at hand; whale-spouts seen from the harbour are tokens of a whaling vessel's approach; and thunder and lightning, happening so seldom as they do, are proof positive that a man-of-war is drawing near.

In short, Jim, the pilot, is quite a character in his way; and no one visits Tahiti without hearing some curious story about him.

CHAPTER XXVII.

A GLANCE AT PAPEETEE--WE ARE SENT ABOARD THE FRIGATE

THE village of Papeetee struck us all very pleasantly. Lying in a semicircle round the bay, the tasteful mansions of the chiefs and foreign residents impart an air of tropical elegance, heightened by the palm-trees waving here and there, and the deep-green groves of the Bread-Fruit in the background. The squalid huts of the common people are out of sight, and there is nothing to mar the prospect.

All round the water extends a wide, smooth beach of mixed pebbles and fragments of coral. This forms the thoroughfare of the village; the handsomest houses all facing it--the fluctuation of the tides being so inconsiderable that they cause no inconvenience.

The Pritchard residence--a fine large building--occupies a site on one side of the bay: a green lawn slopes off to the sea: and in front waves the English flag. Across the water, the tricolour also, and the stars and stripes, distinguish the residences of the other consuls.

What greatly added to the picturesqueness of the bay at this time was the condemned hull of a large ship, which, at the farther end of the harbour, lay bilged upon the beach, its stern settled low in the water, and the other end high and dry. From where we lay, the trees behind seemed to lock their leafy boughs over its bowsprit; which, from its position, looked nearly upright.

She was an American whaler, a very old craft. Having sprung a leak at sea, she had made all sail for the island, to heave down for repairs. Found utterly unseaworthy, however, her oil was taken out and sent home in another vessel; the hull was then stripped and sold for a trifle.

Before leaving Tahiti, I had the curiosity to go over this poor old ship, thus stranded on a strange shore. What were my emotions, when I saw upon her stern the name of a small town on the river Hudson! She was from the noble stream on whose banks I was born; in whose waters I had a hundred times bathed. In an instant, palm-trees and elms--canoes and skiffs--church spires and bamboos--all mingled in one vision of the present and the past.

But we must not leave little Jule.

At last the wishes of many were gratified; and like an aeronaut's grapnel, her rusty little anchor was caught in the coral groves at the bottom of Papeetee Bay. This must have been more than forty days after leaving the Marquesas.

The sails were yet unfurled, when a boat came alongside with our esteemed friend Wilson, the consul.

"How's this, how's this, Mr. Jermin?" he began, looking very savage as he touched the deck. "What brings you in without orders?"

"You did not come off to us, as you promised, sir; and there was no hanging on longer with nobody to work the ship," was the blunt reply.

"So the infernal scoundrels held out--did they? Very good; I'll make them sweat for it," and he eyed the scowling men with unwonted intrepidity. The truth was, he felt safer now, than when outside the reef.

"Muster the mutineers on the quarter-deck," he continued. "Drive them aft, sir, sick and well: I have a word to say to them."

"Now, men," said he, "you think it's all well with you, I suppose. You wished the ship in, and here she is. Captain Guy's ashore, and you think you must go too: but we'll see about that--I'll miserably disappoint you." (These last were his very words.) "Mr. Jermin, call off the names of those who did not refuse duty, and let them go over to the starboard side."

This done, a list was made out of the "mutineers," as he was pleased to call the rest. Among these, the doctor and myself were included; though the former stepped forward, and boldly pleaded the office held by him when the vessel left Sydney. The mate also--who had always been friendly--stated the service rendered by myself two nights previous, as well as my conduct when he announced his intention to enter the harbour. For myself, I stoutly maintained that, according to the tenor of the agreement made with Captain Guy, my time aboard the ship had expired--the cruise being virtually at an end, however it had been brought about--and I claimed my discharge.

But Wilson would hear nothing. Marking something in my manner, nevertheless, he asked my name and country; and then observed with a sneer, "Ah, you are the lad, I see, that wrote the Round Robin; I'll take good care of you, my fine fellow--step back, sir."

As for poor Long Ghost, he denounced him as a "Sydney Flash-Gorger"; though what under heaven he meant by that euphonious title is more than I can tell. Upon this, the doctor gave him such a piece of his mind that the consul furiously commanded him to hold his peace, or he would instantly have him seized into the rigging and flogged. There was no help for either of us--we were judged by the company we kept.

All were now sent forward; not a word being said as to what he intended doing with us.

After a talk with the mate, the consul withdrew, going aboard the French frigate, which lay within a cable's length. We now suspected his object; and since matters had come to this pass, were rejoiced at it. In a day or two the Frenchman was to sail for Valparaiso, the usual place of rendezvous for the English squadron in the Pacific;

and doubtless, Wilson meant to put us on board, and send us thither to be delivered up. Should our conjecture prove correct, all we had to expect, according to our most experienced shipmates, was the fag end of a cruise in one of her majesty's ships, and a discharge before long at Portsmouth.

We now proceeded to put on all the clothes we could--frock over frock, and trousers over trousers--so as to be in readiness for removal at a moment's warning. Armed ships allow nothing superfluous to litter up the deck; and therefore, should we go aboard the frigate, our chests and their contents would have to be left behind.

In an hour's time, the first cutter of the Reine Blanche came alongside, manned by eighteen or twenty sailors, armed with cutlasses and boarding pistols--the officers, of course, wearing their side-arms, and the consul in an official cocked hat borrowed for the occasion. The boat was painted a "pirate black," its crew were a dark, grim-looking set, and the officers uncommonly fierce-looking little Frenchmen. On the whole they were calculated to intimidate--the consul's object, doubtless, in bringing them.

Summoned aft again, everyone's name was called separately; and being solemnly reminded that it was his last chance to escape punishment, was asked if he still refused duty. The response was instantaneous: "Ay, sir, I do." In some cases followed up by divers explanatory observations, cut short by Wilson's ordering the delinquent to the cutter. As a general thing, the order was promptly obeyed--some taking a sequence of hops, skips, and jumps, by way of showing not only their unimpaired activity of body, but their alacrity in complying with all reasonable requests.

Having avowed their resolution not to pull another rope of the Julia's--even if at once restored to perfect health--all the invalids, with the exception of the two to be set ashore, accompanied us into the cutter: They were in high spirits; so much so that something was insinuated about their not having been quite as ill as pretended.

The cooper's name was the last called; we did not hear what he answered, but he stayed behind. Nothing was done about the Mowree.

Shoving clear from the ship, three loud cheers were raised; Flash Jack and others receiving a sharp reprimand for it from the consul.

"Good-bye, Little Jule," cried Navy Bob, as we swept under the bows. "Don't fall overboard, Ropey," said another to the poor landlubber, who, with Wymontoo, the Dane, and others left behind, was looking over at us from the forecastle.

"Give her three more!" cried Salem, springing to his feet and whirling his hat round. "You sacre dam raakeel," shouted the lieutenant of the party, bringing the flat of his sabre across his shoulders, "you now keepy steel."

The doctor and myself, more discreet, sat quietly in the bow of the cutter; and for my own part, though I did not repent what I had done, my reflections were far from being enviable.

CHAPTER XXVIII.

RECEPTION FROM THE FRENCHMAN

IN a few moments, we were paraded in the frigate's gangway; the first lieutenant--an elderly yellow-faced officer, in an ill-cut coat and tarnished gold lace--coming up, and frowning upon us.

This gentleman's head was a mere bald spot; his legs, sticks; in short, his whole physical vigour seemed exhausted in the production of one enormous moustache. Old Gamboge, as he was forthwith christened, now received a paper from the consul; and, opening it, proceeded to compare the goods delivered with the invoice.

After being thoroughly counted, a meek little midshipman was called, and we were soon after given in custody to half-a-dozen sailor-soldiers--fellows with tarpaulins and muskets. Preceded by a pompous functionary (whom we took for one of the ship's corporals, from his ratan and the gold lace on his sleeve), we were now escorted down the ladders to the berth-deck.

Here we were politely handcuffed, all round; the man with the bamboo evincing the utmost solicitude in giving us a good fit from a large basket of the articles of assorted sizes.

Taken by surprise at such an uncivil reception, a few of the party demurred; but all coyness was, at last, overcome; and finally our feet were inserted into heavy anklets of iron, running along a great bar bolted down to the deck. After this, we considered ourselves permanently established in our new quarters.

"The deuce take their old iron!" exclaimed the doctor; "if I'd known this, I'd stayed behind."

"Ha, ha!" cried Flash Jack, "you're in for it, Doctor Long Ghost."

"My hands and feet are, any way," was the reply.

They placed a sentry over us; a great lubber of a fellow, who marched up and down with a dilapidated old cutlass of most extraordinary dimensions. From its length, we had some idea that it was expressly intended to keep a crowd in order--reaching over the heads of half-a-dozen, say, so as to get a cut at somebody behind.

"Mercy!" ejaculated the doctor with a shudder, "what a sensation it must be to be killed by such a tool."

We fasted till night, when one of the boys came along with a couple of "kids" containing a thin, saffron-coloured fluid, with oily particles floating on top. The young wag told us this was soup: it turned out to be nothing more than oleaginous warm water. Such as it was, nevertheless, we were fain to make a meal of it, our sentry being attentive enough to undo our bracelets. The "kids" passed from mouth to mouth, and were soon emptied.

The next morning, when the sentry's back was turned, someone, whom we took for an English sailor, tossed over a few oranges, the rinds of which we afterward used for cups.

On the second day nothing happened worthy of record. On the third, we were amused by the following scene.

A man, whom we supposed a boatswain's mate, from the silver whistle hanging from his neck, came below, driving before him a couple of blubbering boys, and followed by a whole troop of youngsters in tears. The pair, it seemed, were sent down to be punished by command of an officer; the rest had accompanied them out of sympathy.

The boatswain's mate went to work without delay, seizing the poor little culprits by their loose frocks, and using a ratan without mercy. The other boys wept, clasped their hands, and fell on their knees; but in vain; the boatswain's mate only hit out at them; once in a while making them yell ten times louder than ever.

In the midst of the tumult, down comes a midshipman, who, with a great air, orders the man on deck, and running in among the bows, sets them to scampering in all directions.

The whole of this proceeding was regarded with infinite scorn by Navy Bob, who, years before, had been captain of the foretop on board a line-of-battle ship. In his estimation, it was a lubberly piece of business throughout: they did things differently in the English navy.

CHAPTER XXIX.

THE REINE BLANCHE

I CANNOT forbear a brief reflection upon the scene ending the last chapter.

The ratanning of the young culprits, although significant of the imperfect discipline of a French man-of-war, may also be considered as in some measure characteristic of the nation.

In an American or English ship, a boy when flogged is either lashed to the breech of a gun, or brought right up to the gratings, the same way the men are. But as a general rule, he is never punished beyond his strength. You seldom or never draw a cry from the young rogue. He bites his tongue and stands up to it like a hero. If practicable (which is not always the case), he makes a point of smiling under the operation. And so far from his companions taking any compassion on him, they always make merry over his misfortunes. Should he turn baby and cry, they are pretty sure to give him afterward a sly pounding in some dark corner.

This tough training produces its legitimate results. The boy becomes, in time, a thoroughbred tar, equally ready to strip and take a dozen on board his own ship, or, cutlass in hand, dash pell-mell on board the enemy's. Whereas the young Frenchman, as all the world knows, makes but an indifferent seaman; and though, for the most part, he fights well enough, somehow or other he seldom fights well enough to beat.

How few sea-battles have the French ever won! But more: how few ships have they ever carried by the board--that true criterion of naval courage! But not a word against French bravery--there is plenty of it; but not of the right sort. A Yankee's, or an Englishman's, is the downright Waterloo "game." The French fight better on land; and not being essentially a maritime people, they ought to stay there. The best of shipwrights, they are no sailors.

And this carries me back to the Reine Blanche, as noble a specimen of what wood and iron can make as ever floated.

She was a new ship: the present her maiden cruise. The greatest pains having been taken in her construction, she was accounted the "crack" craft in the French navy. She is one of the heavy sixty-gun frigates now in vogue all over the world, and which we Yankees were the first to introduce. In action these are the most murderous vessels ever launched.

The model of the Reine Blanche has all that warlike comeliness only to be seen in a fine fighting ship. Still, there is a good deal of French flummery about her--brass plates and other gewgaws stuck on all over, like baubles on a handsome woman.

Among other things, she carries a stern gallery resting on the uplifted hands of two Caryatides, larger than life. You step out upon this from the commodore's cabin. To behold the rich hangings, and mirrors, and mahogany within, one is almost prepared to see a bevy of ladies trip forth on the balcony for an airing.

But come to tread the gun-deck, and all thoughts like these are put to flight. Such batteries of thunderbolt hurlers! with a sixty-eight-pounder or two thrown in as make-weights. On the spar-deck, also, are carronades of enormous calibre.

Recently built, this vessel, of course, had the benefit of the latest improvements. I was quite amazed to see on what high principles of art some exceedingly simple things were done. But your Gaul is scientific about everything; what other people accomplish by a few hard knocks, he delights in achieving by a complex arrangement of the pulley, lever, and screw.

What demi-semi-quavers in a French air! In exchanging naval courtesies, I have known a French band play "Yankee Doodle" with such a string of variations that no one but a "pretty 'cute" Yankee could tell what they were at.

In the French navy they have no marines; their men, taking turns at carrying the musket, are sailors one moment, and soldiers the next; a fellow running aloft in his line frock to-day, to-morrow stands sentry at the admiral's cabin door. This is fatal to anything like proper sailor pride. To make a man a seaman, he should be put to no other duty. Indeed, a thorough tar is unfit for anything else; and what is more, this fact is the best evidence of his being a true sailor.

On board the Reine Blanche, they did not have enough to eat; and what they did have was not of the right sort. Instead of letting the sailors file their teeth against the rim of a hard sea-biscuit, they baked their bread daily in pitiful little rolls. Then they had no "grog"; as a substitute, they drugged the poor fellows with a thin, sour wine--the juice of a few grapes, perhaps, to a pint of the juice of water-faucets. Moreover, the sailors asked for meat, and they gave them soup; a rascally substitute, as they well knew.

Ever since leaving home, they had been on "short allowance." At the present time, those belonging to the boats--and thus getting an occasional opportunity to run ashore--frequently sold their rations of bread to some less fortunate shipmate for sixfold its real value.

Another thing tending to promote dissatisfaction among the crew was their having such a devil of a fellow for a captain. He was one of those horrid naval bores--a great disciplinarian. In port, he kept them constantly exercising yards and sails, and maneuvering with the boats; and at sea, they were forever at quarters; running in and out the enormous guns, as if their arms were made for nothing else. Then there was the admiral aboard, also; and, no doubt, he too had a paternal eye over them.

In the ordinary routine of duty, we could not but be struck with the listless, slovenly behaviour of these men; there was nothing of the national vivacity in their movements; nothing of the quick precision perceptible on the deck of a thoroughly-disciplined armed vessel.

All this, however, when we came to know the reason, was no matter of surprise; three-fourths of them were pressed men. Some old merchant sailors had been seized the very day they landed from distant voyages; while the landsmen, of whom there were many, had been driven down from the country in herds, and so sent to sea.

At the time, I was quite amazed to hear of press-gangs in a day of comparative peace; but the anomaly is accounted for by the fact that, of late, the French have been building up a great military marine, to take the place of that which Nelson gave to the waves of the sea at Trafalgar. But it is to be hoped that they are not building their ships for the people across the channel to take. In case of a war, what a fluttering of French ensigns there would be!

Though I say the French are no sailors, I am far from seeking to underrate them as a people. They are an ingenious and right gallant nation. And, as an American, I take pride in asserting it.

CHAPTER XXX.

THEY TAKE US ASHORE--WHAT HAPPENED THERE

FIVE days and nights, if I remember right, we were aboard the frigate. On the afternoon of the fifth, we were told that the next morning she sailed for Valparaiso. Rejoiced at this, we prayed for a speedy passage. But, as it turned out, the consul had no idea of letting us off so easily. To our no small surprise, an officer came along toward night, and ordered us out of irons. Being then mustered in the gangway, we were escorted into a cutter alongside, and pulled ashore.

Accosted by Wilson as we struck the beach, he delivered us up to a numerous guard of natives, who at once conducted us to a house near by. Here we were made to sit down under a shade without; and the consul and two elderly European residents passed by us, and entered.

After some delay, during which we were much diverted by the hilarious good-nature of our guard--one of our number was called out for, followed by an order for him to enter the house alone.

On returning a moment after, he told us we had little to encounter. It had simply been asked whether he still continued of the same mind; on replying yes, something was put down upon a piece of paper, and he was waved outside. All being summoned in rotation, my own turn came at last.

Within, Wilson and his two friends were seated magisterially at a table--an inkstand, a pen, and a sheet of paper lending quite a business-like air to the apartment. These three gentlemen, being arrayed in coats and pantaloons, looked respectable, at least in a country where complete suits of garments are so seldom met with. One present essayed a solemn aspect; but having a short neck and full face, only made out to look stupid.

It was this individual who condescended to take a paternal interest in myself. After declaring my resolution with respect to the ship unalterable, I was proceeding to withdraw, in compliance with a sign from the consul, when the stranger turned round to him, saying, "Wait a minute, if you please, Mr. Wilson; let me talk to that youth. Come here, my young friend: I'm extremely sorry to see you associated with these bad men; do you know what it will end in?"

"Oh, that's the lad that wrote the Round Robin," interposed the consul. "He and that rascally doctor are at the bottom of the whole affair--go outside, sir."

I retired as from the presence of royalty; backing out with many bows.

The evident prejudice of Wilson against both the doctor and myself was by no means inexplicable. A man of any education before the mast is always looked upon with dislike by his captain; and, never mind how peaceable he may be, should any disturbance arise, from his intellectual superiority, he is deemed to exert an underhand influence against the officers.

Little as I had seen of Captain Guy, the few glances cast upon me after being on board a week or so were sufficient to reveal his enmity--a feeling quickened by my undisguised companionship with Long Ghost, whom he both feared and cordially hated. Guy's relations with the consul readily explains the latter's hostility.

The examination over, Wilson and his friends advanced to the doorway; when the former, assuming a severe expression, pronounced our perverseness infatuation in the extreme. Nor was there any hope left: our last chance for pardon was gone. Even were we to become contrite and crave permission to return to duty, it would not now be permitted.

"Oh! get along with your gammon, counsellor," exclaimed Black Dan, absolutely indignant that his understanding should be thus insulted.

Quite enraged, Wilson bade him hold his peace; and then, summoning a fat old native to his side, addressed him in Tahitian, giving directions for leading us away to a place of safe keeping.

Hereupon, being marshalled in order, with the old man at our head, we were put in motion, with loud shouts, along a fine pathway, running far on through wide groves of the cocoa-nut and bread-fruit.

The rest of our escort trotted on beside us in high good-humour; jabbering broken English, and in a hundred ways giving us to understand that Wilson was no favourite of theirs, and that we were prime, good fellows for holding out as we did. They seemed to know our whole history.

The scenery around was delightful. The tropical day was fast drawing to a close; and from where we were, the sun looked like a vast red fire burning in the woodlands--its rays falling aslant through the endless ranks of trees, and every leaf fringed with flame. Escaped from the confined decks of the frigate, the air breathed spices to us; streams were heard flowing; green boughs were rocking; and far inland, all sunset flushed, rose the still, steep peaks of the island.

As we proceeded, I was more and more struck by the picturesqueness of the wide, shaded road. In several places, durable bridges of wood were thrown over large water-courses; others were spanned by a single arch of stone. In any part of the road, three horsemen might have ridden abreast.

This beautiful avenue--by far the best thing which civilization has done for the island--is called by foreigners "the Broom Road," though for what reason I do not know. Originally planned for the convenience of the missionaries journeying from one station to another, it almost completely encompasses the larger peninsula; skirting for a distance of at least sixty miles along the low, fertile lands bordering the sea. But on the side next Taiarboo, or the lesser peninsula, it sweeps through a narrow, secluded valley, and thus crosses the island in that direction.

The uninhabited interior, being almost impenetrable from the densely-wooded glens, frightful precipices, and sharp mountain ridges absolutely inaccessible, is but little known, even to the natives themselves; and so, instead of striking directly across from one village to another, they follow the Broom Road round and round.

It is by no means, however, altogether travelled on foot; horses being now quite plentiful. They were introduced from Chili; and possessing all the gaiety, fleetness, and docility of the Spanish breed, are admirably adapted to the tastes of the higher classes, who as equestrians have become very expert. The missionaries and chiefs never think of journeying except in the saddle; and at all hours of the day you see the latter galloping along at full speed. Like the Sandwich Islanders, they ride like Pawnee-Loups.

For miles and miles I have travelled the Broom Road, and never wearied of the continual change of scenery. But wherever it leads you--whether through level woods, across grassy glens, or over hills waving with palms--the bright blue sea on one side, and the green mountain pinnacles on the other, are always in sight.

CHAPTER XXXI.

THE CALABOOZA BERETANEE

ABOUT a mile from the village we came to a halt.

It was a beautiful spot. A mountain stream here flowed at the foot of a verdant slope; on one hand, it murmured along until the waters, spreading themselves upon a beach of small, sparkling shells, trickled into the sea; on the other was a long defile, where the eye pursued a gleaming, sinuous thread, lost in shade and verdure.

The ground next the road was walled in by a low, rude parapet of stones; and, upon the summit of the slope beyond, was a large, native house, the thatch dazzling white, and in shape an oval.

"Calabooza! Calabooza Beretanee!" (the English Jail), cried our conductor, pointing to the building.

For a few months past, having been used by the consul as a house of confinement for his refractory sailors, it was thus styled to distinguish it from similar places in and about Papeetee.

Though extremely romantic in appearance, on a near approach it proved hut ill adapted to domestic comfort. In short, it was a mere shell, recently built, and still unfinished. It was open all round, and tufts of grass were growing here and there under the very roof. The only piece of furniture was the "stocks," a clumsy machine for keeping people in one place, which, I believe, is pretty much out of date in most countries. It is still in use, however, among the Spaniards in South America; from whom, it seems, the Tahitians have borrowed the contrivance, as well as the name by which all places of confinement are known among them.

The stocks were nothing more than two stout timbers, about twenty feet in length, and precisely alike. One was placed edgeways on the ground, and the other, resting on top, left, at regular intervals along the seam, several round holes, the object of which was evident at a glance.

By this time, our guide had informed us that he went by the name of "Capin Bob" (Captain Bob); and a hearty old Bob he proved. It was just the name for him. From the first, so pleased were we with the old man that we cheerfully acquiesced in his authority.

Entering the building, he set us about fetching heaps of dry leaves to spread behind the stocks for a couch. A trunk of a small cocoa-nut tree was then placed for a bolster--rather a hard one, but the natives are used to it. For a pillow, they use a little billet of wood, scooped out, and standing on four short legs--a sort of head-stool.

These arrangements completed, Captain Bob proceeded to "hanna-par," or secure us, for the night. The upper timber of the machine being lifted at one end, and our ankles placed in the semicircular spaces of the lower one, the other beam was then, dropped; both being finally secured together by an old iron hoop at either extremity. This initiation was performed to the boisterous mirth of the natives, and diverted ourselves not a little.

Captain Bob now bustled about, like an old woman seeing the children to bed. A basket of baked "taro," or Indian turnip, was brought in, and we were given a piece all round. Then a great counterpane of coarse, brown "tappa," was stretched over the whole party; and, after sundry injunctions to "moee-moee," and be "maitai"--in other words, to go to sleep, and be good boys--we were left to ourselves, fairly put to bed and tucked in.

Much talk was now had concerning our prospects in life; but the doctor and I, who lay side by side, thinking the occasion better adapted to meditation, kept pretty silent; and, before long, the rest ceased conversing, and, wearied with loss of rest on board the frigate, were soon sound asleep.

After sliding from one reverie into another, I started, and gave the doctor a pinch. He was dreaming, however; and, resolved to follow his example, I troubled him no more.

How the rest managed, I know not; but for my own part, I found it very hard to get to sleep. The consciousness of having one's foot pinned; and the impossibility of getting it anywhere else than just where it was, was most distressing.

But this was not all: there was no way of lying but straight on your back; unless, to be sure, one's limb went round and round in the ankle, like a swivel. Upon getting into a sort of doze, it was no wonder this uneasy posture gave me the nightmare. Under the delusion that I was about some gymnastics or other, I gave my unfortunate member such a twitch that I started up with the idea that someone was dragging the stocks away.

Captain Bob and his friends lived in a little hamlet hard by; and when morning showed in the East, the old gentleman came forth from that direction likewise, emerging from a grove, and saluting us loudly as he approached.

Finding everybody awake, he set us at liberty; and, leading us down to the stream, ordered every man to strip and bathe.

"All han's, my boy, hanna-hanna, wash!" he cried. Bob was a linguist, and had been to sea in his day, as he many a time afterwards told us.

At this moment, we were all alone with him; and it would have been the easiest thing in the world to have given him the slip; but he seemed to have no idea of such a thing; treating us so frankly and cordially, indeed, that even had we thought of running, we should have been ashamed of attempting it. He very well knew, nevertheless (as we ourselves were not slow in finding out), that, for various reasons, any attempt of the kind, without some previously arranged plan for leaving the island, would be certain to fail.

As Bob was a rare one every way, I must give some account of him. There was a good deal of "personal appearance" about him; in short, he was a corpulent giant, over six feet in height, and literally as big round as a hogshead. The enormous bulk of some of the Tahitians has been frequently spoken of by voyagers.

Beside being the English consul's jailer, as it were, he carried on a little Tahitian farming; that is to say, he owned several groves of the bread-fruit and palm, and never hindered their growing. Close by was a "taro" patch of his which he occasionally visited.

Bob seldom disposed of the produce of his lands; it was all needed for domestic consumption. Indeed, for gormandizing, I would have matched him against any three common-council men at a civic feast.

A friend of Bob's told me that, owing to his voraciousness, his visits to other parts of the island were much dreaded; for, according to Tahitian customs, hospitality without charge is enjoined upon everyone; and though it is reciprocal in most cases, in Bob's it was almost out of the question. The damage done to a native larder in one of his morning calls was more than could be made good by his entertainer's spending the holidays with them.

The old man, as I have hinted, had, once upon a time, been a cruise or two in a whaling-vessel; and, therefore, he prided himself upon his English. Having acquired what he knew of it in the forecastle, he talked little else than sailor phrases, which sounded whimsically enough.

I asked him one day how old he was. "Olee?" he exclaimed, looking very profound in consequence of thoroughly understanding so subtile a question--"Oh! very olee--'tousand 'ear--more--big man when Capin Tootee (Captain Cook) heavey in sight." (In sea parlance, came into view.)

This was a thing impossible; but adapting my discourse to the man, I rejoined--"Ah! you see Capin Tootee--well, how you like him?"

"Oh! he maitai: (good) friend of me, and know my wife."

On my assuring him strongly that he could not have been born at the time, he explained himself by saying that he was speaking of his father, all the while. This, indeed, might very well have been.

It is a curious fact that all these people, young and old, will tell

you that they have enjoyed the honour of a personal acquaintance with
the great navigator; and if you listen to them, they will go on and
tell anecdotes without end. This springs from nothing but their great
desire to please; well knowing that a more agreeable topic for a
white man could not be selected. As for the anachronism of the thing,
they seem to have no idea of it: days and years are all the same to
them.

After our sunrise bath, Bob once more placed us in the stocks, almost
moved to tears at subjecting us to so great a hardship; but he could
not treat us otherwise, he said, on pain of the consul's displeasure.
How long we were to be confined, he did not know; nor what was to be
done with us in the end.

As noon advanced, and no signs of a meal were visible, someone
inquired whether we were to be boarded, as well as lodged, at the
Hotel de Calabooza?

"Vast heavey" (avast heaving, or wait a bit)--said Bob--"kow-kow"
(food) "come ship by by."

And, sure enough, along comes Rope Tarn with a wooden bucket of the
Julia's villainous biscuit. With a grin, he said it was a present
from Wilson: it was all we were to get that day. A great cry was now
raised; and well was it for the land-lubber that lie had a pair of
legs, and the men could not use theirs. One and all, we resolved not

to touch the bread, come what come might; and so we told the natives.

Being extravagantly fond of ship-biscuit--the harder the better--they were quite overjoyed; and offered to give us, every day, a small quantity of baked bread-fruit and Indian turnip in exchange for the bread. This we agreed to; and every morning afterward, when the bucket came, its contents were at once handed over to Bob and his friends, who never ceased munching until nightfall.

Our exceedingly frugal meal of bread-fruit over, Captain Bob waddled up to us with a couple of long poles hooked at one end, and several large baskets of woven cocoa-nut branches.

Not far off was an extensive grove of orange-trees in full bearing; and myself and another were selected to go with him, and gather a supply for the party. When we went in among the trees, the sumptuousness of the orchard was unlike anything I had ever seen; while the fragrance shaken from the gently waving boughs regaled our senses most delightfully.

In many places the trees formed a dense shade, spreading overhead a dark, rustling vault, groined with boughs, and studded here and there with the ripened spheres, like gilded balls. In several places, the overladen branches were borne to the earth, hiding the trunk in a tent of foliage. Once fairly in the grove, we could see nothing else; it was oranges all round.

To preserve the fruit from bruising, Bob, hooking the twigs with his pole, let them fall into his basket. But this would not do for us. Seizing hold of a bough, we brought such a shower to the ground that our old friend was fain to run from under. Heedless of remonstrance, we then reclined in the shade, and feasted to our heart's content. Heaping up the baskets afterwards, we returned to our comrades, by whom our arrival was hailed with loud plaudits; and in a marvellously short time, nothing was left of the oranges we brought but the rinds.

While inmates of the Calabooza, we had as much of the fruit as we wanted; and to this cause, and others that might be mentioned, may be ascribed the speedy restoration of our sick to comparative health.

The orange of Tahiti is delicious--small and sweet, with a thin, dry rind. Though now abounding, it was unknown before Cook's time, to whom the natives are indebted for so great a blessing. He likewise introduced several other kinds of fruit; among these were the fig, pineapple, and lemon, now seldom met with. The lime still grows, and some of the poorer natives express the juice to sell to the shipping. It is highly valued as an anti-scorbutic. Nor was the variety of foreign fruits and vegetables which were introduced the only benefit conferred by the first visitors to the Society group. Cattle and sheep were left at various places. More of them anon.

Thus, after all that of late years has been done for these islanders,

Cook and Vancouver may, in one sense at least, be considered their greatest benefactors.

CHAPTER XXXII.

PROCEEDINGS OF THE FRENCH AT TAHITI

AS I happened to arrive at the island at a very interesting period in its political affairs, it may be well to give some little account here of the proceedings of the French, by way of episode to the narrative. My information was obtained at the time from the general reports then rife among the natives, as well as from what I learned upon a subsequent visit, and reliable accounts which I have seen since reaching home.

It seems that for some time back the French had been making repeated ineffectual attempts to plant a Roman Catholic mission here. But, invariably treated with contumely, they sometimes met with open violence; and, in every case, those directly concerned in the enterprise were ultimately forced to depart. In one instance, two priests, Laval and Caset, after enduring a series of persecutions, were set upon by the natives, maltreated, and finally carried aboard a small trading schooner, which eventually put them ashore at Wallis' island--a savage place--some two thousand miles to the westward.

Now, that the resident English missionaries authorized the banishment of these priests is a fact undenied by themselves. I was also repeatedly informed that by their inflammatory harangues they instigated the riots which preceded the sailing of the schooner. At all events, it is certain that their unbounded influence with the natives would easily have enabled them to prevent everything that took place on this occasion, had they felt so inclined.

Melancholy as such an example of intolerance on the part of Protestant missionaries must appear, it is not the only one, and by no means the most flagrant, which might be presented. But I forbear to mention any others; since they have been more than hinted at by recent voyagers, and their repetition here would perhaps be attended with no good effect. Besides, the conduct of the Sandwich Island missionaries in particular has latterly much amended in this respect.

The treatment of the two priests formed the principal ground (and the only justifiable one) upon which Du Petit Thouars demanded satisfaction; and which subsequently led to his seizure of the island. In addition to other things, he also charged that the flag of Merenhout, the consul, had been repeatedly insulted, and the property of a certain French resident violently appropriated by the government. In the latter instance, the natives were perfectly in the right. At that time, the law against the traffic in ardent spirits (every now and then suspended and revived) happened to be in force; and finding a large quantity on the premises of Victor, a low, knavish adventurer from Marseilles, the Tahitians pronounced it forfeit.

For these, and similar alleged outrages, a large pecuniary restitution was demanded (10,000 dollars), which there being no exchequer to supply, the island was forthwith seized, under cover of a mock treaty, dictated to the chiefs on the gun-deck of Du Petit Thouars' frigate.

But, notwithstanding this formality, there seems now little doubt that the downfall of the Pomarees was decided upon at the Tuilleries.

After establishing the Protectorate, so called, the rear-admiral sailed; leaving M. Bruat governor, assisted by Reine and Carpegne, civilians, named members of the Council of Government, and Merenhout, the consul, now made Commissioner Royal. No soldiers, however, were landed until several months afterward. As men, Reine and Carpegne were not disliked by the natives; but Bruat and Merenhout they bitterly detested. In several interviews with the poor queen, the unfeeling governor sought to terrify her into compliance with his demands; clapping his hand upon his sword, shaking his fist in her face, and swearing violently. "Oh, king of a great nation," said Pomaree, in her letter to Louis Philippe, "fetch away this man; I and my people cannot endure his evil doings. He is a shameless man."

Although the excitement among the natives did not wholly subside upon the rear-admiral's departure, no overt act of violence immediately followed. The queen had fled to Imeeo; and the dissensions among the chiefs, together with the ill-advised conduct of the missionaries, prevented a union upon some common plan of resistance. But the great body of the people, as well as their queen, confidently relied upon the speedy interposition of England--a nation bound to them by many ties, and which, more than once, had solemnly guaranteed their independence.

As for the missionaries, they openly defied the French governor, childishly predicting fleets and armies from Britain. But what is the welfare of a spot like Tahiti to the mighty interests of France and England! There was a remonstrance on one side, and a reply on the other; and there the matter rested. For once in their brawling lives, St. George and St. Denis were hand and glove; and they were not going to cross sabres about Tahiti.

During my stay upon the island, so far as I could see, there was little to denote that any change had taken place in the government.

Such laws as they had were administered the same as ever; the missionaries went about unmolested, and comparative tranquillity everywhere prevailed. Nevertheless, I sometimes heard the natives inveighing against the French (no favourites, by the bye, throughout Polynesia), and bitterly regretting that the queen had not, at the outset, made a stand.

In the house of the chief Adeea, frequent discussions took place concerning the ability of the island to cope with the French: the number of fighting men and muskets among the natives were talked of, as well as the propriety of fortifying several heights overlooking Papeetee. Imputing these symptoms to the mere resentment of a recent outrage, and not to any determined spirit of resistance, I little anticipated the gallant, though useless warfare, so soon to follow my departure.

At a period subsequent to my first visit, the island, which before was divided into nineteen districts, with a native chief over each, in capacity of governor and judge, was, by Bruat, divided into four. Over these he set as many recreant chiefs, Kitoti, Tati, Utamai, and Paraita; to whom he paid 1000 dollars each, to secure their assistance in carrying out his evil designs.

The first blood shed, in any regular conflict, was at Mahanar, upon the peninsula of Taraiboo. The fight originated in the seizure of a number of women from the shore by men belonging to one of the French vessels of war. In this affair, the islanders fought desperately, killing about fifty of the enemy, and losing ninety of their own number. The French sailors and marines, who, at the time, were reported to be infuriated with liquor, gave no quarter; and the survivors only saved themselves by fleeing to the mountains. Subsequently, the battles of Hararparpi and Fararar were fought, in which the invaders met with indifferent success.

Shortly after the engagement at Hararparpi, three Frenchmen were waylaid in a pass of the valleys, and murdered by the incensed natives. One was Lefevre, a notorious scoundrel, and a spy, whom Bruat had sent to conduct a certain Major Fergus (said to be a Pole) to the hiding-place of four chiefs, whom the governor wished to seize and execute. This circumstance violently inflamed the hostility of both parties.

About this time, Kitoti, a depraved chief, and the pliant tool of Bruat, was induced by him to give a great feast in the Vale of Paree, to which all his countrymen were invited. The governor's object was to gain over all he could to his interests; he supplied an abundance of wine and brandy, and a scene of bestial intoxication was the natural consequence. Before it came to this, however, several speeches were made by the islanders. One of these, delivered by an aged warrior, who had formerly been at the head of the celebrated Aeorai Society, was characteristic. "This is a very good feast," said the reeling old man, "and the wine also is very good; but you evil-minded Wee-Wees (French), and you false-hearted men of Tahiti, are all very bad."

By the latest accounts, most of the islanders still refuse to submit to the French; and what turn events may hereafter take, it is hard to predict. At any rate, these disorders must accelerate the final extinction of their race.

Along with the few officers left by Du Petit Thouars were several French priests, for whose unobstructed exertions in the dissemination of their faith, the strongest guarantees were provided by an article of the treaty. But no one was bound to offer them facilities; much less a luncheon, the first day they went ashore. True, they had plenty of gold; but to the natives it was anathema--taboo--and, for several hours and some odd minutes, they would not touch it. Emissaries of the Pope and the devil, as the strangers were considered--the smell of sulphur hardly yet shaken out of their canonicals--what islander would venture to jeopardize his soul, and call down a blight on his breadfruit, by holding any intercourse with them! That morning the priests actually picknicked in grove of cocoa-nut trees; but, before night, Christian hospitality--in exchange for a commercial equivalent of hard dollars--was given them in an adjoining house.

Wanting in civility, as the conduct of the English missionaries may be thought, in withholding a decent reception to these persons, the latter were certainly to blame in needlessly placing themselves in so unpleasant a predicament. Under far better auspices, they might have settled upon some one of the thousand unconverted isles of the Pacific, rather than have forced themselves thus upon a people already professedly Christians.

CHAPTER XXXIII.

WE RECEIVE CALLS AT THE HOTEL DE CALABOOZA

OUR place of confinement being open all round, and so near the Broom Road, of course we were in plain sight of everybody passing; and, therefore, we had no lack of visitors among such an idle, inquisitive set as the Tahitians. For a few days, they were coming and going continually; while, thus ignobly fast by the foot, we were fain to give passive audience.

During this period, we were the lions of the neighbourhood; and, no doubt, strangers from the distant villages were taken to see the "Karhowrees" (white men), in the same way that countrymen, in a city, are gallanted to the Zoological Gardens.

All this gave us a fine opportunity of making observations. I was painfully struck by the considerable number of sickly or deformed persons; undoubtedly made so by a virulent complaint, which, under native treatment, almost invariably affects, in the end, the muscles and bones of the body. In particular, there is a distortion of the back, most unsightly to behold, originating in a horrible form of the malady.

Although this, and other bodily afflictions, were unknown before the discovery of the islands by the whites, there are several cases found of the Pa-Fa, or Elephantiasis--a native disease, which seems to have prevailed among them from the earliest antiquity. Affecting the legs and feet alone, it swells them, in some instances, to the girth of a man's body, covering the skin with scales. It might be supposed that one, thus afflicted, would be incapable of walking; but, to all appearance, they seem to be nearly as active as anybody; apparently suffering no pain, and bearing the calamity with a degree of cheerfulness truly marvellous.

The Fa-Fa is very gradual in its approaches, and years elapse before the limb is fully swollen. Its origin is ascribed by the natives to various causes; but the general impression seems to be that it arises, in most cases, from the eating of unripe bread-fruit and Indian turnip. So far as I could find out, it is not hereditary. In no stage do they attempt a cure; the complaint being held incurable.

Speaking of the Fa-Fa reminds me of a poor fellow, a sailor, whom I afterward saw at Roorootoo, a lone island, some two days' sail from Tahiti.

The island is very small, and its inhabitants nearly extinct. We sent a boat off to see whether any yams were to be had, as, formerly, the yams of Roorootoo were as famous among the islands round about, as Sicily oranges in the Mediterranean. Going ashore, to my surprise, I was accosted, near a little shanty of a church, by a white man, who limped forth from a wretched hut. His hair and beard were unshorn, his face deadly pale and haggard, and one limb swelled with the Fa-Fa to an incredible bigness. This was the first instance of a foreigner suffering from it that I had ever seen, or heard of; and the spectacle shocked me accordingly.

He had been there for years. From the first symptoms, he could not believe his complaint to be what it really was, and trusted it would soon disappear. But when it became plain that his only chance for recovery was a speedy change of climate, no ship would receive him as a sailor: to think of being taken as a passenger was idle. This speaks little for the humanity of sea captains; but the truth is that those in the Pacific have little enough of the virtue; and, nowadays, when so many charitable appeals are made to them, they have become callous.

I pitied the poor fellow from the bottom of my heart; but nothing could I do, as our captain was inexorable. "Why," said he, "here we are--started on a six months' cruise--I can't put back; and he is better off on the island than at sea. So on Roorootoo he must die." And probably he did.

I afterwards heard of this melancholy object, from two seamen. His attempts to leave were still unavailing, and his hard fate was fast closing in.

Notwithstanding the physical degeneracy of the Tahitians as a people, among the chiefs, individuals of personable figures are still frequently met with; and, occasionally, majestic-looking men, and diminutive women as lovely as the nymphs who, nearly a century ago, swam round the ships of Wallis. In these instances, Tahitian beauty is quite as seducing as it proved to the crew of the Bounty; the young girls being just such creatures as a poet would picture in the tropics--soft, plump, and dreamy-eyed.

The natural complexion of both sexes is quite light; but the males appear much darker, from their exposure to the sun. A dark complexion, however, in a man, is highly esteemed, as indicating strength of both body and soul. Hence there is a saying, of great antiquity among them.

"If dark the cheek of the mother, The son will sound the war-conch; If strong her frame, he will give laws."

With this idea of manliness, no wonder the Tahitians regarded all pale and tepid-looking Europeans as weak and feminine; whereas, a sailor, with a cheek like the breast of a roast turkey, is held a lad of brawn: to use their own phrase, a "taata tona," or man of bones.

Speaking of bones recalls an ugly custom of theirs, now obsolete--that of making fish-hooks and gimlets out of those of their enemies. This beats the Scandinavians turning people's skulls into cups and saucers.

But to return to the Calabooza Beretanee. Immense was the interest we excited among the throngs that called there; they would stand talking about us by the hour, growing most unnecessarily excited too, and dancing up and down with all the vivacity of their race. They invariably sided with us; flying out against the consul, and denouncing him as "Ita maitai nuee," or very bad exceedingly. They must have borne him some grudge or other.

Nor were the women, sweet souls, at all backward in visiting. Indeed, they manifested even more interest than the men; gazing at us with eyes full of a thousand meanings, and conversing with marvellous rapidity. But, alas! inquisitive though they were, and, doubtless, taking some passing compassion on us, there was little real feeling in them after all, and still less sentimental sympathy. Many of them laughed outright at us, noting only what was ridiculous in our plight.

I think it was the second day of our confinement that a wild, beautiful girl burst into the Calabooza, and, throwing herself into an arch attitude, stood afar off, and gazed at us. She was a heartless one:--tickled to death with Black Dan's nursing his chafed ankle, and indulging in certain moral reflections on the consul and Captain Guy. After laughing her fill at him, she condescended to notice the rest; glancing from one to another in the most methodical and provoking manner imaginable. Whenever anything struck her comically, you saw it like a flash--her finger levelled instantaneously, and, flinging herself back, she gave loose to strange, hollow little notes of laughter, that sounded like the bass of a music-box, playing a lively air with the lid down.

Now, I knew not that there was anything in my own appearance calculated to disarm ridicule; and indeed, to have looked at all heroic, under the circumstances, would have been rather difficult. Still, I could not but feel exceedingly annoyed at the prospect of being screamed at, in turn, by this mischievous young witch, even though she were but an islander. And, to tell a secret, her beauty had something to do with this sort of feeling; and, pinioned as I was to a log, and clad most unbecomingly, I began to grow sentimental.

Ere her glance fell upon me, I had, unconsciously, thrown myself into the most graceful attitude I could assume, leaned my head upon my hand, and summoned up as abstracted an expression as possible. Though my face was averted, I soon felt it flush, and knew that the glance was on me; deeper and deeper grew the flush, and not a sound of laughter.

Delicious thought! she was moved at the sight of me. I could stand it no longer, but started up. Lo! there she was; her great hazel eyes rounding and rounding in her head, like two stars, her whole frame in a merry quiver, and an expression about the mouth that was sudden and violent death to anything like sentiment.

The next moment she spun round, and, bursting from peal to peal of laughter, went racing out of the Calabooza; and, in mercy to me, never returned.

CHAPTER XXXIV.

LIFE AT THE CALABOOZA

A FEW days passed; and, at last, our docility was rewarded by some indulgence on the part of Captain Bob.

He allowed the entire party to be at large during the day; only enjoining upon us always to keep within hail. This, to be sure, was in positive disobedience to Wilson's orders; and so, care had to be taken that he should not hear of it. There was little fear of the natives telling him; but strangers travelling the Broom Road might. By way of precaution, boys were stationed as scouts along the road. At sight of a white man, they sounded the alarm! when we all made for our respective holes (the stocks being purposely left open): the beam then descended, and we were prisoners. As soon as the traveller was out of sight, of course, we were liberated.

Notwithstanding the regular supply of food which we obtained from Captain Bob and his friends, it was so small that we often felt most intolerably hungry. We could not blame them for not bringing us more, for we soon became aware that they had to pinch themselves in order to give us what they did; besides, they received nothing for their kindness but the daily bucket of bread.

Among a people like the Tahitians, what we call "hard times" can only be experienced in the scarcity of edibles; yet, so destitute are many of the common people that this most distressing consequence of civilization may be said, with them, to be ever present. To be sure, the natives about the Calabooza had abundance of limes and oranges; but what were these good for, except to impart a still keener edge to appetites which there was so little else to gratify? During the height of the bread-fruit season, they fare better; but, at other times, the demands of the shipping exhaust the uncultivated resources of the island; and the lands being mostly owned by the chiefs, the inferior orders have to suffer for their cupidity. Deprived of their nets, many of them would starve.

As Captain Bob insensibly remitted his watchfulness, and we began to stroll farther and farther from the Calabooza, we managed, by a systematic foraging upon the country round about, to make up some of our deficiencies. And fortunate it was that the houses of the wealthier natives were just as open to us as those of the most destitute; we were treated as kindly in one as the other.

Once in a while, we came in at the death of a chiefs pig; the noise of whose slaughtering was generally to be heard at a great distance. An occasion like this gathers the neighbours together, and they have a bit of a feast, where a stranger is always welcome. A good loud squeal, therefore, was music in our ears. It showed something going on in that direction.

Breaking in upon the party tumultuously, as we did, we always created a sensation. Sometimes, we found the animal still alive and struggling; in which case, it was generally dropped at our approach.

To provide for these emergencies, Flash Jack generally repaired to the scene of operations with a sheath-knife between his teeth, and a club in his hand. Others were exceedingly officious in singeing off the bristles, and disembowelling. Doctor Long Ghost and myself, however, never meddled with these preliminaries, but came to the feast itself with unimpaired energies.

Like all lank men, my long friend had an appetite of his own. Others occasionally went about seeking what they might devour, but he was always on the alert.

He had an ingenious way of obviating an inconvenience which we all experienced at times. The islanders seldom use salt with their food; so he begged Rope Yarn to bring him some from the ship; also a little pepper, if he could; which, accordingly, was done. This he placed in a small leather wallet--a "monkey bag" (so called by sailors)--usually worn as a purse about the neck.

"In my opinion," said Long Ghost, as he tucked the wallet out of sight, "it behooves a stranger, in Tahiti, to have his knife in readiness, and his castor slung."

CHAPTER XXXV.

VISIT FROM AN OLD ACQUAINTANCE

WE had not been many days ashore, when Doctor Johnson was espied coming along the Broom Road.

We had heard that he meditated a visit, and suspected what he was after. Being upon the consul's hands, all our expenses were of course payable by him in his official capacity; and, therefore, as a friend of Wilson, and sure of good pay, the shore doctor had some idea of allowing us to run up a bill with him. True, it was rather awkward to ask us to take medicines which, on board the ship, he told us were not needed. However, he resolved to put a bold face on the matter, and give us a call.

His approach was announced by one of the scouts, upon which someone suggested that we should let him enter, and then put him in the stocks. But Long Ghost proposed better sport. What it was, we shall presently see.

Very bland and amiable, Doctor Johnson advanced, and, resting his cane on the stocks, glanced to right and left, as we lay before him.
"Well, my lads"--he began--"how do you find yourselves to-day?"

Looking very demure, the men made some rejoinder; and he went on.

"Those poor fellows I saw the other day--the sick, I mean--how are they?" and he scrutinized the company. At last, he singled out one who was assuming a most unearthly appearance, and remarked that he looked as if he were extremely ill. "Yes," said the sailor dolefully, "I'm afeard, doctor, I'll soon be losing the number of my mess!" (a sea phrase, for departing this life) and he closed his eyes, and moaned.

"What does he say?" said Johnson, turning round eagerly.

"Why," exclaimed Flash Jack, who volunteered as interpreter, "he means he's going to croak" (die).

"Croak! and what does that mean, applied to a patient?"

"Oh! I understand," said he, when the word was explained; and he stepped over the stocks, and felt the man's pulse.

"What's his name?" he asked, turning this time to old Navy Bob.

"We calls him Jingling Joe," replied that worthy.

"Well then, men, you must take good care of poor Joseph; and I will send him a powder, which must be taken according to the directions. Some of you know how to read, I presume?"

"That ere young cove does," replied Bob, pointing toward the place where I lay, as if he were directing attention to a sail at sea.

After examining the rest--some of whom were really invalids, but convalescent, and others only pretending to be labouring under divers maladies, Johnson turned round, and addressed the party.

"Men," said he, "if any more of you are ailing, speak up, and let me know. By order of the consul, I'm to call every day; so if any of you are at all sick, it's my duty to prescribe for you. This sudden change from ship fare to shore living plays the deuce with you sailors, so be cautious about eating fruit. Good-day! I'll send you the medicines the first thing in the morning."

Now, I am inclined to suspect that with all his want of understanding, Johnson must have had some idea that we were quizzing him. Still, that was nothing, so long as it answered his purpose; and therefore, if he did see through us, he never showed it.

Sure enough, at the time appointed, along came a native lad with a small basket of cocoa-nut stalks, filled with powders, pill-boxes, and-vials, each with names and directions written in a large, round hand. The sailors, one and all, made a snatch at the collection, under the strange impression that some of the vials were seasoned with spirits. But, asserting his privilege as physician to the first reading of the labels, Doctor Long Ghost was at last permitted to take possession of the basket.

The first thing lighted upon was a large vial, labelled--"For William--rub well in."

This vial certainly had a spirituous smell; and upon handing it to the patient, he made a summary internal application of its contents. The doctor looked aghast.

There was now a mighty commotion. Powders and pills were voted mere drugs in the market, and the holders of vials were pronounced lucky dogs. Johnson must have known enough of sailors to make some of his medicines palatable--this, at least, Long Ghost suspected. Certain it was, everyone took to the vials; if at all spicy, directions were unheeded, their contents all going one road.

The largest one of all, quite a bottle indeed, and having a sort of burnt brandy odour, was labelled--"For Daniel, drink freely, and until relieved." This Black Dan proceeded to do; and would have made an end of it at once, had not the bottle, after a hard struggle, been snatched from his hands, and passed round, like a jovial decanter. The old tar had complained of the effects of an immoderate eating of fruit.

Upon calling the following morning, our physician found his precious row of patients reclining behind the stocks, and doing "as well as could be expected."

But the pills and powders were found to have been perfectly inactive: probably because none had been taken. To make them efficacious, it was suggested that, for the future, a bottle of Pisco should be sent along with them. According to Flash Jack's notions, unmitigated medical compounds were but dry stuff at the best, and needed something good to wash them down.

Thus far, our own M.D., Doctor Long Ghost, after starting the frolic, had taken no further part in it; but on the physician's third visit, he took him to one side, and had a private confabulation. What it was, exactly, we could not tell; but from certain illustrative signs and gestures, I fancied that he was describing the symptoms of some mysterious disorganization of the vitals, which must have come on within the hour. Assisted by his familiarity with medical terms, he seemed to produce a marked impression. At last, Johnson went his way, promising aloud that he would send Long Ghost what he desired.

When the medicine boy came along the following morning, the doctor was the first to accost him, walking off with a small purple vial. This time, there was little else in the basket but a case-bottle of the burnt brandy cordial, which, after much debate, was finally disposed of by someone pouring the contents, little by little, into the half of a cocoa-nut shell, and so giving all who desired a glass. No further medicinal cheer remaining, the men dispersed.

An hour or two passed, when Flash Jack directed attention to my long friend, who, since the medicine boy left, had not been noticed till now. With eyes closed, he was lying behind the stocks, and Jack was lifting his arm and letting it fall as if life were extinct. On running up with the rest, I at once connected the phenomenon with the mysterious vial. Searching his pocket, I found it, and holding it up, it proved to be laudanum. Flash Jack, snatching it from my hand in a rapture, quickly informed all present what it was; and with much glee, proposed a nap for the company. Some of them not comprehending him exactly, the apparently defunct Long Ghost--who lay so still that I a little suspected the genuineness of his sleep--was rolled about as an illustration of the virtues of the vial's contents. The idea tickled everybody mightily; and throwing themselves down, the magic draught was passed from hand to hand. Thinking that, as a matter of course, they must at once become insensible, each man, upon taking his sip, fell back, and closed his eyes.

There was little fear of the result, since the narcotic was equally distributed. But, curious to see how it would operate, I raised myself gently after a while, and looked around. It was about noon, and perfectly still; and as we all daily took the siesta, I was not much surprised to find everyone quiet. Still, in one or two instances, I thought I detected a little peeping.

Presently, I heard a footstep, and saw Doctor Johnson approaching.

And perplexed enough did he look at the sight of his prostrate file of patients, plunged, apparently, in such unaccountable slumbers.

"Daniel," he cried, at last, punching in the side with his cane the individual thus designated--"Daniel, my good fellow, get up! do you hear?"

But Black Dan was immovable; and he poked the next sleeper.

"Joseph, Joseph! come, wake up! it's me, Doctor Johnson."

But Jingling Joe, with mouth open, and eyes shut, was not to be started.

"Bless my soul!" he exclaimed, with uplifted hands and cane, "what's got into 'em? I say, men"--he shouted, running up and down--"come to life, men! what under the sun's the matter with you?" and he struck the stocks, and bawled with increased vigour.

At last he paused, folded his hands over the head of his cane, and steadfastly gazed upon us. The notes of the nasal orchestra were rising and falling upon his ear, and a new idea suggested itself.

"Yes, yes; the rascals must have been getting boozy. Well, it's none of my business--I'll be off;" and off he went.

No sooner was he out of sight, than nearly all started to their feet, and a hearty laugh ensued.

Like myself, most of them had been watching the event from under a sly eyelid. By this time, too, Doctor Long Ghost was as wide awake as anybody. What were his reasons for taking laudanum,--if, indeed, he took any whatever,--is best known to himself; and, as it is neither mine nor the reader's business, we will say no more about it.

CHAPTER XXXVI.

WE ARE CARRIED BEFORE THE CONSUL AND CAPTAIN

WE HAD been inmates of the Calabooza Beretanee about two weeks, when, one morning, Captain Bob, coming from the bath, in a state of utter nudity, brought into the building an armful of old tappa, and began to dress to go out.

The operation was quite simple. The tappa--of the coarsest kind--was in one long, heavy piece; and, fastening one end to a column of Habiscus wood supporting the Calabooza, he went off a few paces, and putting the other about his waist, wound himself right up to the post. This unique costume, in rotundity something like a farthingale, added immensely to his large hulk; so much so that he fairly waddled in his gait. But he was only adhering to the fashion of his fathers; for, in the olden time, the "Kihee," or big girdle, was quite the mode for both sexes. Bob, despising recent innovations, still clung to it. He was a gentleman of the old school--one of the last of the Kihees.

He now told us that he had orders to take us before the consul. Nothing loth, we formed in procession; and, with the old man at our head, sighing and labouring like an engine, and flanked by a guard of some twenty natives, we started for the village.

Arrived at the consular office, we found Wilson there, and four or five Europeans, seated in a row facing us; probably with the view of presenting as judicial an appearance as possible.

On one side was a couch, where Captain Guy reclined. He looked convalescent; and, as we found out, intended soon to go aboard his ship. He said nothing, but left everything to the consul.

The latter now rose, and, drawing forth a paper from a large roll tied with red tape, commenced reading aloud.

It purported to be, "the affidavit of John Jennin, first officer of the British Colonial Barque Julia; Guy, Master;" and proved to be a long statement of matters, from the time of leaving Sydney, down to our arrival in the harbour. Though artfully drawn up so as to bear hard against every one of us, it was pretty correct in the de-. tails; excepting that it was wholly silent as to the manifold derelictions of the mate himself--a fact which imparted unusual significance to the concluding sentence, "And furthermore, this deponent sayeth not."

No comments were made, although we all looked round for the mate to see whether it was possible that he could have authorized this use of his name. But he was not present.

The next document produced was the deposition of the captain himself.

As on all other occasions, however, he had very little to say for himself, and it was soon set aside.

The third affidavit was that of the seamen remaining aboard the vessel, including the traitor Bungs, who, it seemed, had turned ship's evidence. It was an atrocious piece of exaggeration, from beginning to end; and those who signed it could not have known what they were about. Certainly Wymontoo did not, though his mark was there. In vain the consul commanded silence during the reading of this paper; comments were shouted out upon every paragraph.

The affidavits read, Wilson, who, all the while, looked as stiff as a poker, solemnly drew forth the ship's articles from their tin case. This document was a discoloured, musty, bilious-looking affair, and hard to read. When finished, the consul held it up; and, pointing to the marks of the ship's company, at the bottom, asked us, one by one, whether we acknowledged the same for our own.

"What's the use of asking that?" said Black Dan; "Captain Guy there knows as well as we they are."

"Silence, sir!" said Wilson, who, intending to produce a suitable impression by this ridiculous parade, was not a little mortified by the old sailor's bluntness.

A pause of a few moments now ensued; during which the bench of judges communed with Captain Guy, in a low tone, and the sailors canvassed the motives of the consul in having the affidavits taken.

The general idea seemed to be that it was done with a view of "bouncing," or frightening us into submission. Such proved to be the case; for Wilson, rising to his feet again, addressed us as follows:--

"You see, men, that every preparation has been made to send you to Sydney for trial. The Rosa (a small Australian schooner, lying in the harbour) will sail for that place in the course of ten days, at farthest. The Julia sails on a cruise this day week. Do you still refuse duty?"

We did.

Hereupon the consul and captain exchanged glances; and the latter looked bitterly disappointed.

Presently I noticed Guy's eye upon me; and, for the first time, he spoke, and told me to come near. I stepped forward.

"Was it not you that was taken off the island?"

"It was."

"It was you then who owe your life to my humanity. Yet this is the gratitude of a sailor, Mr. Wilson!"

"Not so, sir." And I at once gave him to understand that I was perfectly acquainted with his motives in sending a boat into the bay; his crew was reduced, and he merely wished to procure the sailor whom he expected to find there. The ship was the means of my deliverance, and no thanks to the benevolence of its captain.

Doctor Long Ghost also had a word to say. In two masterly sentences he summed up Captain Guy's character, to the complete satisfaction of every seaman present.

Matters were now growing serious; especially as the sailors became riotous, and talked about taking the consul and the captain back to the Calabooza with them.

The other judges fidgeted, and loudly commanded silence. It was at length restored; when Wilson, for the last time addressing us, said something more about the Rose and Sydney, and concluded by reminding us that a week would elapse ere the Julia sailed.

Leaving these hints to operate for themselves, he dismissed the party, ordering Captain Bob and his friends to escort us back whence we came.

CHAPTER XXXVII.

THE FRENCH PRIESTS PAY THEIR RESPECTS

A DAY or two after the events just related, we were lounging in the Calabooza Beretanee, when we were honoured by a visit from three of the French Priests; and as about the only notice ever taken of us by the English missionaries was their leaving their cards for us, in the shape of a package of tracts, we could not help thinking that the Frenchmen, in making a personal call, were at least much better bred.

By this time they had settled themselves down quite near our habitation. A pleasant little stroll down the Broom Road, and a rustic cross peeped through the trees; and soon you came to as charming a place as one would wish to see: a soft knoll, planted with old breadfruit trees; in front, a savannah, sloping to a grove of palms, and, between these, glimpses of blue, sunny waves.

On the summit of the knoll was a rude chapel, of bamboos; quite small, and surmounted by the cross. Between the canes, at nightfall, the natives stole peeps at a small portable altar; a crucifix to correspond, and gilded candlesticks and censers. Their curiosity carried them no further; nothing could induce them to worship there. Such queer ideas as they entertained of the hated strangers. Masses and chants were nothing more than evil spells. As for the priests themselves, they were no better than diabolical sorcerers; like those who, in old times, terrified their fathers.

Close by the chapel was a range of native houses; rented from a chief, and handsomely furnished. Here lived the priests; and very comfortably, too. They looked sanctimonious enough abroad; but that went for nothing; since, at home, in their retreat, they were a club of Friar Tucks; holding priestly wassail over many a good cup of red brandy, and rising late in the morning.

Pity it was they couldn't marry--pity for the ladies of the island, I mean, and the cause of morality; for what business had the ecclesiastical old bachelors with such a set of trim little native handmaidens? These damsels were their first converts; and devoted ones they were.

The priests, as I have said before, were accounted necromancers: the appearance of two of our three visitors might have justified the conceit.

They were little, dried-up Frenchmen, in long, straight gowns of black cloth, and unsightly three-cornered hats--so preposterously big that, in putting them on, the reverend fathers seemed to extinguish themselves.

Their companion was dressed differently. He wore a sort of yellow, flannel morning gown, and a broad-brimmed Manilla hat. Large and portly, he was also hale and fifty; with a complexion like an autumnal leaf--handsome blue eyes--fine teeth, and a racy Milesian brogue. In short, he was an Irishman; Father Murphy, by name; and, as such, pretty well known, and very thoroughly disliked, throughout all the Protestant missionary settlements in Polynesia. In early youth, he had been sent to a religious seminary in France; and, taking orders there, had but once or twice afterwards revisited his native land.

Father Murphy marched up to us briskly; and the first words he uttered were, to ask whether there were any of his countrymen among us. There were two of them; one, a lad of sixteen--a bright, curly-headed rascal--and, being a young Irishman, of course, his name was Pat. The other was an ugly, and rather melancholy-looking scamp; one M'Gee, whose prospects in life had been blasted by a premature transportation to Sydney. This was the report, at least, though it might have been scandal.

In most of my shipmates were some redeeming qualities; but about M'Gee, there was nothing of the kind; and forced to consort with him, I could not help regretting, a thousand times, that the gallows had been so tardy. As if impelled, against her will, to send him into the world, Nature had done all she could to insure his being taken for what he was. About the eyes there was no mistaking him; with a villainous cast in one, they seemed suspicious of each other.

Glancing away from him at once, the bluff priest rested his gaze on the good-humoured face of Pat, who, with a pleasant roguishness, was "twigging" the enormous hats (or "Hytee Belteezers," as land beavers are called by sailors), from under which, like a couple of snails, peeped the two little Frenchmen.

Pat and the priest were both from the same town in Meath; and, when this was found out, there was no end to the questions of the latter. To him, Pat seemed a letter from home, and said a hundred times as much.

After a long talk between these two, and a little broken English from the Frenchmen, our visitors took leave; but Father Murphy had hardly gone a dozen rods when back he came, inquiring whether we were in want of anything.

"Yes," cried one, "something to eat." Upon this he promised to send us some fresh wheat bread, of his own baking; a great luxury in Tahiti.

We all felicitated Pat upon picking up such a friend, and told him his fortune was made.

The next morning, a French servant of the priest's made his appearance with a small bundle of clothing for our young Hibernian; and the promised bread for the party. Pat being out at the knees and elbows, and, like the rest of us, not full inside, the present was acceptable all round.

In the afternoon, Father Murphy himself came along; and, in addition to his previous gifts, gave Pat a good deal of advice: said he was sorry to see him in limbo, and that he would have a talk with the consul about having him set free.

We saw nothing more of him for two or three days; at the end of which time he paid us another call, telling Pat that Wilson was inexorable, having refused to set him at liberty, unless to go aboard the ship. This, the priest now besought him to do forthwith; and so escape the punishment which, it seems, Wilson had been hinting at to his intercessor. Pat, however, was staunch against entreaties; and, with all the ardour of a sophomorean sailor, protested his intention to hold out to the last. With none of the meekness of a good little boy about him, the blunt youngster stormed away at such a rate that it was hard to pacify him; and the priest said no more.

How it came to pass--whether from Murphy's speaking to the consul, or otherwise, we could not tell--but the next day, Pat was sent for by Wilson, and being escorted to the village by our good old keeper, three days elapsed before he returned.

Bent upon reclaiming him, they had taken him on board the ship; feasted him in the cabin; and, finding that of no avail, down they thrust him into the hold, in double irons, and on bread and water.

All would not do; and so he was sent back to the Calabooza. Boy that he was, they must have counted upon his being more susceptible to discipline than the rest.

The interest felt in Pat's welfare, by his benevolent countryman, was very serviceable to the rest of us; especially as we all turned Catholics, and went to mass every morning, much to Captain Bob's consternation. Upon finding it out, he threatened to keep us in the stocks if we did not desist. He went no farther than this, though; and so, every few days, we strolled down to the priest's residence, and had a mouthful to eat, and something generous to drink. In particular, Dr. Long Ghost and myself became huge favourites with Pat's friend; and many a time he regaled us from a quaint-looking travelling case for spirits, stowed away in one corner of his dwelling. It held four square flasks, which, somehow or other, always contained just enough to need emptying. In truth, the fine old Irishman was a rosy fellow in canonicals. His countenance and his soul were always in a glow. It may be ungenerous to reveal his failings, but he often talked thick, and sometimes was perceptibly eccentric in his gait.

I never drink French brandy but I pledge Father Murphy. His health again! And many jolly proselytes may he make in Polynesia!

CHAPTER XXXVIII.

LITTLE JULIA SAILS WITHOUT US

TO MAKE good the hint thrown out by the consul upon the conclusion of the Farce of the Affidavits, we were again brought before him within the time specified.

It was the same thing over again: he got nothing out of us, and we were remanded; our resolute behaviour annoying him prodigiously.

What we observed led us to form the idea that, on first learning the state of affairs on board the Julia, Wilson must have addressed his invalid friend, the captain, something in the following style:

"Guy, my poor fellow, don't worry yourself now about those rascally sailors of yours. I'll dress them out for you--just leave it all to me, and set your mind at rest."

But handcuffs and stocks, big looks, threats, dark hints, and depositions, had all gone for nought.

Conscious that, as matters now stood, nothing serious could grow out of what had happened; and never dreaming that our being sent home for trial had ever been really thought of, we thoroughly understood Wilson, and laughed at him accordingly.

Since leaving the Julia, we had caught no glimpse of the mate; but we often heard of him.

It seemed that he remained on board, keeping house in the cabin for himself and Viner; who, going to see him according to promise, was induced to remain a guest. These two cronies now had fine times; tapping the captain's quarter-casks, playing cards on the transom, and giving balls of an evening to the ladies ashore. In short, they cut up so many queer capers that the missionaries complained of them to the consul; and Jermin received a sharp reprimand.

This so affected him that he still drank more freely than before; and one afternoon, when mellow as a grape, he took umbrage at a canoe full of natives, who, on being hailed from the deck to come aboard and show their papers, got frightened, and paddled for the shore.

Lowering a boat instantly, he equipped Wymontoo and the Dane with a cutlass apiece, and seizing another himself, off they started in pursuit, the ship's ensign flying in the boat's stern. The alarmed islanders, beaching their canoe, with loud cries fled through the village, the mate after them, slashing his naked weapon to right and left. A crowd soon collected; and the "Karhowree toonee," or crazy stranger, was quickly taken before Wilson.

Now, it so chanced that, in a native house hard by, the consul and

Captain Guy were having a quiet game at cribbage by themselves, a decanter on the table standing sentry. The obstreperous Jermin was brought in; and finding the two thus pleasantly occupied, it had a soothing effect upon him; and he insisted upon taking a hand at the cards, and a drink of the brandy. As the consul was nearly as tipsy as himself, and the captain dared not object for fear of giving offence, at it they went--all three of them--and made a night of it; the mate's delinquencies being summarily passed over, and his captors sent away.

An incident worth relating grew out of this freak.

There wandered about Papeetee, at this time, a shrivelled little fright of an Englishwoman, known among sailors as "Old Mother Tot." From New Zealand to the Sandwich Islands, she had been all over the South Seas; keeping a rude hut of entertainment for mariners, and supplying them with rum and dice. Upon the missionary islands, of course, such conduct was severely punishable; and at various places, Mother Tot's establishment had been shut up, and its proprietor made to quit in the first vessel that could be hired to land her elsewhere. But, with a perseverance invincible, wherever she went she always started afresh; and so became notorious everywhere.

By some wicked spell of hers, a patient, one-eyed little cobbler followed her about, mending shoes for white men, doing the old woman's cooking, and bearing all her abuse without grumbling. Strange to relate, a battered Bible was seldom out of his sight; and whenever he had leisure, and his mistress' back was turned, he was forever poring over it. This pious propensity used to enrage the old crone past belief; and oftentimes she boxed his ears with the book, and tried to burn it. Mother Tot and her man Josy were, indeed, a curious pair.

But to my story.

A week or so after our arrival in the harbour, the old lady had once again been hunted down, and forced for the time to abandon her nefarious calling. This was brought about chiefly by Wilson, who, for some reason unknown, had contracted the most violent hatred for her; which, on her part, was more than reciprocated.

Well: passing, in the evening, where the consul and his party were making merry, she peeped through the bamboos of the house; and straightway resolved to gratify her spite.

The night was very dark; and providing herself with a huge ship's lantern, which usually swung in her hut, she waited till they came forth. This happened about midnight; Wilson making his appearance, supported by two natives, holding him up by the arms. These three went first; and just as they got under a deep shade, a bright light was thrust within an inch of Wilson's nose. The old hag was kneeling before him, holding the lantern with uplifted hands.

"Ha, ha! my fine counsellor," she shrieked; "ye persecute a lone old body like me for selling rum--do ye? And here ye are, carried home drunk--Hoot! ye villain, I scorn ye!" And she spat upon him.

Terrified at the apparition, the poor natives--arrant believers in ghosts--dropped the trembling consul, and fled in all directions. After giving full vent to her rage, Mother Tot hobbled away, and left the three revellers to stagger home the best way they could.

The day following our last interview with Wilson, we learned that Captain Guy had gone on board his vessel for the purpose of shipping a new crew. There was a round bounty offered; and a heavy bag of Spanish dollars, with the Julia's articles ready for signing, were laid on the capstan-head.

Now, there was no lack of idle sailors ashore, mostly "Beachcombers," who had formed themselves into an organized gang, headed by one Mack, a Scotchman, whom they styled the Commodore. By the laws of the fraternity, no member was allowed to ship on board a vessel unless granted permission by the rest. In this way the gang controlled the port, all discharged seamen being forced to join them.

To Mack and his men our story was well known; indeed, they had several times called to see us; and of course, as sailors and congenial spirits, they were hard against Captain Guy.

Deeming the matter important, they came in a body to the Calabooza, and wished to know whether, all things considered, we thought it best for any of them to join the Julia.

Anxious to pack the ship off as soon as possible, we answered, by all means. Some went so far as to laud the Julia to the skies as the best and fastest of ships. Jermin too, as a good fellow, and a sailor every inch, came in for his share of praise; and as for the captain--quiet man, he would never trouble anyone. In short, every inducement we could think of was presented; and Plash Jack ended by assuring the beachcombers solemnly that, now we were all well and hearty, nothing but a regard to principle prevented us from returning on board ourselves.

The result was that a new crew was finally obtained, together with a steady New Englander for second mate, and three good whalemen for harpooners. In part, what was wanting for the ship's larder was also supplied; and as far as could be done in a place like Tahiti, the damages the vessel had sustained were repaired. As for the Mowree, the authorities refusing to let him be put ashore, he was carried to sea in irons, down in the hold. What eventually became of him we never heard.

Ropey, poor poor Ropey, who a few days previous had fallen sick, was left ashore at the sailor hospital at Townor, a small place upon the beach between Papeetee and Matavai. Here, some time after, he breathed his last. No one knew his complaint: he must have died of hard times. Several of us saw him interred in the sand, and I planted a rude post to mark his resting-place.

The cooper, and the rest who had remained aboard from the first, of course, composed part of the Julia's new crew.

To account for the conduct, all along, of the consul and captain, in trying so hard to alter our purpose with respect to the ship, the following statement is all that is requisite. Beside an advance of from fifteen to twenty-five dollars demanded by every sailor shipping at Tahiti, an additional sum for each man so shipped has to be paid into the hands of the government, as a charge of the port. Beside this, the men--with here and there an exception--will only ship for one cruise, thus becoming entitled to a discharge before the vessel reaches home; which, in time, creates the necessity of obtaining other men, at a similar cost. Now, the Julia's exchequer was at low-water mark, or rather, it was quite empty; and to meet these expenses, a good part of what little oil there was aboard had to be sold for a song to a merchant of Papeetee.

It was Sunday in Tahiti and a glorious morning, when Captain Bob, waddling into the Calabooza, startled us by announcing "Ah--my boy--shippy you, harre--maky sail!" In other words, the Julia was off.

The beach was quite near, and in this quarter altogether uninhabited; so down we ran, and, at cable's length, saw little Jule gliding past--top-gallant-sails hoisting, and a boy aloft with one leg thrown over the yard, loosing the fore-royal. The decks were all life and commotion; the sailors on the forecastle singing "Ho, cheerly men!" as they catted the anchor; and the gallant Jennin, bare-headed as his wont, standing up on the bowsprit, and issuing his orders. By the man at the helm stood Captain Guy, very quiet and gentlemanly, and smoking a cigar.

Soon the ship drew near the reef, and, altering her course, glided out through the break, and went on her way.

Thus disappeared little Jule, about three weeks after entering the harbour: and nothing more have I ever heard of her.

CHAPTER XXXIX.

JERMIN SERVES US A GOOD TURN--FRIENDSHIPS IN POLYNESIA

THE ship out of the way, we were quite anxious to know what was going to be done with us. On this head, Captain Bob could tell us nothing; no further, at least, than that he still considered himself responsible for our safe-keeping. However, he never put us to bed any more; and we had everything our own way.

The day after the Julia left, the old man came up to us in great tribulation, saying that the bucket of bread was no longer forthcoming, and that Wilson had refused to send anything in its place. One and all, we took this for a hint to disperse quietly, and go about our business. Nevertheless, we were not to be shaken off so easily; and taking a malicious pleasure in annoying our old enemy, we resolved, for the present, to stay where we were. For the part he had been acting, we learned that the consul was the laughing-stock of all the foreigners ashore, who frequently twitted him upon his hopeful proteges of the Calabooza Beretanee.

As we were wholly without resources, so long as we remained on the island no better place than Captain Bob's could be selected for an abiding-place. Beside, we heartily loved the old gentleman, and could not think of leaving him; so, telling him to give no thought as to wherewithal we should be clothed and fed, we resolved, by extending and systematizing our foraging operations, to provide for ourselves.

We were greatly assisted by a parting legacy of Jermin's. To him we were indebted for having all our chests sent ashore, and everything left therein. They were placed in the custody of a petty chief living near by, who was instructed by the consul not to allow them to be taken away; but we might call and make our toilets whenever we pleased.

We went to see Mahinee, the old chief; Captain Bob going along, and stoutly insisting upon having the chattels delivered up. At last this was done; and in solemn procession the chests were borne by the natives to the Calabooza. Here, we disposed them about quite tastefully; and made such a figure that, in the eyes of old Bob and his friends, the Calabooza Beretanee was by far the most sumptuously furnished saloon in Tahiti.

Indeed, so long as it remained thus furnished, the native courts of the district were held there; the judge, Mahinee, and his associates, sitting upon one of the chests, and the culprits and spectators thrown at full length upon the ground, both inside of the building and under the shade of the trees without; while, leaning over the stocks as from a gallery, the worshipful crew of the Julia looked on, and canvassed the proceedings.

I should have mentioned before that, previous to the vessel's departure, the men had bartered away all the clothing they could possibly spare; but now, it was resolved to be more provident.

The contents of the chests were of the most miscellaneous description:--sewing utensils, marling-spikes, strips of calico, bits of rope, jack-knives; nearly everything, in short, that a seaman could think of. But of wearing apparel, there was little but old frocks, remnants of jackets, and legs of trousers, with now and then the foot of a stocking.

These, however, were far from being valueless; for, among the poorer Tahitians, everything European is highly esteemed. They come from "Beretanee, Fenooa Pararee" (Britain, Land of Wonders), and that is enough.

The chests themselves were deemed exceedingly precious, especially those with unfractured looks, which would absolutely click, and enable the owner to walk off with the key. Scars, however, and bruises, were considered great blemishes. One old fellow, smitten with the doctor's large mahogany chest (a well-filled one, by the bye), and finding infinite satisfaction in merely sitting thereon, was detected in the act of applying a healing ointment to a shocking scratch which impaired the beauty of the lid.

There is no telling the love of a Tahitian for a sailor's trunk. So ornamental is it held as an article of furniture in the hut, that the women are incessantly tormenting their husbands to bestir themselves and make them a present of one. When obtained, no pier-table just placed in a drawing-room is regarded with half the delight. For these reasons, then, our coming into possession of our estate at this time was an important event.

The islanders are much like the rest of the world; and the news of our good fortune brought us troops of "tayos," or friends, eager to form an alliance after the national custom, and do our slightest bidding.

The really curious way in which all the Polynesians are in the habit of making bosom friends at the shortest possible notice is deserving of remark. Although, among a people like the Tahitians, vitiated as they are by sophisticating influences, this custom has in most cases degenerated into a mere mercenary relation, it nevertheless had its origin in a fine, and in some instances, heroic sentiment, formerly entertained by their fathers.

In the annals of the island are examples of extravagant friendships, unsurpassed by the story of Damon and Pythias: in truth, much more wonderful; for, notwithstanding the devotion--even of life in some cases--to which they led, they were frequently entertained at first sight for some stranger from another island.

Filled with love and admiration for the first whites who came among them, the Polynesians could not testify the warmth of their emotions more strongly than by instantaneously making their abrupt proffer of friendship. Hence, in old voyages we read of chiefs coming off from the shore in their canoes, and going through with strange antics, expressive of the desire. In the same way, their inferiors accosted the seamen; and thus the practice has continued in some islands down to the present day.

There is a small place, not many days' sail from Tahiti, and seldom visited by shipping, where the vessel touched to which I then happened to belong.

Of course, among the simple-hearted natives, We had a friend all round. Mine was Poky, a handsome youth, who never could do enough for me. Every morning at sunrise, his canoe came alongside loaded with fruits of all kinds; upon being emptied, it was secured by a line to the bowsprit, under which it lay all day long, ready at any time to carry its owner ashore on an errand.

Seeing him so indefatigable, I told Poky one day that I was a virtuoso in shells and curiosities of all kinds. That was enough; away he paddled for the head of the bay, and I never saw him again for twenty-four hours. The next morning, his canoe came gliding slowly along the shore with the full-leaved bough of a tree for a sail. For the purpose of keeping the things dry, he had also built a sort of platform just behind the prow, railed in with green wicker-work; and here was a heap of yellow bananas and cowree shells; young cocoa-nuts

and antlers of red coral; two or three pieces of carved wood; a
little pocket-idol, black as jet, and rolls of printed tappa.

We were given a holiday; and upon going ashore, Poky, of course, was
my companion and guide. For this, no mortal could be better
qualified; his native country was not large, and he knew every inch
of it. Gallanting me about, everyone was stopped and ceremoniously
introduced to Poty's "tayo karhowree nuee" or his particular white
friend.

He showed me all the lions; but more than all, he took me to see a
charming lioness--a young damsel--the daughter of a chief--the
reputation of whose charms had spread to the neighbouring islands,
and even brought suitors therefrom. Among these was Tooboi, the heir
of Tamatory, King of Eaiatair, one of the Society Isles. The girl was
certainly fair to look upon. Many heavens were in her sunny eyes; and
the outline of that arm of hers, peeping forth from a capricious
tappa robe, was the very curve of beauty.

Though there was no end to Poky's attentions, not a syllable did he
ever breathe of reward; but sometimes he looked very knowing. At last
the day came for sailing, and with it, also, his canoe, loaded down
to the gunwale with a sea stock of fruits. Giving him all I could
spare from my chest, I went on deck to take my place at the windlass;
for the anchor was weighing. Poky followed, and heaved with me at the
same handspike.

The anchor was soon up; and away we went out of the bay with more than twenty shallops towing astern. At last they left us; but long as I could see him at all, there was Poky, standing alone and motionless in the bow of his canoe.

PART II

CHAPTER XL.

WE TAKE UNTO OURSELVES FRIENDS

THE arrival of the chests made my friend, the doctor, by far the wealthiest man of the party. So much the better for me, seeing that I had little or nothing myself; though, from our intimacy, the natives courted my favour almost as much as his.

Among others, Kooloo was a candidate for my friendship; and being a comely youth, quite a buck in his way, I accepted his overtures. By this, I escaped the importunities of the rest; for be it known that, though little inclined to jealousy in love matters, the Tahitian will hear of no rivals in his friendship.

Kooloo, running over his qualifications as a friend, first of all informed me that he was a "Mickonaree," thus declaring his communion with the church.

The way this "tayo" of mine expressed his regard was by assuring me over and over again that the love he bore me was "nuee, nuee, nuee," or infinitesimally extensive. All over these seas, the word "nuee" is significant of quantity. Its repetition is like placing ciphers at the right hand of a numeral; the more places you carry it out to, the greater the sum. Judge, then, of Kooloo's esteem. Nor is the allusion to the ciphers at all inappropriate, seeing that, in themselves, Kooloo's profession turned out to be worthless. He was, alas! as sounding brass and a tinkling cymbal; one of those who make no music unless the clapper be silver.

In the course of a few days, the sailors, like the doctor and myself, were cajoled out of everything, and our "tayos," all round, began to cool off quite sensibly. So remiss did they become in their attentions that we could no longer rely upon their bringing us the daily supply of food, which all of them had faithfully promised.

As for Kooloo, after sponging me well, he one morning played the part of a retrograde lover; informing me that his affections had undergone a change; he had fallen in love at first sight with a smart sailor, who had just stepped ashore quite flush from a lucky whaling-cruise.

It was a touching interview, and with it, our connection dissolved. But the sadness which ensued would soon have been dissipated, had not my sensibilities been wounded by his indelicately sporting some of my gifts very soon after this transfer of his affections. Hardly a day passed that I did not meet him on the Broom Road, airing himself in a regatta shirt which I had given him in happier hours.

He went by with such an easy saunter too, looking me pleasantly in the eye, and merely exchanging the cold salute of the road:--"Yar onor, boyoee," a mere sidewalk how d'ye do. After several experiences like this, I began to entertain a sort of respect for Kooloo, as quite a man of the world. In good sooth, he turned out to be one; in one week's time giving me the cut direct, and lounging by without even nodding. He must have taken me for part of the landscape.

Before the chests were quite empty, we had a grand washing in the stream of our best raiment, for the purpose of looking tidy, and visiting the European chapel in the village. Every Sunday morning it is open for divine service, some member of the mission officiating. This was the first time we ever entered Papeetee unattended by an escort.

In the chapel there were about forty people present, including the officers of several ships in harbour. It was an energetic discourse, and the pulpit cushion was well pounded. Occupying a high seat in the synagogue, and stiff as a flagstaff, was our beloved guardian, Wilson. I shall never forget his look of wonder when his interesting wards filed in at the doorway, and took up a seat directly facing him.

Service over, we waited outside in hopes of seeing more of him; but sorely annoyed at the sight of us, he reconnoitred from the window, and never came forth until we had started for home.

CHAPTER XLI.

WE LEVY CONTRIBUTIONS ON THE SHIPPING

SCARCELY a week went by after the Julia's sailing, when, with the proverbial restlessness of sailors, some of the men began to grow weary of the Calabooza Beretanee, and resolved to go boldly among the vessels in the bay, and offer to ship.

The thing was tried; but though strongly recommended by the commodore of the beachcombers, in the end they were invariably told by the captains to whom they applied that they bore an equivocal character ashore, and would not answer. So often were they repulsed that we pretty nearly gave up all thoughts of leaving the island in this way; and growing domestic again, settled down quietly at Captain Bob's.

It was about this time that the whaling-ships, which have their regular seasons for cruising, began to arrive at Papeetee; and of course their crews frequently visited us. This is customary all over the Pacific. No sailor steps ashore, but he straightway goes to the "Calabooza," where he is almost sure to find some poor fellow or other in confinement for desertion, or alleged mutiny, or something of that sort. Sympathy is proffered, and if need be, tobacco. The latter, however, is most in request; as a solace to the captive, it is invaluable.

Having fairly carried the day against both consul and captain, we were objects of even more than ordinary interest to these philanthropists; and they always cordially applauded our conduct. Besides, they invariably brought along something in the way of refreshments; occasionally smuggling in a little Pisco. Upon one occasion, when there was quite a number present, a calabash was passed round, and a pecuniary collection taken up for our benefit.

One day a newcomer proposed that two or three of us should pay him a sly, nocturnal visit aboard his ship; engaging to send us away well freighted with provisions. This was not a bad idea; nor were we at all backward in acting upon it. Right after night every vessel in the harbour was visited in rotation, the foragers borrowing Captain Bob's canoe for the purpose. As we all took turns at this--two by two--in due course it came to Long Ghost and myself, for the sailors invariably linked us together. In such an enterprise, I somewhat distrusted the doctor, for he was no sailor, and very tall; and a canoe is the most ticklish of navigable things. However, it could not be helped; and so we went.

But a word about the canoes before we go any further. Among the Society Islands, the art of building them, like all native accomplishments, has greatly deteriorated; and they are now the most inelegant, as well as the most insecure of any in the South Seas. In Cook's time, according to his account, there was at Tahiti a royal fleet of seventeen hundred and twenty large war canoes, handsomely carved, and otherwise adorned. At present, those used are quite small; nothing more than logs hollowed out, sharpened at one end, and then launched into the water.

To obviate a certain rolling propensity, the Tahitians, like all Polynesians, attach to them what sailors call an "outrigger." It consists of a pole floating alongside, parallel to the canoe, and connected with it by a couple of cross sticks, a yard or more in length. Thus equipped, the canoe cannot be overturned, unless you overcome the buoyancy of the pole, or lift it entirely out of the water.

Now, Captain Bob's "gig" was exceedingly small; so small, and of such a grotesque shape, that the sailors christened it the Pill Box; and by this appellation it always went. In fact, it was a sort of "sulky," meant for a solitary paddler, but, on an emergency, capable of floating two or three. The outrigger was a mere switch, alternately rising in air, and then depressed in the water.

Assuming the command of the expedition, upon the strength of my being a sailor, I packed the Long Doctor with a paddle in the bow, and then shoving off, leaped into the stern; thus leaving him to do all the work, and reserving to myself the dignified sinecure of steering. All would have gone on well, were it not that my paddler made such clumsy work that the water spattered, and showered down upon us without ceasing. Continuing to ply his tool, however, quite energetically, I thought he would improve after a while, and so let him alone. But by and bye, getting wet through with this little storm we were raising, and seeing no signs of its clearing off, I conjured him, in mercy's name, to stop short, and let me wring myself out. Upon this, he suddenly turned round, when the canoe gave a roll, the outrigger flew overhead, and the next moment came rap on the doctor's skull, and we were both in the water.

Fortunately, we were just over a ledge of coral, not half-a-fathom under the surface. Depressing one end of the filled canoe, and letting go of it quickly, it bounced up, and discharged a great part of its contents; so that we easily baled out the remainder, and again embarked. This time, my comrade coiled himself away in a very small space; and enjoining upon him not to draw a single unnecessary breath, I proceeded to urge the canoe along by myself. I was astonished at his docility, never speaking a word, and stirring neither hand nor foot; but the secret was, he was unable to swim, and in case we met with a second mishap, there were no more ledges beneath to stand upon. "Crowning's but a shabby way of going out of the world," he exclaimed, upon my rallying him; "and I'm not going to be guilty of it."

At last, the ship was at hand, and we approached with much caution, wishing to avoid being hailed by anyone from the quarter-deck. Dropping silently under her bows, we heard a low whistle--the signal agreed upon--and presently a goodly-sized bag was lowered over to us.

We cut the line, and then paddled away as fast as we could, and made the best of our way home. Here, we found the rest waiting impatiently.

The bag turned out to be well filled with sweet potatoes boiled, cubes of salt beef and pork, and a famous sailors' pudding, what they call "duff," made of flour and water, and of about the consistence of an underdone brick. With these delicacies, and keen appetites, we went out into the moonlight, and had a nocturnal picnic.

CHAPTER XLII.

MOTOO-OTOO A TAHITIAN CASUIST

THE Pill Box was sometimes employed for other purposes than that described in the last chapter. We sometimes went a-pleasuring in it.

Right in the middle of Papeetee harbour is a bright, green island, one circular grove of waving palms, and scarcely a hundred yards across. It is of coral formation; and all round, for many rods out, the bay is so shallow that you might wade anywhere. Down in these waters, as transparent as air, you see coral plants of every hue and shape imaginable:--antlers, tufts of azure, waving reeds like stalks of grain, and pale green buds and mosses. In some places, you look through prickly branches down to a snow-white floor of sand, sprouting with flinty bulbs; and crawling among these are strange shapes:--some bristling with spikes, others clad in shining coats of mail, and here and there, round forms all spangled with eyes.

The island is called Hotoo-Otoo; and around Hotoo-Otoo have I often paddled of a white moonlight night, pausing now and then to admire the marine gardens beneath.

The place is the private property of the queen, who has a residence there--a melancholy-looking range of bamboo houses--neglected and falling to decay among the trees.

Commanding the harbour as it does, her majesty has done all she could to make a fortress of the island. The margin has been raised and levelled, and built up with a low parapet of hewn Hocks of coral. Behind the parapet are ranged, at wide intervals, a number of rusty old cannon, of all fashions and calibres. They are mounted upon lame, decrepit-looking carriages, ready to sink under the useless burden of bearing them up. Indeed, two or three have given up the ghost altogether, and the pieces they sustained lie half buried among their bleaching bones. Several of the cannon are spiked; probably with a view of making them more formidable; as they certainly must be to anyone undertaking to fire them off.

Presented to Pomaree at various times by captains of British armed ships, these poor old "dogs of war," thus toothless and turned out to die, formerly bayed in full pack as the battle-hounds of Old England.

There was something about Hotoo-Otoo that struck my fancy; and I registered a vow to plant my foot upon its soil, notwithstanding an old bareheaded sentry menaced me in the moonlight with an unsightly musket. As my canoe drew scarcely three inches of water, I could paddle close up to the parapet without grounding; but every time I came near, the old man ran toward me, pushing his piece forward, but never clapping it to his shoulder. Thinking he only meant to frighten me, I at last dashed the canoe right Up to the wall, purposing a leap. It was the rashest act of my life; for never did cocoa-nut come nearer getting demolished than mine did then. With the stock of his gun, the old warder fetched a tremendous blow, which I managed to dodge; and then falling back, succeeded in paddling out of harm's reach.

He must have been dumb; for never a word did he utter; but grinning from ear to ear, and with his white cotton robe streaming in the moonlight, he looked more like the spook of the island than anything mortal.

I tried to effect my object by attacking him in the rear--but he was all front; running about the place as I paddled, and presenting his confounded musket wherever I went. At last I was obliged to retreat; and to this day my vow remains unfulfilled.

It was a few days after my repulse from before the walls of Hotoo-Otoo that I heard a curious case of casuistry argued between one of the most clever and intelligent natives I ever saw in Tahiti, a man by the name of Arheetoo, and our learned Theban of a doctor.

It was this:--whether it was right and lawful for anyone, being a native, to keep the European Sabbath, in preference to the day set apart as such by the missionaries, and so considered by the islanders in general.

It must be known that the missionaries of the good ship Duff, who more than half-a-century ago established the Tahitian reckoning, came hither by the way of the Cape of Good Hope; and by thus sailing to the eastward, lost one precious day of their lives all round, getting about that much in advance of Greenwich time. For this reason, vessels coming round Cape Horn--as they most all do nowadays--find it Sunday in Tahiti, when, according to their own view of the matter, it ought to be Saturday. But as it won't do to alter the log, the sailors keep their Sabbath, and the islanders theirs.

This confusion perplexes the poor natives mightily; and it is to no purpose that you endeavour to explain so incomprehensible a phenomenon. I once saw a worthy old missionary essay to shed some light on the subject; and though I understood but a few of the words employed, I could easily get at the meaning of his illustrations. They were something like the following:

"Here," says he, "you see this circle" (describing a large one on the ground with a stick); "very good; now you see this spot here" (marking a point in the perimeter): "well; this is Beretanee (England), and I'm going to sail round to Tahiti. Here I go, then (following the circle round), and there goes the sun (snatching up another stick, and commissioning a bandy-legged native to travel round with it in a contrary direction). Now then, we are both off, and both going away from each other; and here you see I have arrived at Tahiti (making a sudden stop); and look now where Bandy Legs is!"

But the crowd strenuously maintained that Bandy Legs ought to be somewhere above them in the atmosphere; for it was a traditionary fact that the people from the Duff came ashore when the sun was high overhead. And here the old gentleman, being a very good sort of man, doubtless, but no astronomer, was obliged to give up.

Arheetoo, the casuist alluded to, though a member of the church, and extremely conscientious about what Sabbath he kept, was more liberal in other matters. Learning that I was something of a "mick-onaree" (in this sense, a man able to read, and cunning in the use of the pen), he desired the slight favour of my forging for him a set of papers; for which, he said, he would be much obliged, and give me a good dinner of roast pig and Indian turnip in the bargain.

Now, Arheetoo was one of those who board the shipping for their washing; and the competition being very great (the proudest chiefs not disdaining to solicit custom in person, though the work is done by their dependants), he had decided upon a course suggested by a knowing sailor, a friend of his. He wished to have manufactured a set of certificates, purporting to come from certain man-of-war and merchant captains, known to have visited the island; recommending him as one of the best getters up of fine linen in all Polynesia.

At this time, Arheetoo had known me but two hours; and, as he made the proposition very coolly, I thought it rather presumptuous, and told him so. But as it was quite impossible to convey a hint, and there was a slight impropriety in the thing, I did not resent the insult, but simply declined.

CHAPTER XLIII.

ONE IS JUDGED BY THE COMPANY HE KEEPS

ALTHOUGH, from its novelty, life at Captain Bob's was pleasant enough, for the time; there were some few annoyances connected with it anything but agreeable to a "soul of sensibility."

Prejudiced against us by the malevolent representations of the consul and others, many worthy foreigners ashore regarded us as a set of lawless vagabonds; though, truth to speak, better behaved sailors never stepped on the island, nor any who gave less trouble to the natives. But, for all this, whenever we met a respectably-dressed European, ten to one he shunned us by going over to the other side of the road. This was very unpleasant, at least to myself; though, certes, it did not prey upon the minds of the others.

To give an instance.

Of a fine evening in Tahiti--but they are all fine evenings there--you may see a bevy of silk bonnets and parasols passing along the Broom Road: perhaps a band of pale, little white urchins--sickly exotics--and, oftener still, sedate, elderly gentlemen, with canes; at whose appearance the natives, here and there, slink into their huts. These are the missionaries, their wives, and children, taking a family airing. Sometimes, by the bye, they take horse, and ride down to Point Venus and back; a distance of several miles. At this place is settled the only survivor of the first missionaries that landed--an old, white-headed, saint-like man, by the name of Wilson, the father of our friend, the consul.

The little parties on foot were frequently encountered; and, recalling, as they did, so many pleasant recollections of home and the ladies, I really longed for a dress coat and beaver that I might step up and pay my respects. But, situated as I was, this was out of the question. On one occasion, however, I received a kind, inquisitive glance from a matron in gingham. Sweet lady! I have not forgotten her: her gown was a plaid.

But a glance, like hers, was not always bestowed.

One evening, passing the verandah of a missionary's dwelling, the dame, his wife, and a pretty, blonde young girl, with ringlets, were sitting there, enjoying the sea-breeze, then coming in, all cool and refreshing, from the spray of the reef. As I approached, the old lady peered hard at me; and her very cap seemed to convey a prim rebuke. The blue, English eyes, by her side, were also bent on me. But, oh Heavens! what a glance to receive from such a beautiful creature! As for the mob cap, not a fig did I care for it; but, to be taken for anything but a cavalier, by the ringleted one, was absolutely unendurable.

I resolved on a courteous salute, to show my good-breeding, if nothing more. But, happening to wear a sort of turban--hereafter to be particularly alluded to--there was no taking it off and putting it on again with anything like dignity. At any rate, then, here goes a bow. But, another difficulty presented itself; my loose frock was so voluminous that I doubted whether any spinal curvature would be perceptible.

"Good evening, ladies," exclaimed I, at last, advancing winningly; "a delightful air from the sea, ladies."

Hysterics and hartshorn! who would have thought it? The young lady screamed, and the old one came near fainting. As for myself, I retreated in double-quick time; and scarcely drew breath until safely housed in the Calabooza.

CHAPTER XLIV.

CATHEDRAL OF PAPOAR--THE CHURCH OF THE COCOA-NUTS

ON Sundays I always attended the principal native church, on the outskirts of the village of Papeetee, and not far from the Calabooza Beretanee. It was esteemed the best specimen of architecture in Tahiti.

Of late, they have built their places of worship with more reference to durability than formerly. At one time, there were no less than thirty-six on the island--mere barns, tied together with thongs, which went to destruction in a very few years.

One, built many years ago in this style, was a most remarkable structure. It was erected by Pomaree II., who, on this occasion, showed all the zeal of a royal proselyte. The building was over seven hundred feet in length, and of a proportionate width; the vast ridge-pole was at intervals supported by a row of thirty-six cylindrical trunks of the bread-fruit tree; and, all round, the wall-plates rested on shafts of the palm. The roof--steeply inclining to within a man's height of the ground--was thatched with leaves, and the sides of the edifice were open. Thus spacious was the Royal Mission Chapel of Papoar.

At its dedication, three distinct sermons were, from different pulpits, preached to an immense concourse gathered from all parts of the island.

As the chapel was built by the king's command, nearly as great a multitude was employed in its construction as swarmed over the scaffolding of the great temple of the Jews. Much less time, however, was expended. In less than three weeks from planting the first post, the last tier of palmetto-leaves drooped from the eaves, and the work was done.

Apportioned to the several chiefs and their dependants, the labour, though immense, was greatly facilitated by everyone's bringing his post, or his rafter, or his pole strung with thatching, ready for instant use. The materials thus prepared being afterwards secured together by thongs, there was literally "neither hammer, nor axe, nor any tool of iron heard in the house while it was building."

But the most singular circumstance connected with this South Sea cathedral remains to be related. As well for the beauty as the advantages of such a site, the islanders love to dwell near the mountain streams; and so, a considerable brook, after descending from the hills and watering the valley, was bridged over in three places, and swept clean through the chapel.

Flowing waters! what an accompaniment to the songs of the sanctuary; mingling with them the praises and thanksgivings of the green solitudes inland.

But the chapel of the Polynesian Solomon has long since been deserted. Its thousand rafters of habiscus have decayed, and fallen to the ground; and now, the stream murmurs over them in its bed.

The present metropolitan church of Tahiti is very unlike the one just described. It is of moderate dimensions, boarded over, and painted white. It is furnished also with blinds, but no sashes; indeed, were it not for the rustic thatch, it would remind one of a plain chapel at home.

The woodwork was all done by foreign carpenters, of whom there are always several about Papeetee.

Within, its aspect is unique, and cannot fail to interest a stranger. The rafters overhead are bound round with fine matting of variegated dyes; and all along the ridge-pole these trappings hang pendent, in alternate bunches of tassels and deep fringes of stained grass. The floor is composed of rude planks. Regular aisles run between ranges of native settees, bottomed with crossed braids of the cocoa-nut fibre, and furnished with backs.

But the pulpit, made of a dark, lustrous wood, and standing at one end, is by far the most striking object. It is preposterously lofty; indeed, a capital bird's-eye view of the congregation ought to be had from its summit.

Nor does the church lack a gallery, which runs round on three sides, and is supported by columns of the cocoa-nut tree.

Its facings are here and there daubed over with a tawdry blue; and in other places (without the slightest regard to uniformity), patches of the same colour may be seen. In their ardour to decorate the sanctuary, the converts must have borrowed each a brush full of paint, and zealously daubed away at the first surface that offered.

As hinted, the general impression is extremely curious. Little light being admitted, and everything being of a dark colour, there is an indefinable Indian aspect of duskiness throughout. A strange, woody smell, also--more or less pervading every considerable edifice in Polynesia--is at once perceptible. It suggests the idea of worm-eaten idols packed away in some old lumber-room at hand.

For the most part, the congregation attending this church is composed of the better and wealthier orders--the chiefs and their retainers; in short, the rank and fashion of the island. This class is infinitely superior in personal beauty and general healthfulness to the "marenhoar," or common people; the latter having been more exposed to the worst and most debasing evils of foreign intercourse. On Sundays, the former are invariably arrayed in their finery; and thus appear to the best advantage. Nor are they driven to the chapel, as some of their inferiors are to other places of worship; on the contrary, capable of maintaining a handsome exterior, and possessing greater intelligence, they go voluntarily.

In respect of the woodland colonnade supporting its galleries, I called this chapel the Church of the Cocoa-nuts.

It was the first place for Christian worship in Polynesia that I had seen; and the impression upon entering during service was all the stronger. Majestic-looking chiefs whose fathers had hurled the battle-club, and old men who had seen sacrifices smoking upon the altars of Oro, were there. And hark! hanging from the bough of a bread-fruit tree without, a bell is being struck with a bar of iron by a native lad. In the same spot, the blast of the war-conch had often resounded. But to the proceedings within.

The place is well filled. Everywhere meets the eye the gay calico draperies worn on great occasions by the higher classes, and forming a strange contrast of patterns and colours. In some instances, these are so fashioned as to resemble as much as possible European garments. This is in excessively bad taste. Coats and pantaloons, too, are here and there seen; but they look awkwardly enough, and take away from the general effect.

But it is the array of countenances that most strikes you. Each is suffused with the peculiar animation of the Polynesians, when thus collected in large numbers. Every robe is rustling, every limb in motion, and an incessant buzzing going on throughout the assembly. The tumult is so great that the voice of the placid old missionary, who now rises, is almost inaudible. Some degree of silence is at length obtained through the exertions of half-a-dozen strapping fellows, in white shirts and no pantaloons. Running in among the settees, they are at great pains to inculcate the impropriety of making a noise by creating a most unnecessary racket themselves. This part of the service was quite comical.

There is a most interesting Sabbath School connected with the church; and the scholars, a vivacious, mischievous set, were in one part of the gallery. I was amused by a party in a corner. The teacher sat at one end of the bench, with a meek little fellow by his side. When the others were disorderly, this young martyr received a rap; intended, probably, as a sample of what the rest might expect, if they didn't amend.

Standing in the body of the church, and leaning against a pillar, was an old man, in appearance very different from others of his countrymen. He wore nothing but a coarse, scant mantle of faded tappa; and from his staring, bewildered manner, I set him down as an aged bumpkin from the interior, unaccustomed to the strange sights and sounds of the metropolis. This old worthy was sharply reprimanded for standing up, and thus intercepting the view of those behind; but not comprehending exactly what was said to him, one of the white-liveried gentry made no ceremony of grasping him by the shoulders, and fairly crushing him down into a seat.

During all this, the old missionary in the pulpit--as well as his associates beneath, never ventured to interfere--leaving everything to native management. With South Sea islanders, assembled in any numbers, there is no other way of getting along.

CHAPTER XLV.

MISSIONARY'S SERMON; WITH SOME REFLECTIONS

SOME degree of order at length restored, the service was continued, by singing. The choir was composed of twelve or fifteen ladies of the mission, occupying a long bench to the left of the pulpit. Almost the entire congregation joined in.

The first air fairly startled me; it was the brave tune of Old Hundred, adapted to a Tahitian psalm. After the graceless scenes I had recently passed through, this circumstance, with all its accessories, moved me forcibly.

Many voices around were of great sweetness and compass. The singers, also, seemed to enjoy themselves mightily; some of them pausing, now and then, and looking round, as if to realize the scene more fully. In truth, they sang right joyously, despite the solemnity of the tune.

The Tahitians have much natural talent for singing; and, on all occasions, are exceedingly fond of it. I have often heard a stave or two of psalmody, hummed over by rakish young fellows, like a snatch from an opera.

With respect to singing, as in most other matters, the Tahitians widely differ from the people of the Sandwich Islands; where the parochial flocks may be said rather to Heat than sing.

The psalm concluded, a prayer followed. Very considerately, the good old missionary made it short; for the congregation became fidgety and inattentive as soon as it commenced.

A chapter of the Tahitian Bible was now read; a text selected; and the sermon began. It was listened to with more attention than I had anticipated.

Having been informed, from various sources, that the discourses of the missionaries, being calculated to engage the attention of their simple auditors, were, naturally enough, of a rather amusing description to strangers; in short, that they had much to say about steamboats, lord mayor's coaches, and the way fires are put out in London, I had taken care to provide myself with a good interpreter, in the person of an intelligent Hawaiian sailor, whose acquaintance I had made.

"Now, Jack," said I, before entering, "hear every word, and tell me what you can as the missionary goes on."

Jack's was not, perhaps, a critical version of the discourse; and at the time, I took no notes of what he said. Nevertheless, I will here venture to give what I remember of it; and, as far as possible, in

Jack's phraseology, so as to lose nothing by a double translation.

"Good friends, I glad to see you; and I very well like to have some talk with you to-day. Good friends, very bad times in Tahiti; it make me weep. Pomaree is gone--the island no more yours, but the Wee-wees' (French). Wicked priests here, too; and wicked idols in woman's clothes, and brass chains.

"Good friends, no you speak, or look at them--but I know you won't--they belong to a set of robbers--the wicked Wee-wees. Soon these bad men be made to go very quick. Beretanee ships of thunder come and away they go. But no more 'bout this now. I speak more by by.

"Good friends, many whale-ships here now; and many bad men come in 'em. No good sailors living--that you know very well. They come here, 'cause so bad they no keep 'em home.

"My good little girls, no run after sailors--no go where they go; they harm you. Where they come from, no good people talk to 'em--just like dogs. Here, they talk to Pomaree, and drink arva with great Poofai.

"Good friends, this very small island, but very wicked, and very poor; these two go together. Why Beretanee so great? Because that island good island, and send mickonaree to poor kannaka In Beretanee, every man rich: plenty things to buy; and plenty things to sell. Houses bigger than Pomaree's, and more grand. Everybody, too, ride about in coaches, bigger than hers; and wear fine tappa every day. (Several luxurious appliances of civilization were here enumerated, and described.)

"Good friends, little to eat left at my house. Schooner from Sydney no bring bag of flour: and kannaka no bring pig and fruit enough. Mickonaree do great deal for kannaka; kannaka do little for mickonaree. So, good friends, weave plenty of cocoa-nut baskets, fill 'em, and bring 'em to-morrow."

Such was the substance of great part of this discourse; and, whatever may be thought of it, it was specially adapted to the minds of the islanders: who are susceptible to no impressions, except from things palpable, or novel and striking. To them, a dry sermon would be dry indeed.

The Tahitians can hardly ever be said to reflect: they are all impulse; and so, instead of expounding dogmas, the missionaries give them the large type, pleasing cuts, and short and easy lessons of the primer. Hence, anything like a permanent religious impression is seldom or never produced.

In fact, there is, perhaps, no race upon earth, less disposed, by nature, to the monitions of Christianity, than the people of the South Seas. And this assertion is made with full knowledge of what is called the "Great Revival at the Sandwich Islands," about the year

1836; when several thousands were, in the course of a few weeks, admitted into the bosom of the Church. But this result was brought about by no sober moral convictions; as an almost instantaneous relapse into every kind of licentiousness soon after testified. It was the legitimate effect of a morbid feeling, engendered by the sense of severe physical wants, preying upon minds excessively prone to superstition; and, by fanatical preaching, inflamed into the belief that the gods of the missionaries were taking vengeance upon the wickedness of the land.

It is a noteworthy fact that those very traits in the Tahitians, which induced the London Missionary Society to regard them as the most promising subjects for conversion, and which led, moreover, to the selection of their island as the very first field for missionary labour, eventually proved the most serious obstruction. An air of softness in their manners, great apparent ingenuousness and docility, at first misled; but these were the mere accompaniments of an indolence, bodily and mental; a constitutional voluptuousness; and an aversion to the least restraint; which, however fitted for the luxurious state of nature, in the tropics, are the greatest possible hindrances to the strict moralities of Christianity.

Added to all this is a quality inherent in Polynesians; and more akin to hypocrisy than anything else. It leads them to assume the most passionate interest in matters for which they really feel little or none whatever; but in which, those whose power they dread, or whose favour they court, they believe to be at all affected. Thus, in their heathen state, the Sandwich Islanders actually knocked out their teeth, tore their hair, and mangled their bodies with shells, to testify their inconsolable grief at the demise of a high chief, or member of the royal family. And yet, Vancouver relates that, on such an occasion, upon which he happened to be present, those apparently the most abandoned to their feelings, immediately assumed the utmost light-heartedness on receiving the present of a penny whistle, or a Dutch looking-glass. Similar instances, also, have come under my own observation.

The following is an illustration of the trait alluded to, as occasionally manifested among the converted Polynesians.

At one of the Society Islands--Baiatair, I believe--the natives, for special reasons, desired to commend themselves particularly to the favour of the missionaries. Accordingly, during divine service, many of them behaved in a manner, otherwise unaccountable, and precisely similar to their behaviour as heathens. They pretended to be wrought up to madness by the preaching which they heard. They rolled their eyes; foamed at the mouth; fell down in fits; and so were carried home. Yet, strange to relate, all this was deemed the evidence of the power of the Most High; and, as such, was heralded abroad.

But, to return to the Church of the Cocoa-nuts. The blessing pronounced, the congregation disperse; enlivening the Broom Road with their waving mantles. On either hand, they disappear down the shaded pathways, which lead off from the main route, conducting to hamlets in the groves, or to the little marine villas upon the beach. There is considerable hilarity; and you would suppose them just from an old-fashioned "hevar," or jolly heathen dance. Those who carry Bibles swing them carelessly from their arms by cords of sinnate.

The Sabbath is no ordinary day with the Tahitians. So far as doing any work is concerned, it is scrupulously observed. The canoes are hauled up on the beach; the nets are spread to dry. Passing by the hen-coop huts on the roadside, you find their occupants idle, as usual; but less disposed to gossip. After service, repose broods over the whole island; the valleys reaching inland look stiller than ever.

In short, it is Sunday--their "Taboo Day"; the very word formerly expressing the sacredness of their pagan observances now proclaiming the sanctity of the Christian Sabbath.

CHAPTER XLVI.

SOMETHING ABOUT THE KANNAKIPPERS

A WORTHY young man, formerly a friend of mine (I speak of Kooloo with all possible courtesy, since after our intimacy there would be an impropriety in doing otherwise)--this worthy youth, having some genteel notions of retirement, dwelt in a "maroo boro," or bread-fruit shade, a pretty nook in a wood, midway between the Calabooza Beretanee and the Church of Cocoa-nuts. Hence, at the latter place, he was one of the most regular worshippers.

Kooloo was a blade. Standing up in the congregation in all the bravery of a striped calico shirt, with the skirts rakishly adjusted over a pair of white sailor trousers, and hair well anointed with cocoa-nut oil, he ogled the ladies with an air of supreme satisfaction. Nor were his glances unreturned.

But such looks as the Tahitian belles cast at each other: frequently turning up their noses at the advent of a new cotton mantle recently imported in the chest of some amorous sailor. Upon one occasion, I observed a group of young girls, in tunics of course, soiled sheeting, disdainfully pointing at a damsel in a flaming red one. "Oee tootai owree!" said they with ineffable scorn, "itai maitai!" (You are a good-for-nothing huzzy, no better than you should be).

Now, Kooloo communed with the church; so did all these censorious young ladies. Yet after eating bread-fruit at the Eucharist, I knew several of them, the same night, to be guilty of some sad derelictions.

Puzzled by these things, I resolved to find out, if possible, what ideas, if any, they entertained of religion; but as one's spiritual concerns are rather delicate for a stranger to meddle with, I went to work as adroitly as I could.

Farnow, an old native who had recently retired from active pursuits, having thrown up the business of being a sort of running footman to the queen, had settled down in a snug little retreat, not fifty rods from Captain Bob's. His selecting our vicinity for his residence may have been with some view to the advantages it afforded for introducing his three daughters into polite circles. At any rate, not averse to receiving the attentions of so devoted a gallant as the doctor, the sisters (communicants, be it remembered) kindly extended to him free permission to visit them sociably whenever he pleased.

We dropped in one evening, and found the ladies at home. My long friend engaged his favourites, the two younger girls, at the game of "Now," or hunting a stone under three piles of tappa. For myself, I lounged on a mat with Ideea the eldest, dallying with her grass fan, and improving my knowledge of Tahitian.

The occasion was well adapted to my purpose, and I began.

"Ah, Ideea, mickonaree oee?" the same as drawling out--"By the bye, Miss Ideea, do you belong to the church?"

"Yes, me mickonaree," was the reply.

But the assertion was at once qualified by certain, reservations; so curious that I cannot forbear their relation.

"Mickonaree ena" (church member here), exclaimed she, laying her hand upon her mouth, and a strong emphasis on the adverb. In the same way, and with similar exclamations, she touched her eyes and hands. This done, her whole air changed in an instant; and she gave me to understand, by unmistakable gestures, that in certain other respects she was not exactly a "mickonaree." In short, Ideea was

"A sad good Christian at the heart--A very heathen in the carnal part."

The explanation terminated in a burst of laughter, in which all three sisters joined; and for fear of looking silly, the doctor and myself. As soon as good-breeding would permit, we took leave.

The hypocrisy in matters of religion, so apparent in all Polynesian converts, is most injudiciously nourished in Tahiti by a zealous and in many cases, a coercive superintendence over their spiritual well-being. But it is only manifested with respect to the common people, their superiors being exempted.

On Sunday mornings, when the prospect is rather small for a full house in the minor churches, a parcel of fellows are actually sent out with ratans into the highways and byways as whippers-in of the congregation. This is a sober fact.

These worthies constitute a religious police; and you always know them by the great white diapers they wear. On week days they are quite as busy as on Sundays; to the great terror of the inhabitants, going all over the island, and spying out the wickedness thereof.

Moreover, they are the collectors of fines--levied generally in grass mats--for obstinate non-attendance upon divine worship, and other offences amenable to the ecclesiastical judicature of the missionaries.

Old Bob called these fellows "kannakippers" a corruption, I fancy, of our word constable.

He bore them a bitter grudge; and one day, drawing near home, and learning that two of them were just then making a domiciliary visit at his house, he ran behind a bush; and as they came forth, two green bread-fruit from a hand unseen took them each between the shoulders.

The sailors in the Calabooza were witnesses to this, as well as several natives; who, when the intruders were out of sight, applauded Captain Bob's spirit in no measured terms; the ladies present vehemently joining in. Indeed, the kannakippers have no greater enemies than the latter. And no wonder: the impertinent varlets, popping into their houses at all hours, are forever prying into their peccadilloes.

Kooloo, who at times was patriotic and pensive, and mourned the evils under which his country was groaning, frequently inveighed against the statute which thus authorized an utter stranger to interfere with domestic arrangements. He himself--quite a ladies' man--had often been annoyed thereby. He considered the kannakippers a bore.

Beside their confounded inquisitiveness, they add insult to injury, by making a point of dining out every day at some hut within the limits of their jurisdiction. As for the gentleman of the house, his meek endurance of these things is amazing. But "good easy man," there is nothing for him but to be as hospitable as possible.

These gentry are indefatigable. At the dead of night prowling round the houses, and in the daytime hunting amorous couples in the groves. Yet in one instance the chase completely baffled them.

It was thus.

Several weeks previous to our arrival at the island, someone's husband and another person's wife, having taken a mutual fancy for each other, went out for a walk. The alarm was raised, and with hue and cry they were pursued; but nothing was seen of them again until the lapse of some ninety days; when we were called out from the Calabooza to behold a great mob inclosing the lovers, and escorting them for trial to the village.

Their appearance was most singular. The girdle excepted, they were quite naked; their hair was long, burned yellow at the ends, and entangled with burrs; and their bodies scratched and scarred in all directions. It seems that, acting upon the "love in a cottage" principle, they had gone right into the interior; and throwing up a hut in an uninhabited valley, had lived there, until in an unlucky stroll they were observed and captured.

They were subsequently condemned to make one hundred fathoms of Broom Road--a six months' work, if not more.

Often, when seated in a house, conversing quietly with its inmates, I have known them betray the greatest confusion at the sudden announcement of a kannakipper's being in sight. To be reported by one of these officials as a "Tootai Owree" (in general, signifying a bad person or disbeliever in Christianity), is as much dreaded as the forefinger of Titus Gates was, levelled at an alleged papist.

But the islanders take a sly revenge upon them. Upon entering a dwelling, the kannakippers oftentimes volunteer a pharisaical prayer-meeting: hence, they go in secret by the name of "Boora-Artuas," literally, "Pray-to-Gods."

CHAPTER XLVII.

HOW THEY DRESS IN TAHITI

EXCEPT where the employment of making "tappa" is inflicted as a punishment, the echoes of the cloth-mallet have long since died away in the listless valleys of Tahiti. Formerly, the girls spent their mornings like ladies at their tambour frames; now, they are lounged away in almost utter indolence. True, most of them make their own garments; but this comprises but a stitch or two; the ladies of the mission, by the bye, being entitled to the credit of teaching them to sew.

The "kihee whihenee," or petticoat, is a mere breadth of white cotton, or calico; loosely enveloping the person, from the waist to the feet. Fastened simply by a single tuck, or by twisting the upper corners together, this garment frequently becomes disordered; thus affording an opportunity of being coquettishly adjusted. Over the "kihee," they wear a sort of gown, open in front, very loose, and as negligent as you please. The ladies here never dress for dinner.

But what shall be said of those horrid hats! Fancy a bunch of straw, plaited into the shape of a coal-scuttle, and stuck, bolt upright, on the crown; with a yard or two of red ribbon flying about like kite-strings. Milliners of Paris, what would ye say to them! Though made by the natives, they are said to have been first contrived and recommended by the missionaries' wives; a report which, I really trust, is nothing but scandal.

Curious to relate, these things for the head are esteemed exceedingly becoming. The braiding of the straw is one of the few employments of the higher classes; all of which but minister to the silliest vanity.

The young girls, however, wholly eschew the hats; leaving those dowdy old souls, their mothers, to make frights of themselves.

As for the men, those who aspire to European garments seem to have no perception of the relation subsisting between the various parts of a gentleman's costume. To the wearer of a coat, for instance, pantaloons are by no means indispensable; and a bell-crowned hat and a girdle are full dress. The young sailor, for whom Kooloo deserted me, presented him with a shaggy old pea-jacket; and with this buttoned up to his chin, under a tropical sun, he promenaded the Broom Road, quite elated. Doctor Long Ghost, who saw him thus, ran away with the idea that he was under medical treatment at the time--in the act of taking, what the quacks call, a "sweat."

A bachelor friend of Captain Bob rejoiced in the possession of a full European suit; in which he often stormed the ladies' hearts. Having a military leaning, he ornamented the coat with a great scarlet patch on the breast; and mounted it also, here and there, with several regimental buttons, slyly cut from the uniform of a parcel of drunken marines sent ashore on a holiday from a man-of-war. But, in spite of the ornaments, the dress was not exactly the thing. From the tightness of the cloth across the shoulders, his elbows projected from his sides, like an ungainly rider's; and his ponderous legs were jammed so hard into his slim, nether garments that the threads of every seam showed; and, at every step, you looked for a catastrophe.

In general, there seems to be no settled style of dressing among the males; they wear anything they can get; in some cases, awkwardly modifying the fashions of their fathers so as to accord with their own altered views of what is becoming.

But ridiculous as many of them now appear, in foreign habiliments, the Tahitians presented a far different appearance in the original national costume; which was graceful in the extreme, modest to all but the prudish, and peculiarly adapted to the climate. But the short kilts of dyed tappa, the tasselled maroes, and other articles formerly worn, are, at the present day, prohibited by law as indecorous. For what reason necklaces and garlands of flowers, among the women, are also forbidden, I never could learn; but, it is said, that they were associated, in some way, with a forgotten heathen observance.

Many pleasant, and, seemingly, innocent sports and pastimes, are likewise interdicted. In old times, there were several athletic games practised, such as wrestling, foot-racing, throwing the javelin, and archery. In all these they greatly excelled; and, for some, splendid festivals were instituted. Among their everyday amusements were dancing, tossing the football, kite-flying, flute-playing, and singing traditional ballads; now, all punishable offences; though most of them have been so long in disuse that they are nearly forgotten.

In the same way, the "Opio," or festive harvest-home of the breadfruit, has been suppressed; though, as described to me by Captain Bob, it seemed wholly free from any immoral tendency. Against tattooing, of any kind, there is a severe law.

That this abolition of their national amusements and customs was not willingly acquiesced in, is shown in the frequent violation of many of the statutes inhibiting them; and, especially, in the frequency with which their "hevars," or dances, are practised in secret.

Doubtless, in thus denationalizing the Tahitians, as it were, the missionaries were prompted by a sincere desire for good; but the effect has been lamentable. Supplied with no amusements in place of those forbidden, the Tahitians, who require more recreation than other people, have sunk into a listlessness, or indulge in sensualities, a hundred times more pernicious than all the games ever celebrated in the Temple of Tanee.

CHAPTER XLVIII.

TAHITI AS IT IS

AS IN the last few chapters, several matters connected with the general condition of the natives have been incidentally touched upon, it may be well not to leave so important a subject in a state calculated to convey erroneous impressions. Let us bestow upon it, therefore, something more than a mere cursory glance.

But in the first place, let it be distinctly understood that, in all I have to say upon this subject, both here and elsewhere, I mean no harm to the missionaries nor their cause; I merely desire to set forth things as they actually exist.

Of the results which have flowed from the intercourse of foreigners with the Polynesians, including the attempts to civilize and Christianize them by the missionaries, Tahiti, on many accounts, is obviously the fairest practical example. Indeed, it may now be asserted that the experiment of Christianizing the Tahitians, and improving their social condition by the introduction of foreign customs, has been fully tried. The present generation have grown up under the auspices of their religious instructors. And although it may be urged that the labours of the latter have at times been more or less obstructed by unprincipled foreigners, still, this in no wise renders Tahiti any the less a fair illustration; for, with obstacles like these, the missionaries in Polynesia must always, and everywhere struggle.

Nearly sixty years have elapsed since the Tahitian mission was started; and, during this period, it has received the unceasing prayers and contributions of its friends abroad. Nor has any enterprise of the kind called forth more devotion on the part of those directly employed in it.

It matters not that the earlier labourers in the work, although strictly conscientious, were, as a class, ignorant, and, in many cases, deplorably bigoted: such traits have, in some degree, characterized the pioneers of all faiths. And although in zeal and disinterestedness the missionaries now on the island are, perhaps, inferior to their predecessors, they have, nevertheless, in their own way at least, laboured hard to make a Christian people of their charge.

Let us now glance at the most obvious changes wrought in their condition.

The entire system of idolatry has been done away; together with several barbarous practices engrafted thereon. But this result is not so much to be ascribed to the missionaries, as to the civilizing effects of a long and constant intercourse with whites of all nations; to whom, for many years, Tahiti has been one of the principal places of resort in the South Seas. At the Sandwich Islands, the potent institution of the Taboo, together with the entire paganism of the land, was utterly abolished by a voluntary act of the natives some time previous to the arrival of the first missionaries among them.

The next most striking change in the Tahitians is this. From the permanent residence among them of influential and respectable foreigners, as well as from the frequent visits of ships-of-war, recognizing the nationality of the island, its inhabitants are no longer deemed fit subjects for the atrocities practised upon mere savages; and hence, secure from retaliation, vessels of all kinds now enter their harbours with perfect safety.

But let us consider what results are directly ascribable to the missionaries alone.

In all cases, they have striven hard to mitigate the evils resulting from the commerce with the whites in general. Such attempts, however, have been rather injudicious, and often ineffectual: in truth, a barrier almost insurmountable is presented in the dispositions of the people themselves. Still, in this respect, the morality of the islanders is, upon the whole, improved by the presence of the missionaries.

But the greatest achievement of the latter, and one which in itself is most hopeful and gratifying, is that they have translated the entire Bible into the language of the island; and I have myself known several who were able to read it with facility. They have also established churches, and schools for both children and adults; the latter, I regret to say, are now much neglected: which must be ascribed, in a great measure, to the disorders growing out of the proceedings of the French.

It were unnecessary here to enter diffusely into matters connected with the internal government of the Tahitian churches and schools. Nor, upon this head, is my information copious enough to warrant me in presenting details. But we do not need them. We are merely considering general results, as made apparent in the moral and religious condition of the island at large.

Upon a subject like this, however, it would be altogether too assuming for a single individual to decide; and so, in place of my own random observations, which may be found elsewhere, I will here present those of several known authors, made under various circumstances, at different periods, and down to a comparative late date. A few very brief extracts will enable the reader to mark for himself what progressive improvement, if any, has taken place.

Nor must it be overlooked that, of these authorities, the two first in order are largely quoted by the Right Reverend M. Kussell, in a work composed for the express purpose of imparting information on the subject of Christian missions in Polynesia. And he frankly acknowledges, moreover, that they are such as "cannot fail to have great weight with the public."

After alluding to the manifold evils entailed upon the natives by foreigners, and their singularly inert condition; and after somewhat too severely denouncing the undeniable errors of the mission, Kotzebue, the Russian navigator, says, "A religion like this, which forbids every innocent pleasure, and cramps or annihilates every mental power, is a libel on the divine founder of Christianity. It is true that the religion of the missionaries has, with a great deal of evil, effected some good. It has restrained the vices of theft and incontinence; but it has given birth to ignorance, hypocrisy, and a hatred of all other modes of faith, which was once foreign to the open and benevolent character of the Tahitian."

Captain Beechy says that, while at Tahiti, he saw scenes "which must have convinced the great sceptic of the thoroughly immoral condition of the people, and which would force him to conclude, as Turnbull did, many years previous, that their intercourse with the Europeans had tended to debase, rather than exalt their condition."

About the year 1834, Daniel Wheeler, an honest-hearted Quaker, prompted by motives of the purest philanthropy, visited, in a vessel of his own, most of the missionary settlements in the South Seas. He remained some time at Tahiti; receiving the hospitalities of the missionaries there, and, from time to time, exhorting the natives.

After bewailing their social condition, he frankly says of their religious state, "Certainly, appearances are unpromising; and however unwilling to adopt such a conclusion, there is reason to apprehend that Christian principle is a great rarity."

Such, then, is the testimony of good and unbiassed men, who have been upon the spot; but, how comes it to differ so widely from impressions of others at home? Simply thus: instead of estimating the result of missionary labours by the number of heathens who have actually been made to understand and practise (in some measure at least) the precepts of Christianity, this result has been unwarrantably inferred from the number of those who, without any understanding of these things, have in any way been induced to abandon idolatry and conform to certain outward observances.

By authority of some kind or other, exerted upon the natives through their chiefs, and prompted by the hope of some worldly benefit to the latter, and not by appeals to the reason, have conversions in Polynesia been in most cases brought about.

Even in one or two instances--so often held up as wonderful examples of divine power--where the natives have impulsively burned their idols, and rushed to the waters of baptism, the very suddenness of the change has but indicated its unsoundness. Williams, the martyr of

Erromanga, relates an instance where the inhabitants of an island professing Christianity voluntarily assembled, and solemnly revived all their heathen customs.

All the world over, facts are more eloquent than words; the following will show in what estimation the missionaries themselves hold the present state of Christianity and morals among the converted Polynesians.

On the island of Imeeo (attached to the Tahitian mission) is a seminary under the charge of the Rev. Mr. Simpson and wife, for the education of the children of the missionaries, exclusively. Sent home--in many cases, at a very early age--to finish their education, the pupils here are taught nothing but the rudiments of knowledge; nothing more than may be learned in the native schools. Notwithstanding this, the two races are kept as far as possible from associating; the avowed reason being to preserve the young whites from moral contamination. The better to insure this end, every effort is made to prevent them from acquiring the native language.

They went even further at the Sandwich Islands; where, a few years ago, a playground for the children of the missionaries was inclosed with a fence many feet high, the more effectually to exclude the wicked little Hawaiians.

And yet, strange as it may seem, the depravity among the Polynesians, which renders precautions like these necessary, was in a measure unknown before their intercourse with the whites. The excellent Captain Wilson, who took the first missionaries out to Tahiti, affirms that the people of that island had, in many things, "more refined ideas of decency than ourselves." Vancouver, also, has some noteworthy ideas on this subject, respecting the Sandwich Islanders.

That the immorality alluded to is continually increasing is plainly shown in the numerous, severe, and perpetually violated laws against licentiousness of all kinds in both groups of islands.

It is hardly to be expected that the missionaries would send home accounts of this state of things. Hence, Captain Beechy, in alluding to the "Polynesian Researches" of Ellis, says that the author has impressed his readers with a far more elevated idea of the moral condition of the Tahitians, and the degree of civilization to which they have attained, than they deserve; or, at least, than the facts which came under his observation authorized. He then goes on to say that, in his intercourse with the islanders, "they had no fear of him, and consequently acted from the impulse of their natural feeling; so that he was the better enabled to obtain a correct knowledge of their real disposition and habits."

Prom my own familiar intercourse with the natives, this last reflection still more forcibly applies to myself.

CHAPTER XLIX.

SAME SUBJECT CONTINUED

WE have glanced at their moral and religious condition; let us see how it is with them socially, and in other respects.

It has been said that the only way to civilize a people is to form in them habits of industry. Judged by this principle, the Tahitians are less civilized now than formerly. True, their constitutional indolence is excessive; but surely, if the spirit of Christianity is among them, so unchristian a vice ought to be, at least, partially remedied. But the reverse is the fact. Instead of acquiring new occupations, old ones have been discontinued.

As previously remarked, the manufacture of tappa is nearly obsolete in many parts of the island. So, too, with that of the native tools and domestic utensils; very few of which are now fabricated, since the superiority of European wares has been made so evident.

This, however, would be all very well were the natives to apply themselves to such occupations as would enable them to supply the few articles they need. But they are far from doing so; and the majority being unable to obtain European substitutes for many things before made by themselves, the inevitable consequence is seen in the present wretched and destitute mode of life among the common people. To me so recently from a primitive valley of the Marquesas, the aspect of most of the dwellings of the poorer Tahitians, and their general habits, seemed anything but tidy; nor could I avoid a comparison, immeasurably to the disadvantage of these partially civilized islanders.

In Tahiti, the people have nothing to do; and idleness, everywhere, is the parent of vice. "There is scarcely anything," says the good old Quaker Wheeler, "so striking, or pitiable, as their aimless, nerveless mode of spending life."

Attempts have repeatedly been made to rouse them from their sluggishness; but in vain. Several years ago, the cultivation of cotton was introduced; and, with their usual love of novelty, they went to work with great alacrity; but the interest excited quickly subsided, and now, not a pound of the article is raised.

About the same time, machinery for weaving was sent out from London; and a factory was started at Afrehitoo, in Imeeo. The whiz of the wheels and spindles brought in volunteers from all quarters, who deemed it a privilege to be admitted to work: yet, in six months, not a boy could be hired; and the machinery was knocked down, and packed off to Sydney.

It was the same way with the cultivation of the sugar-cane, a plant indigenous to the island; peculiarly fitted to the soil and climate, and of so excellent a quality that Bligh took slips of it to the West Indies. All the plantations went on famously for a while; the natives swarming in the fields like ants, and making a prodigious stir. What few plantations now remain are owned and worked by whites; who would rather pay a drunken sailor eighteen or twenty Spanish dollars a month, than hire a sober native for his "fish and tarro."

It is well worthy remark here, that every evidence of civilization among the South Sea Islands directly pertains to foreigners; though the fact of such evidence existing at all is usually urged as a proof of the elevated condition of the natives. Thus, at Honolulu, the capital of the Sandwich Islands, there are fine dwelling-houses, several hotels, and barber-shops, ay, even billiard-rooms; but all these are owned and used, be it observed, by whites. There are tailors, and blacksmiths, and carpenters also; but not one of them is a native.

The fact is, that the mechanical and agricultural employment of civilized life require a kind of exertion altogether too steady and sustained to agree with an indolent people like the Polynesians. Calculated for a state of nature, in a climate providentially adapted to it, they are unfit for any other. Nay, as a race, they cannot otherwise long exist.

The following statement speaks for itself.

About the year 1777, Captain Cook estimated the population of Tahiti at about two hundred thousand. By a regular census, taken some four or five years ago, it was found to be only nine thousand. This amazing decrease not only shows the malignancy of the evils necessary to produce it; but, from the fact, the inference unavoidably follows that all the wars, child murders, and other depopulating causes, alleged to have existed in former times, were nothing in comparison to them.

These evils, of course, are solely of foreign origin. To say nothing of the effects of drunkenness, the occasional inroads of the small-pox, and other things which might be mentioned, it is sufficient to allude to a virulent disease which now taints the blood of at least two-thirds of the common people of the island; and, in some form or other, is transmitted from father to son.

Their first horror and consternation at the earlier ravages of this scourge were pitiable in the extreme. The very name bestowed upon it is a combination of all that is horrid and unmentionable to a civilized being.

Distracted with their sufferings, they brought forth their sick before the missionaries, when they were preaching, and cried out, "Lies, lies! you tell us of salvation; and, behold, we are dying. We want no other salvation than to live in this world. Where are there any saved through your speech? Pomaree is dead; and we are all dying with your cursed diseases. When will you give over?"

At present, the virulence of the disorder, in individual cases, has somewhat abated; but the poison is only the more widely diffused.

"How dreadful and appalling," breaks forth old Wheeler, "the consideration that the intercourse of distant nations should have entailed upon these poor, untutored islanders a curse unprecedented, and unheard of, in the annals of history."

In view of these things, who can remain blind to the fact that, so far as mere temporal felicity is concerned, the Tahitians are far worse off now, than formerly; and although their circumstances, upon the whole, are bettered by the presence of the missionaries, the benefits conferred by the latter become utterly insignificant when confronted with the vast preponderance of evil brought about by other means.

Their prospects are hopeless. Nor can the most devoted efforts now exempt them from furnishing a marked illustration of a principle which history has always exemplified. Years ago brought to a stand, where all that is corrupt in barbarism and civilization unite, to the exclusion of the virtues of either state; like other uncivilized beings, brought into contact with Europeans, they must here remain stationary until utterly extinct.

The islanders themselves are mournfully watching their doom.

Several years since, Pomaree II. said to Tyreman and Bennet, the deputies of the London Missionary Society, "You have come to see me at a very bad time. Your ancestors came in the time of men, when Tahiti was inhabited: you are come to behold just the remnant of my people."

Of like import was the prediction of Teearmoar, the high-priest of Paree; who lived over a hundred years ago. I have frequently heard it chanted, in a low, sad tone, by aged Tahitiana:--

"A harree ta fow,
A toro ta farraro,
A now tatararta."

"The palm-tree shall grow,
The coral shall spread,
But man shall cease."

CHAPTER L.

SOMETHING HAPPENS TO LONG GHOST

WE will now return to the narrative.

The day before the Julia sailed, Dr. Johnson paid his last call. He was not quite so bland as usual. All he wanted was the men's names to a paper, certifying to their having received from him sundry medicaments therein mentioned. This voucher, endorsed by Captain Guy, secured his pay. But he would not have obtained for it the sailors' signs manual, had either the doctor or myself been present at the time.

Now, my long friend wasted no love upon Johnson; but, for reasons of his own, hated him heartily: all the same thing in one sense; for either passion argues an object deserving thereof. And so, to be hated cordially, is only a left-handed compliment; which shows how foolish it is to be bitter against anyone.

For my own part, I merely felt a cool, purely incidental, and passive contempt for Johnson, as a selfish, mercenary apothecary, and hence, I often remonstrated with Long Ghost when he flew out against him, and heaped upon him all manner of scurrilous epithets. In his professional brother's presence, however, he never acted thus; maintaining an amiable exterior, to help along the jokes which were played.

I am now going to tell another story in which my long friend figures with the physician: I do not wish to bring one or the other of them too often upon the stage; but as the thing actually happened, I must relate it.

A few days after Johnson presented his bill, as above mentioned, the doctor expressed to me his regret that, although he (Johnson) 'had apparently been played off for our entertainment, yet, nevertheless, he had made money out of the transaction. And I wonder, added the doctor, if that now he cannot expect to receive any further pay, he could be induced to call again.

By a curious coincidence, not five minutes after making this observation, Doctor Long Ghost himself fell down in an unaccountable fit; and without asking anybody's leave, Captain Bob, who was by, at once dispatched a boy, hot foot, for Johnson.

Meanwhile, we carried him into the Calabooza; and the natives, who assembled in numbers, suggested various modes of treatment. One rather energetic practitioner was for holding the patient by the shoulders, while somebody tugged at his feet. This resuscitatory operation was called the "Potata"; but thinking our long comrade sufficiently lengthy without additional stretching, we declined potataing him.

Presently the physician was spied coming along the Broom Road at a great rate, and so absorbed in the business of locomotion, that he heeded not the imprudence of being in a hurry in a tropical climate. He was in a profuse perspiration; which must have been owing to the warmth of his feelings, notwithstanding we had supposed him a man of no heart. But his benevolent haste upon this occasion was subsequently accounted for: it merely arose from professional curiosity to behold a case most unusual in his Polynesian practice. Now, under certain circumstances, sailors, generally so frolicsome, are exceedingly particular in having everything conducted with the strictest propriety. Accordingly, they deputed me, as his intimate friend, to sit at Long Ghost's head, so as to be ready to officiate as "spokesman" and answer all questions propounded, the rest to keep silent.

"What's the matter?" exclaimed Johnson, out of breath, and bursting into the Calabooza: "how did it happen?--speak quick!" and he looked at Long Ghost.

I told him how the fit came on.

"Singular"--he observed--"very: good enough pulse;" and he let go of it, and placed his hand upon the heart.

"But what's all that frothing at the mouth?" he continued; "and bless me! look at the abdomen!"

The region thus denominated exhibited the most unaccountable symptoms. A low, rumbling sound was heard; and a sort of undulation was discernible beneath the thin cotton frock.

"Colic, sir?" suggested a bystander.

"Colic be hanged!" shouted the physician; "who ever heard of anybody in a trance of the colic?"

During this, the patient lay upon his back, stark and straight, giving no signs of life except those above mentioned.

"I'll bleed him!" cried Johnson at last--"run for a calabash, one of you!"

"Life ho!" here sung out Navy Bob, as if he had just spied a sail.

"What under the sun's the matter with him!" cried the physician, starting at the appearance of the mouth, which had jerked to one side, and there remained fixed.

"Pr'aps it's St. Witus's hornpipe," suggested Bob.

"Hold the calabash!"--and the lancet was out in a moment.

But before the deed could be done, the face became natural;--a sigh was heaved;--the eyelids quivered, opened, closed; and Long Ghost, twitching all over, rolled on his side, and breathed audibly. By degrees, he became sufficiently recovered to speak.

After trying to get something coherent out of him, Johnson withdrew; evidently disappointed in the scientific interest of the case. Soon after his departure, the doctor sat up; and upon being asked what upon earth ailed him, shook his head mysteriously. He then deplored the hardship of being an invalid in such a place, where there was not the slightest provision for his comfort. This awakened the compassion of our good old keeper, who offered to send him to a place where he would be better cared for. Long Ghost acquiesced; and being at once mounted upon the shoulders of four of Captain Bob's men, was marched off in state, like the Grand Lama of Thibet.

Now, I do not pretend to account for his remarkable swoon; but his reason for suffering himself to be thus removed from the Calabooza was strongly suspected to be nothing more than a desire to insure more regularity in his dinner-hour; hoping that the benevolent native to whom he was going would set a good table.

The next morning, we were all envying his fortune; when, of a sudden, he bolted in upon us, looking decidedly out of humour.

"Hang it!" he cried; "I'm worse off than ever; let me have some breakfast!" We lowered our slender bag of ship-stores from a rafter, and handed him a biscuit. While this was being munched, he went on and told us his story.

"After leaving here, they trotted me back into a valley, and left me in a hut, where an old woman lived by herself. This must be the nurse, thought I; and so I asked her to kill a pig, and bake it; for I felt my appetite returning. 'Ha! Hal--oee mattee--mattee nuee'--(no, no; you too sick). 'The devil mattee ye,' said I--'give me something to eat!' But nothing could be had. Night coming on, I had to stay. Creeping into a corner, I tried to sleep; but it was to no purpose;--the old crone must have had the quinsy, or something else; and she kept up such a wheezing and choking that at last I sprang up, and groped after her; but she hobbled away like a goblin; and that was the last of her. As soon as the sun rose, I made the best of my way back; and here I am." He never left us more, nor ever had a second fit.

CHAPTER LI.

WILSON GIVES US THE CUT--DEPARTURE FOR IMEEO

ABOUT three weeks after the Julia's sailing, our conditions began to be a little precarious. We were without any regular supply of food; the arrival of ships was growing less frequent; and, what was worse yet, all the natives but good old Captain Bob began to tire of us. Nor was this to be wondered at; we were obliged to live upon their benevolence, when they had little enough for themselves. Besides, we were sometimes driven to acts of marauding; such as kidnapping pigs, and cooking them in the groves; at which their proprietors were by no means pleased.

In this state of affairs, we determined to march off to the consul in a body; and, as he had brought us to these straits, demand an adequate maintenance.

On the point of starting, Captain Bob's men raised the most outrageous cries, and tried to prevent us. Though hitherto we had strolled about wherever we pleased, this grand conjunction of our whole force, upon one particular expedition, seemed to alarm them. But we assured them that we were not going to assault the village; and so, after a good deal of gibberish, they permitted us to leave.

We went straight to the Pritchard residence, where the consul dwelt.

This house--to which I have before referred--is quite commodious. It has a wide verandah, glazed windows, and other appurtenances of a civilized mansion. Upon the lawn in front are palm-trees standing erect here and there, like sentinels. The Consular Office, a small building by itself, is inclosed by the same picket which fences in the lawn.

We found the office closed; but, in the verandah of the dwelling-house, was a lady performing a tonsorial operation on the head of a prim-looking, elderly European, in a low, white cravat;--the most domestic little scene I had witnessed since leaving home. Bent upon an interview with Wilson, the sailors now deputed the doctor to step forward as a polite inquirer after his health.

The pair stared very hard as he advanced; but no ways disconcerted, he saluted them gravely, and inquired for the consul.

Upon being informed that he had gone down to the beach, we proceeded in that direction; and soon met a native, who told us that, apprised of our vicinity, Wilson was keeping out of the way. We resolved to meet him; and passing through the village, he suddenly came walking toward us; having apparently made up his mind that any attempt to elude us would be useless.

"What do you want of me, you rascals?" he cried--a greeting which provoked a retort in no measured terms. At this juncture, the natives began to crowd round, and several foreigners strolled along. Caught in the very act of speaking to such disreputable acquaintances, Wilson now fidgeted, and moved rapidly toward his office; the men following. Turning upon them incensed, he bade them be off--he would have nothing more to say to us; and then, hurriedly addressing Captain Bob in Tahitian, he hastened on, and never stopped till the postern of Pritchard's wicket was closed behind him.

Our good old keeper was now highly excited, bustling about in his huge petticoats, and conjuring us to return to the Calabooza. After a little debate, we acquiesced.

This interview was decisive. Sensible that none of the charges brought against us would stand, yet unwilling formally to withdraw them, the consul now wished to get rid of us altogether; but without being suspected of encouraging our escape. Thus only could we account for his conduct.

Some of the party, however, with a devotion to principle truly heroic, swore they would never leave him, happen what might. For my own part, I began to long for a change; and as there seemed to be no getting away in a ship, I resolved to hit upon some other expedient. But first, I cast about for a comrade; and of course the long doctor was chosen. We at once laid our heads together; and for the present, resolved to disclose nothing to the rest.

A few days previous, I had fallen in with a couple of Yankee lads, twins, who, originally deserting their ship at Tanning's Island (an uninhabited spot, but exceedingly prolific in fruit of all kinds), had, after a long residence there, roved about among the Society group. They were last from Imeeo--the island immediately adjoining--where they had been in the employ of two foreigners who had recently started a plantation there. These persons, they said, had charged them to send over from Papeetee, if they could, two white men for field-labourers.

Now, all but the prospect of digging and delving suited us exactly; but the opportunity for leaving the island was not to be slighted; and so we held ourselves in readiness to return with the planters; who, in a day or two, were expected to visit Papeetee in their boat.

At the interview which ensued, we were introduced to them as Peter and Paul; and they agreed to give Peter and Paul fifteen silver dollars a month, promising something more should we remain with them permanently. What they wanted was men who would stay. To elude the natives--many of whom, not exactly understanding our relations with the consul, might arrest us, were they to see us departing--the coming midnight was appointed for that purpose.

When the hour drew nigh, we disclosed our intention to the rest. Some upbraided us for deserting them; others applauded, and said that, on the first opportunity, they would follow our example. At last, we bade them farewell. And there would now be a serene sadness in thinking over the scene--since we never saw them again--had not all been dashed by M'Gee's picking the doctor's pocket of a jack-knife, in the very act of embracing him.

We stole down to the beach, where, under the shadow of a grove, the boat was waiting. After some delay, we shipped the oars, and pulling outside of the reef, set the sail; and with a fair wind, glided away for Imeeo.

It was a pleasant trip. The moon was up--the air, warm--the waves, musical--and all above was the tropical night, one purple vault hung round with soft, trembling stars.

The channel is some five leagues wide. On one hand, you have the three great peaks of Tahiti lording it over ranges of mountains and valleys; and on the other, the equally romantic elevations of Imeeo, high above which a lone peak, called by our companions, "the Marling-pike," shot up its verdant spire.

The planters were quite sociable. They had been sea-faring men, and this, of course, was a bond between us. To strengthen it, a flask of wine was produced, one of several which had been procured in person from the French admiral's steward; for whom the planters, when on a former visit to Papeetee, had done a good turn, by introducing the amorous Frenchman to the ladies ashore. Besides this, they had a calabash filled with wild boar's meat, baked yams, bread-fruit, and Tombez potatoes. Pipes and tobacco also were produced; and while regaling ourselves, plenty of stories were told about the neighbouring islands.

At last we heard the roar of the Imeeo reef; and gliding through a break, floated over the expanse within, which was smooth as a young girl's brow, and beached the boat.

CHAPTER LII.

THE VALLEY OF MARTAIR

WE went up through groves to an open space, where we heard voices, and a light was seen glimmering from out a bamboo dwelling. It was the planters' retreat; and in their absence, several girls were keeping house, assisted by an old native, who, wrapped up in tappa, lay in the corner, smoking.

A hasty meal was prepared, and after it we essayed a nap; but, alas! a plague, little anticipated, prevented. Unknown in Tahiti, the mosquitoes here fairly eddied round us. But more of them anon.

We were up betimes, and strolled out to view the country. We were in the valley of Martair; shut in, on both sides, by lofty hills. Here and there were steep cliffs, gay with flowering shrubs, or hung with pendulous vines, swinging blossoms in the air. Of considerable width at the sea, the vale contracts as it runs inland; terminating, at the distance of several miles, in a range of the most grotesque elevations, which seem embattled with turrets and towers, grown over with verdure, and waving with trees. The valley itself is a wilderness of woodland; with links of streams flashing through, and narrow pathways fairly tunnelled through masses of foliage.

All alone, in this wild place, was the abode of the planters; the only one back from the beach--their sole neighbours, the few fishermen and their families, dwelling in a small grove of cocoa-nut trees whose roots were washed by the sea.

The cleared tract which they occupied comprised some thirty acres, level as a prairie, part of which was under cultivation; the whole being fenced in by a stout palisade of trunks and boughs of trees staked firmly in the ground. This was necessary as a defence against the wild cattle and hogs overrunning the island.

Thus far, Tombez potatoes were the principal crop raised; a ready sale for them being obtained among the shipping touching at Papeetee. There was a small patch of the taro, or Indian turnip, also; another of yams; and in one corner, a thrifty growth of the sugar-cane, just ripening.

On the side of the inclosure next the sea was the house; newly built of bamboos, in the native style. The furniture consisted of a couple of sea-chests, an old box, a few cooking utensils, and agricultural tools; together with three fowling-pieces, hanging from a rafter; and two enormous hammocks swinging in opposite corners, and composed of dried bullocks' hides, stretched out with poles.

The whole plantation was shut in by a dense forest; and, close by the house, a dwarfed "Aoa," or species of banian-tree, had purposely been left twisting over the palisade, in the most grotesque manner, and thus made a pleasant shade. The branches of this curious tree afforded low perches, upon which the natives frequently squatted, after the fashion of their race, and smoked and gossiped by the hour.

We had a good breakfast of fish--speared by the natives, before sunrise, on the reef--pudding of Indian turnip, fried bananas, and roasted bread-fruit.

During the repast, our new friends were quite sociable and communicative. It seems that, like nearly all uneducated foreigners, residing in Polynesia, they had, some time previous, deserted from a ship; and, having heard a good deal about the money to be made by raising supplies for whaling-vessels, they determined upon embarking in the business. Strolling about, with this intention, they, at last, came to Martair; and, thinking the soil would suit, set themselves to work. They began by finding out the owner of the particular spot coveted, and then making a "tayo" of him.

He turned out to be Tonoi, the chief of the fishermen: who, one day, when exhilarated with brandy, tore his meagre tappa from his loins, and gave me to know that he was allied by blood with Pomaree herself; and that his mother came from the illustrious race of pontiffs, who, in old times, swayed their bamboo crosier over all the pagans of Imeeo. A regal, and right reverend lineage! But, at the time I speak of, the dusky noble was in decayed circumstances, and, therefore, by no means unwilling to alienate a few useless acres. As an equivalent, he received from the strangers two or three rheumatic old muskets, several red woollen shirts, and a promise to be provided for in his old age: he was always to find a home with the planters.

Desirous of living on the cosy footing of a father-in-law, he frankly offered his two daughters for wives; but as such, they were politely declined; the adventurers, though not averse to courting, being unwilling to entangle themselves in a matrimonial alliance, however splendid in point of family.

Tonoi's men, the fishermen of the grove, were a sad set. Secluded, in a great measure, from the ministrations of the missionaries, they gave themselves up to all manner of lazy wickedness. Strolling among the trees of a morning, you came upon them napping on the shady side of a canoe hauled up among the bushes; lying on a tree smoking; or, more frequently still, gambling with pebbles; though, a little tobacco excepted, what they gambled for at their outlandish games, it would be hard to tell. Other idle diversions they had also, in which they seemed to take great delight. As for fishing, it employed but a small part of their time. Upon the whole, they were a merry, indigent, godless race.

Tonoi, the old sinner, leaning against the fallen trunk of a cocoa-nut tree, invariably squandered his mornings at pebbles; a gray-headed rook of a native regularly plucking him of every other stick of tobacco obtained from his friends, the planters. Toward afternoon, he strolled back to their abode; where he tarried till the next morning, smoking and snoozing, and, at times, prating about the hapless fortunes of the House of Tonoi. But like any other easy-going old dotard, he seemed for the most part perfectly content with cheerful board and lodging.

On the whole, the valley of Martair was the quietest place imaginable. Could the mosquitoes be induced to emigrate, one might spend the month of August there quite pleasantly. But this was not the case with the luckless Long Ghost and myself; as will presently be seen.

CHAPTER LIII.

FARMING IN POLYNESIA

THE planters were both whole-souled fellows; but, in other respects, as unlike as possible.

One was a tall, robust Yankee, hern in the backwoods of Maine, sallow, and with a long face;--the other was a short little Cockney, who had first clapped his eyes on the Monument.

The voice of Zeke, the Yankee, had a twang like a cracked viol; and Shorty (as his comrade called him), clipped the aspirate from every word beginning with one. The latter, though not the tallest man in the world, was a good-looking young fellow of twenty-five. His cheeks were dyed with the fine Saxon red, burned deeper from his roving life: his blue eye opened well, and a profusion of fair hair curled over a well-shaped head.

But Zeke was no beauty. A strong, ugly man, he was well adapted for manual labour; and that was all. His eyes were made to see with, and not for ogling. Compared with the Cockney, he was grave, and rather taciturn; but there was a deal of good old humour bottled up in him, after all. For the rest, he was frank, good-hearted, shrewd, and resolute; and like Shorty, quite illiterate.

Though a curious conjunction, the pair got along together famously. But, as no two men were ever united in any enterprise without one getting the upper hand of the other, so in most matters Zeke had his own way. Shorty, too, had imbibed from him a spirit of invincible industry; and Heaven only knows what ideas of making a fortune on their plantation.

We were much concerned at this; for the prospect of their setting us, in their own persons, an example of downright hard labour, was anything but agreeable. But it was now too late to repent what we had done.

The first day--thank fortune--we did nothing. Having treated us as guests thus far, they no doubt thought it would be wanting in delicacy to set us to work before the compliments of the occasion were well over. The next morning, however, they both looked business-like, and we were put to.

"Wall, b'ys" (boys), said Zeke, knocking the ashes out of his pipe, after breakfast--"we must get at it. Shorty, give Peter there (the doctor), the big hoe, and Paul the other, and let's be off." Going to a corner, Shorty brought forth three of the implements; and distributing them impartially, trudged on after his partner, who took the lead with something in the shape of an axe.

For a moment left alone in the house, we looked at each other, quaking. We were each equipped with a great, clumsy piece of a tree, armed at one end with a heavy, flat mass of iron.

The cutlery part--especially adapted to a primitive soil--was an importation from Sydney; the handles must have been of domestic manufacture. "Hoes"--so called--we had heard of, and seen; but they were harmless in comparison with the tools in our hands.

"What's to be done with them?" inquired I of Peter.

"Lift them up and down," he replied; "or put them in motion some way or other. Paul, we are in a scrape--but hark! they are calling;" and shouldering the hoes, off we marched.'

Our destination was the farther side of the plantation, where the ground, cleared in part, had not yet been broken up; but they were now setting about it. Upon halting, I asked why a plough was not used; some of the young wild steers might be caught and trained for draught.

Zeke replied that, for such a purpose, no cattle, to his knowledge, had ever been used in any part of Polynesia. As for the soil of Martair, so obstructed was it with roots, crossing and recrossing each other at all points, that no kind of a plough could be used to advantage. The heavy Sydney hoes were the only thing for such land.

Our work was now before us; but, previous to commencing operations, I endeavoured to engage the Yankee in a little further friendly chat concerning the nature of virgin soils in general, and that of the valley of Martair in particular. So masterly a stratagem made Long Ghost brighten up; and he stood by ready to join in. But what our friend had to say about agriculture all referred to the particular part of his plantation upon which we stood; and having communicated enough on this head to enable us to set to work to the best advantage, he fell to, himself; and Shorty, who had been looking on, followed suit.

The surface, here and there, presented closely amputated branches of what had once been a dense thicket. They seemed purposely left projecting, as if to furnish a handle whereby to drag out the roots beneath. After loosening the hard soil, by dint of much thumping and pounding, the Yankee jerked one of the roots this way and that, twisting it round and round, and then tugging at it horizontally.

"Come! lend us a hand!" he cried, at last; and running up, we all four strained away in concert. The tough obstacle convulsed the surface with throes and spasms; but stuck fast, notwithstanding.

"Dumn it!" cried Zeke, "we'll have to get a rope; run to the house, Shorty, and fetch one."

The end of this being attached, we took plenty of room, and strained away once more.

"Give us a song, Shorty," said the doctor; who was rather sociable, on a short acquaintance. Where the work to be accomplished is any way difficult, this mode of enlivening toil is quite efficacious among sailors. So willing to make everything as cheerful as possible, Shorty struck up, "Were you ever in Dumbarton?" a marvellously inspiring, but somewhat indecorous windlass chorus.

At last, the Yankee cast a damper on his enthusiasm by exclaiming, in a pet, "Oh! dumn your singing! keep quiet, and pull away!" This we now did, in the most uninteresting silence; until, with a jerk that made every elbow hum, the root dragged out; and most inelegantly, we all landed upon the ground. The doctor, quite exhausted, stayed there; and, deluded into believing that, after so doughty a performance, we would be allowed a cessation of toil, took off his hat, and fanned himself.

"Rayther a hard customer, that, Peter," observed the Yankee, going up to him: "but it's no use for any on 'em to hang back; for I'm dumned if they hain't got to come out, whether or no. Hurrah! let's get at it agin!"

"Mercy!" ejaculated the doctor, rising slowly, and turning round. "He'll be the death of us!"

Falling to with our hoes again, we worked singly, or together, as occasion required, until "Nooning Time" came.

The period, so called by the planters, embraced about three hours in the middle of the day; during which it was so excessively hot, in this still, brooding valley, shut out from the Trades, and only open toward the leeward side of the island, that labour in the sun was out of the question. To use a hyperbolical phrase of Shorty's, "It was 'ot enough to melt the nose h'off a brass monkey."

Returning to the house, Shorty, assisted by old Tonoi, cooked the dinner; and, after we had all partaken thereof, both the Cockney and Zeke threw themselves into one of the hammocks, inviting us to occupy the other. Thinking it no bad idea, we did so; and, after skirmishing with the mosquitoes, managed to fall into a doze. As for the planters, more accustomed to "Nooning," they, at once, presented a nuptial back to each other; and were soon snoring away at a great rate. Tonoi snoozed on a mat, in one corner.

At last, we were roused by Zeke's crying out, "Up b'ys; up! rise, and shine; time to get at it agin!"

Looking at the doctor, I perceived, very plainly, that he had decided upon something.

In a languid voice, he told Zeke that he was not very well: indeed, that he had not been himself for some time past; though a little rest, no doubt, would recruit him. The Yankee thinking, from this, that our valuable services might be lost to him altogether, were he too hard upon us at the outset, at once begged us both to consult our own feelings, and not exert ourselves for the present, unless we felt like it. Then--without recognizing the fact that my comrade claimed to be actually unwell--he simply suggested that, since he was so tired, he had better, perhaps, swing in his hammock for the rest of the day. If agreeable, however, I myself might accompany him upon a little bullock-hunting excursion in the neighbouring hills. In this proposition, I gladly acquiesced; though Peter, who was a great sportsman, put on a long face. The muskets and ammunition were forthwith got from overhead; and, everything being then ready, Zeke cried out, "Tonoi! come; aramai! (get up) we want you for pilot. Shorty, my lad, look arter things, you know; and if you likes, why, there's them roots in the field yonder."

Having thus arranged his domestic affairs to please himself, though little to Shorty's satisfaction, I thought, he slung his powder-horn over his shoulder, and we started. Tonoi was, at once, sent on in advance; and leaving the plantation, he struck into a path which led toward the mountains.

After hurrying through the thickets for some time, we came out into the sunlight, in an open glade, just under the shadow of the hills. Here, Zeke pointed aloft to a beetling crag far distant, where a bullock, with horns thrown back, stood like a statue.

CHAPTER LIV.

SOME ACCOUNT OF THE WILD CATTLE IN POLYNESIA

BEFORE we proceed further, a word or two concerning these wild cattle, and the way they came on the island.

Some fifty years ago, Vancouver left several bullocks, sheep and goats, at various places in the Society group. He instructed the natives to look after the animals carefully; and by no means to slaughter any until a considerable stock had accumulated.

The sheep must have died off: for I never saw a solitary fleece in any part of Polynesia. The pair left were an ill-assorted couple, perhaps; separated in disgust, and died without issue.

As for the goats, occasionally you come across a black, misanthropic ram, nibbling the scant herbage of some height inaccessible to man, in preference to the sweet grasses of the valley below. The goats are not very numerous.

The bullocks, coming of a prolific ancestry, are a hearty set, racing over the island of Imeeo in considerable numbers, though in Tahiti but few of them are seen. At the former place, the original pair must have scampered off to the interior since it is now so thickly populated by their wild progeny. The herds are the private property of Queen Pomaree; from whom the planters had obtained permission to shoot for their own use as many as they pleased.

The natives stand in great awe of these cattle; and for this reason are excessively timid in crossing the island, preferring rather to sail round to an opposite village in their canoes.

Tonoi abounded in bullock stories; most of which, by the bye, had a spice of the marvellous. The following is one of these.

Once upon a time, he was going over the hills with a brother--now no more--when a great bull came bellowing out of a wood, and both took to their heels. The old chief sprang into a tree; his companion, flying in an opposite direction, was pursued, and, in the very act of reaching up to a bough, trampled underfoot. The unhappy man was then gored--tossed in the air--and finally run away with on the bull's horns. More dead than alive, Tonoi waited till all was over, and then made the best of his way home. The neighbours, armed with two or three muskets, at once started to recover, if possible, his unfortunate brother's remains. At nightfall, they returned without discovering any trace of him; but the next morning, Tonoi himself caught a glimpse of the bullock, marching across the mountain's brow, with a long dark object borne aloft on his horns.

Having referred to Vancouver's attempts to colonize the islands with useful quadrupeds, we may as well say something concerning his success upon Hawaii, one of the largest islands in the whole Polynesian Archipelago; and which gives the native name to the well-known cluster named by Cook in honour of Lord Sandwich.

Hawaii is some one hundred leagues in circuit, and covers an area of over four thousand miles. Until within a few years past, its interior was almost unknown, even to the inhabitants themselves, who, for ages, had been prevented from wandering thither by certain strange superstitions. Pelee, the terrific goddess of the volcanoes Mount Eoa and Mount Kea, was supposed to guard all the passes to the extensive valleys lying round their base. There are legends of her having chased with streams of fire several impious adventurers. Near Hilo, a jet-black cliff is shown, with the vitreous torrent apparently pouring over into the sea: just as it cooled after one of these supernatural eruptions.

To these inland valleys, and the adjoining hillsides, which are clothed in the most luxuriant vegetation, Vancouver's bullocks soon wandered; and unmolested for a long period, multiplied in vast herds.

Some twelve or fifteen years ago, the natives lost sight of their superstitions, and learning the value of the hides in commerce, began hunting the creatures that wore them; but being very fearful and awkward in a business so novel, their success was small; and it was not until the arrival of a party of Spanish hunters, men regularly trained to their calling upon the plains of California, that the work of slaughter was fairly begun.

The Spaniards were showy fellows, tricked out in gay blankets, leggings worked with porcupine quills, and jingling spurs. Mounted upon trained Indian mares, these heroes pursued their prey up to the very base of the burning mountains; making the profoundest solitudes ring with their shouts, and flinging the lasso under the very nose of the vixen goddess Pelee. Hilo, a village upon the coast, was their place of resort; and thither flocked roving whites from all the islands of the group. As pupils of the dashing Spaniards, many of these dissipated fellows, quaffing too freely of the stirrup-cup, and riding headlong after the herds, when they reeled in the saddle, were unhorsed and killed.

This was about the year 1835, when the present king, Tammahamaha III., was a lad. With royal impudence laying claim to the sole property of the cattle, he was delighted with the idea of receiving one of every two silver dollars paid down for their hides; so, with no thought for the future, the work of extermination went madly on. In three years' time, eighteen thousand bullocks were slain, almost entirely upon the single island of Hawaii.

The herds being thus nearly destroyed, the sagacious young prince imposed a rigorous "taboo" upon the few surviving cattle, which was to remain in force for ten years. During this period--not yet expired--all hunting is forbidden, unless directly authorized by the king.

The massacre of the cattle extended to the hapless goats. In one year, three thousand of their skins were sold to the merchants of Honolulu, fetching a quartila, or a shilling sterling apiece.

After this digression, it is time to run on after Tonoi and the Yankee.

CHAPTER LV.

A HUNTING RAMBLE WITH ZEKE

AT THE foot of the mountain, a steep path went up among rocks and clefts mantled with verdure. Here and there were green gulfs, down which it made one giddy to peep. At last we gained an overhanging, wooded shelf of land which crowned the heights; and along this, the path, well shaded, ran like a gallery.

In every direction the scenery was enchanting. There was a low, rustling breeze; and below, in the vale, the leaves were quivering; the sea lay, blue and serene, in the distance; and inland the surface swelled up, ridge after ridge, and peak upon peak, all bathed in the Indian haze of the Tropics, and dreamy to look upon. Still valleys, leagues away, reposed in the deep shadows of the mountains; and here and there, waterfalls lifted up their voices in the solitude. High above all, and central, the "Marling-spike" lifted its finger. Upon the hillsides, small groups of bullocks were seen; some quietly browsing; others slowly winding into the valleys.

We went on, directing our course for a slope of these hills, a mile or two further, where the nearest bullocks were seen.

We were cautious in keeping to the windward of them; their sense of smell and hearing being, like those of all wild creatures, exceedingly acute.

As there was no knowing that we might not surprise some other kind of game in the coverts through which we were passing, we crept along warily.

The wild hogs of the island are uncommonly fierce; and as they often attack the natives, I could not help following Tonoi's example of once in a while peeping in under the foliage. Frequent retrospective glances also served to assure me that our retreat was not cut off.

As we rounded a clump of bushes, a noise behind them, like the crackling of dry branches, broke the stillness. In an instant, Tonoi's hand was on a bough, ready for a spring, and Zeke's finger touched the trigger of his piece. Again the stillness was broken; and thinking it high time to get ready, I brought my musket to my shoulder.

"Look sharp!" cried the Yankee; and dropping on one knee, he brushed the twigs aside. Presently, off went his piece; and with a wild snort, a black, bristling boar--his cherry red lip curled up by two glittering tusks--dashed, unharmed, across the path, and crashed through the opposite thicket. I saluted him with a charge as he disappeared; but not the slightest notice was taken of the civility.

By this time, Tonoi, the illustrious descendant of the Bishops of

Imeeo, was twenty feet from the ground. "Aramai! come down, you old fool!" cried the Yankee; "the pesky critter's on t'other side of the island aforethis."

"I rayther guess," he continued, as we began reloading, "that we've spoiled sport by firing at that 'ere tarnal hog. Them bullocks heard the racket, and are flinging their tails about now on the keen jump. Quick, Paul, and let's climb that rock yonder, and see if so be there's any in sight."

But none were to be seen, except at such a distance that they looked like ants.

As evening was now at hand, my companion proposed our returning home forthwith; and then, after a sound night's rest, starting in the morning upon a good day's hunt with the whole force of the plantation.

Following another pass in descending into the valley, we passed through some nobly wooded land on the face of the mountain.

One variety of tree particularly attracted my attention. The dark mossy stem, over seventy feet high, was perfectly branchless for many feet above the ground, when it shot out in broad boughs laden with lustrous leaves of the deepest green. And all round the lower part of the trunk, thin, slab-like buttresses of bark, perfectly smooth, and radiating from a common centre, projected along the ground for at least two yards. From below, these natural props tapered upward until gradually blended with the trunk itself. There were signs of the wild cattle having sheltered themselves behind them. Zeke called this the canoe tree; as in old times it supplied the navies of the Kings of Tahiti. For canoe building, the woods is still used. Being extremely dense, and impervious to worms, it is very durable.

Emerging from the forest, when half-way down the hillside, we came upon an open space, covered with ferns and grass, over which a few lonely trees were casting long shadows in the setting sun. Here, a piece of ground some hundred feet square, covered with weeds and brambles, and sounding hollow to the tread, was inclosed by a ruinous wall of stones. Tonoi said it was an almost forgotten burial-place, of great antiquity, where no one had been interred since the islanders had been Christians. Sealed up in dry, deep vaults, many a dead heathen was lying here.

Curious to prove the old man's statement, I was anxious to get a peep at the catacombs; but hermetically overgrown with vegetation as they were, no aperture was visible.

Before gaining the level of the valley, we passed by the site of a village, near a watercourse, long since deserted. There was nothing but stone walls, and rude dismantled foundations of houses, constructed of the same material. Large trees and brushwood were growing rankly among them.

I asked Tonoi how long it was since anyone had lived here. "Me, tammaree (boy)--plenty kannaker (men) Martair," he replied. "Now, only poor pehe kannaka (fishermen) left--me born here."

Going down the valley, vegetation of every kind presented a different aspect from that of the high land.

Chief among the trees of the plain on this island is the "Ati," large and lofty, with a massive trunk, and broad, laurel-shaped leaves. The wood is splendid. In Tahiti, I was shown a narrow, polished plank fit to make a cabinet for a king. Taken from the heart of the tree, it was of a deep, rich scarlet, traced with yellow veins, and in some places clouded with hazel.

In the same grove with the regal "AH" you may see the beautiful flowering "Hotoo"; its pyramid of shining leaves diversified with numberless small, white blossoms.

Planted with trees as the valley is almost throughout its entire length, I was astonished to observe so very few which were useful to the natives: not one in a hundred was a cocoa-nut or bread-fruit tree.

But here Tonoi again enlightened me. In the sanguinary religious hostilities which ensued upon the conversion of Christianity of the first Pomaree, a war-party from Tahiti destroyed (by "girdling" the bark) entire groves of these invaluable trees. For some time afterwards they stood stark and leafless in the sun; sad monuments of the fate which befell the inhabitants of the valley.

CHAPTER LVI.

MOSQUITOES

THE NIGHT following the hunting trip, Long Ghost and myself, after a valiant defence, had to fly the house on account of the mosquitoes.

And here I cannot avoid relating a story, rife among the natives, concerning the manner in which these insects were introduced upon the island.

Some years previous, a whaling captain, touching at an adjoining bay, got into difficulty with its inhabitants, and at last carried his complaint before one of the native tribunals; but receiving no satisfaction, and deeming himself aggrieved, he resolved upon taking signal revenge. One night, he towed a rotten old water-cask ashore, and left it in a neglected Taro patch where the ground was warm and moist. Hence the mosquitoes.

I tried my best to learn the name of this man; and hereby do what I can to hand it down to posterity. It was Coleman--Nathan Cole-man. The ship belonged to Nantucket.

When tormented by the mosquitoes, I found much relief in coupling the word "Coleman" with another of one syllable, and pronouncing them together energetically.

The doctor suggested a walk to the beach, where there was a long, low shed tumbling to pieces, but open lengthwise to a current of air which he thought might keep off the mosquitoes. So thither we went.

The ruin partially sheltered a relic of times gone by, which, a few days after, we examined with much curiosity. It was an old war-canoe, crumbling to dust. Being supported by the same rude blocks upon which, apparently, it had years before been hollowed out, in all probability it had never been afloat.

Outside, it seemed originally stained of a green colour, which, here and there, was now changed into a dingy purple. The prow terminated in a high, blunt beak; both sides were covered with carving; and upon the stern, was something which Long Ghost maintained to be the arms of the royal House of Pomaree. The device had an heraldic look, certainly--being two sharks with the talons of hawks clawing a knot left projecting from the wood.

The canoe was at least forty feet long, about two wide, and four deep. The upper part--consisting of narrow planks laced together with cords of sinnate--had in many places fallen off, and lay decaying upon the ground. Still, there were ample accommodations left for sleeping; and in we sprang--the doctor into the bow, and I into the stern. I soon fell asleep; but waking suddenly, cramped in every joint from my constrained posture, I thought, for an instant, that I must have been prematurely screwed down in my coffin.

Presenting my compliments to Long Ghost, I asked how it fared with him.

"Bad enough," he replied, as he tossed about in the outlandish rubbish lying in the bottom of our couch. "Pah! how these old mats smell!"

As he continued talking in this exciting strain for some time, I at last made no reply, having resumed certain mathematical reveries to induce repose. But finding the multiplication table of no avail, I summoned up a grayish image of chaos in a sort of sliding fluidity, and was just falling into a nap on the strength of it, when I heard a solitary and distinct buzz. The hour of my calamity was at hand. One blended hum, the creature darted into the canoe like a small swordfish; and I out of it.

Upon getting into the open air, to my surprise, there was Long Ghost, fanning himself wildly with an old paddle. He had just made a noiseless escape from a swarm which had attacked his own end of the canoe.

It was now proposed to try the water; so a small fishing canoe, hauled up near by, was quickly launched; and paddling a good distance off, we dropped overboard the native contrivance for an anchor--a heavy stone, attached to a cable of braided bark. At this part of the island the encircling reef was close to the shore, leaving the water within smooth, and extremely shallow.

It was a blessed thought! We knew nothing till sunrise, when the motion of our aquatic cot awakened us. I looked up, and beheld Zeke wading toward the shore, and towing us after him by the bark cable. Pointing to the reef, he told us we had had a narrow escape.

It was true enough; the water-sprites had rolled our stone out of its noose, and we had floated away.

CHAPTER LVII.

THE SECOND HUNT IN THE MOUNTAINS

FAIR dawned, over the hills of Martair, the jocund morning of our hunt.

Everything had been prepared for it overnight; and, when we arrived at the house, a good breakfast was spread by Shorty: and old Tonoi was bustling about like an innkeeper. Several of his men, also, were in attendance to accompany us with calabashes of food; and, in case we met with any success, to officiate as bearers of burdens on our return.

Apprised, the evening previous, of the meditated sport, the doctor had announced his willingness to take part therein.

Now, subsequent events made us regard this expedition as a shrewd device of the Yankee's. Once get us off on a pleasure trip, and with what face could we afterward refuse to work? Beside, he enjoyed all the credit of giving us a holiday. Nor did he omit assuring us that, work or play, our wages were all the while running on.

A dilapidated old musket of Tonoi's was borrowed for the doctor. It was exceedingly short and heavy, with a clumsy lock, which required a strong finger to pull the trigger. On trying the piece by firing at a mark, Long Ghost was satisfied that it could not fail of doing execution: the charge went one way, and he the other.

Upon this, he endeavoured to negotiate an exchange of muskets with Shorty; but the Cockney was proof against his blandishments; at last, he intrusted his weapon to one of the natives to carry for him.

Marshalling our forces, we started for the head of the valley; near which a path ascended to a range of high land, said to be a favourite resort of the cattle.

Shortly after gaining the heights, a small herd, some way off, was perceived entering a wood. We hurried on; and, dividing our party, went in after them at four different points; each white man followed by several natives.

I soon found myself in a dense covert; and, after looking round, was just emerging into a clear space, when I heard a report, and a bullet knocked the bark from a tree near by. The same instant there was a trampling and crashing; and five bullocks, nearly abreast, broke into View across the opening, and plunged right toward the spot where myself and three of the islanders were standing.

They were small, black, vicious-looking creatures; with short, sharp horns, red nostrils, and eyes like coals of fire. On they came--their dark woolly heads hanging down.

By this time my island backers were roosting among the trees. Glancing round, for an instant, to discover a retreat in case of emergency, I raised my piece, when a voice cried out, from the wood, "Right between the 'orns, Paul! right between the 'orns!" Down went my barrel in range with a small white tuft on the forehead of the headmost one; and, letting him have it, I darted to one side. As I turned again, the five bullocks shot by like a blast, making the air eddy in their wake.

The Yankee now burst into view, and saluted them in flank. Whereupon, the fierce little bull with the tufted forehead flirted his long tail over his buttocks; kicked out with his hind feet, and shot forward a full length. It was nothing but a graze; and, in an instant, they were out of sight, the thicket into which they broke rocking overhead, and marking their progress.

The action over, the heavy artillery came up, in the person of the Long Doctor with the blunderbuss.

"Where are they?" he cried, out of breath.

"A mile or two h'off, by this time," replied the Cockney. "Lord, Paul! you ought to've sent an 'ailstone into that little black 'un."

While excusing my want of skill, as well as I could, Zeke, rushing forward, suddenly exclaimed, "Creation! what are you 'bout there, Peter?"

Peter, incensed at our ill luck, and ignorantly imputing it to the cowardice of our native auxiliaries, was bringing his piece to bear upon his trembling squire--the musket-carrier--now descending a tree.

Pulling trigger, the bullet went high over his head; and, hopping to the ground, bellowing like a calf, the fellow ran away as fast as his heels could carry him. The rest followed us, after this, with fear and trembling.

After forming our line of march anew, we went on for several hours without catching a glimpse of the game; the reports of the muskets having been heard at a great distance. At last, we mounted a craggy height, to obtain a wide view of the country. Prom this place, we beheld three cattle quietly browsing in a green opening of a wood below; the trees shutting them in all round.

A general re-examination of the muskets now took place, followed by a hasty lunch from the calabashes: we then started. As we descended the mountainside the cattle were in plain sight until we entered the forest, when we lost sight of them for a moment; but only to see them again, as we crept close up to the spot where they grazed.

They were a bull, a cow, and a calf. The cow was lying down in the shade, by the edge of the wood; the calf, sprawling out before her in the grass, licking her lips; while old Taurus himself stood close by, casting a paternal glance at this domestic little scene, and conjugally elevating his nose in the air.

"Now then," said Zeke, in a whisper, "let's take the poor creeturs while they are huddled together. Crawl along, b'ys; crawl along. Fire together, mind; and not till I say the word."

We crept up to the very edge of the open ground, and knelt behind a clump of bushes; resting our levelled barrels among the branches. The slight rustling was heard. Taurus turned round, dropped his head to the ground, and sent forth a low, sullen bellow; then snuffed the air. The cow rose on her foreknees, pitched forward alannedly, and stood upon her legs; while the calf, with ears pricked, got right underneath her. All three were now grouped, and in an instant would be off.

"I take the bull," cried our leader; "fire!"

The calf fell like a clod; its dam uttered a cry, and thrust her head into the thicket; but she turned, and came moaning up to the lifeless calf, going round and round it, snuffing fiercely with her bleeding nostrils. A crashing in the wood, and a loud roar, announced the flying bull.

Soon, another shot was fired, and the cow fell. Leaving some of the natives to look after the dead cattle, the rest of us hurried on after the bull; his dreadful bellowing guiding us to the spot where he lay. Wounded in the shoulder, in his fright and agony he had bounded into the wood; but when we came up to him, he had sunk to the earth in a green hollow, thrusting his black muzzle into a pool of his own blood, and tossing it over his hide in clots.

The Yankee brought his piece to a rest; and, the next instant, the wild brute sprang into the air, and with his forelegs crouching under him, fell dead.

Our island friends were now in high spirits; all courage and alacrity. Old Tonoi thought nothing of taking poor Taurus himself by the horns, and peering into his glazed eyes.

Our ship knives were at once in request; and, skinning the cattle, we hung them high up by cords of bark from the boughs of a tree. Withdrawing into a covert, we there waited for the wild hogs; which, according to Zeke, would soon make their appearance, lured by the smell of blood. Presently we heard them coming, in two or three different directions; and, in a moment, they were tearing the offal to pieces.

As only one shot at these creatures could be relied on, we intended firing simultaneously; but, somehow or other, the doctor's piece went off by itself, and one of the hogs dropped. The others then breaking into the thicket, the rest of us sprang after them; resolved to have another shot at all hazards.

The Cockney darted among some bushes; and, a few moments after, we heard the report of his musket, followed by a quick cry. On running up, we saw our comrade doing battle with a young devil of a boar, as black as night, whose snout had been partly torn away. Firing when the game was in full career, and coming directly toward him, Shorty had been assailed by the enraged brute; it was now crunching the breech of the musket, with which he had tried to club it; Shorty holding fast to the barrel, and fingering his waist for a knife.
Being in advance of the others, I clapped my gun to the boar's head, and so put an end to the contest.

Evening now coming on, we set to work loading our carriers. The cattle were so small that a stout native could walk off with an entire quarter; brushing through thickets, and descending rocks without an apparent effort; though, to tell the truth, no white man present could have done the thing with any ease. As for the wild hogs, none of the islanders could be induced to carry Shorty's; some invincible superstition being connected with its black colour. We were, therefore, obliged to leave it. The other, a spotted one, being slung by green thongs to a pole, was marched off with by two young natives.

With our bearers of burdens ahead, we then commenced our return down the valley. Half-way home, darkness overtook us in the woods; and torches became necessary. We stopped, and made them of dry palm branches; and then, sending two lads on in advance for the purpose of gathering fuel to feed the flambeaux, we continued our journey.

It was a wild sight. The torches, waved aloft, flashed through the forest; and, where the ground admitted, the islanders went along on a brisk trot, notwithstanding they bent forward under their loads. Their naked backs were stained with blood; and occasionally, running by each other, they raised wild cries which startled the hillsides.

CHAPTER LVIII.

THE HUNTING-FEAST; AND A VISIT TO AFREHITOO

TWO BULLOCKS and a boar! No bad trophies of our day's sport. So by torchlight we marched into the plantation, the wild hog rocking from its pole, and the doctor singing an old hunting-song--Tally-ho! the chorus of which swelled high above the yells of the natives.

We resolved to make a night of it. Kindling a great fire just outside the dwelling, and hanging one of the heifer's quarters from a limb of the banian-tree, everyone was at liberty to cut and broil for himself. Baskets of roasted bread-fruit, and plenty of taro pudding; bunches of bananas, and young cocoa-nuts, had also been provided by the natives against our return.

The fire burned bravely, keeping off the mosquitoes, and making every man's face glow like a beaker of Port. The meat had the true wild-game flavour, not at all impaired by our famous appetites, and a couple of flasks of white brandy, which Zeke, producing from his secret store, circulated freely.

There was no end to my long comrade's spirits. After telling his stories, and singing his songs, he sprang to his feet, clasped a young damsel of the grove round the waist, and waltzed over the grass with her. But there's no telling all the pranks he played that night.

The natives, who delight in a wag, emphatically pronounced him "maitai."

It was long after midnight ere we broke up; but when the rest had retired, Zeke, with the true thrift of a Yankee, salted down what was left of the meat.

The next day was Sunday; and at my request, Shorty accompanied me to Afrehitoo--a neighbouring bay, and the seat of a mission, almost directly opposite Papeetee. In Afrehitoo is a large church and school-house, both quite dilapidated; and planted amid shrubbery on a fine knoll, stands a very tasteful cottage, commanding a view across the channel. In passing, I caught sight of a graceful calico skirt disappearing from the piazza through a doorway. The place was the residence of the missionary.

A trim little sail-boat was dancing out at her moorings, a few yards from the beach.

Straggling over the low lands in the vicinity were several native huts--untidy enough--but much better every way than most of those in Tahiti.

We attended service at the church, where we found but a small congregation; and after what I had seen in Papeetee, nothing very interesting took place. But the audience had a curious, fidgety look, which I knew not how to account for until we ascertained that a sermon with the eighth commandment for a text was being preached.

It seemed that there lived an Englishman in the district, who, like our friends, the planters, was cultivating Tombez potatoes for the Papeetee market.

In spite of all his precautions, the natives were in the habit of making nocturnal forays into his inclosure, and carrying off the potatoes. One night he fired a fowling-piece, charged with pepper and salt, at several shadows which he discovered stealing across his premises. They fled. But it was like seasoning anything else; the knaves stole again with a greater relish than ever; and the very next night, he caught a party in the act of roasting a basketful of potatoes under his own cooking-shed. At last, he stated his grievances to the missionary; who, for the benefit of his congregation, preached the sermon we heard.

Now, there were no thieves in Martair; but then, the people of the valley were bribed to be honest. It was a regular business transaction between them and the planters. In consideration of so many potatoes "to them in hand, duly paid," they were to abstain from all depredations upon the plantation. Another security against roguery was the permanent residence upon the premises of their chief, Tonoi.

On our return to Martair in the afternoon, we found the doctor and

Zeke making themselves comfortable. The latter was reclining on the ground, pipe in mouth, watching the doctor, who, sitting like a Turk, before a large iron kettle, was slicing potatoes and Indian turnip, and now and then shattering splinters from a bone; all of which, by turns, were thrown into the pot. He was making what he called "Bullock broth."

In gastronomic affairs, my friend was something of an artist; and by way of improving his knowledge, did nothing the rest of the day but practise in what might be called Experimental Cookery: broiling and grilling, and deviling slices of meat, and subjecting them to all sorts of igneous operations. It was the first fresh beef that either of us had tasted in more than a year.

"Oh, ye'll pick up arter a while, Peter," observed Zeke toward night, as Long Ghost was turning a great rib over the coals--"what d'ye think, Paul?"

"He'll get along, I dare say," replied I; "he only wants to get those cheeks of his tanned." To tell the truth, I was not a little pleased to see the doctor's reputation as an invalid fading away so fast; especially as, on the strength of his being one, he had promised to have such easy times of it, and very likely, too, at my expense.

CHAPTER LIX.

THE MURPHIES

DOZING in our canoe the next morning about daybreak, we were awakened by Zeke's hailing us loudly from the beach.

Upon paddling up, he told us that a canoe had arrived overnight, from Papeetee, with an order from a ship lying there for a supply of his potatoes; and as they must be on board the vessel by noon, he wanted us to assist in bringing them down to his sail-boat.

My long comrade was one of those who, from always thrusting forth the wrong foot foremost when they rise, or committing some other indiscretion of the limbs, are more or less crabbed or sullen before breakfast. It was in vain, therefore, that the Yankee deplored the urgency of the case which obliged him to call us up thus early:--the doctor only looked the more glum, and said nothing in reply.

At last, by way of getting up a little enthusiasm for the occasion, the Yankee exclaimed quite spiritedly, "What d'ye say, then, b'ys, shall we get at it?"

"Yes, in the devil's name!" replied the doctor, like a snapping turtle; and we moved on to the house. Notwithstanding his ungracious answer, he probably thought that, after the gastronomic performance of the day previous, it would hardly do to hang back. At the house, we found Shorty ready with the hoes; and we at once repaired to the farther side of the inclosure, where the potatoes had yet to be taken out of the ground.

The rich, tawny soil seemed specially adapted to the crop; the great yellow murphies rolling out of the hills like eggs from a nest.

My comrade really surprised me by the zeal with which he applied himself to his hoe. For my own part, exhilarated by the cool breath of the morning, I worked away like a good fellow. As for Zeke and the Cockney, they seemed mightily pleased at this evidence of our willingness to exert ourselves.

It was not long ere all the potatoes were turned out; and then came the worst of it: they were to be lugged down to the beach, a distance of at least a quarter of a mile. And there being no such thing as a barrow, or cart, on the island, there was nothing for it but spinal-marrows and broad shoulders. Well knowing that this part of the business would be anything but agreeable, Zeke did his best to put as encouraging a face upon it as possible; and giving us no time to indulge in desponding thoughts, gleefully directed our attention to a pile of rude baskets--made of stout stalks--which had been provided for the occasion. So, without more ado, we helped ourselves from the heap: and soon we were all four staggering along under our loads.

The first trip down, we arrived at the beach together: Zeke's enthusiastic cries proving irresistible. A trip or two more, however, and my shoulders began to grate in their sockets; while the doctor's tall figure acquired an obvious stoop. Presently, we both threw down our baskets, protesting we could stand it no longer. But our employers, bent, as it Were, upon getting the work out of us by a silent appeal to our moral sense, toiled away without pretending to notice us. It was as much as to say, "There, men, we've been boarding and lodging ye for the last three days; and yesterday ye did nothing earthly but eat; so stand by now, and look at us working, if ye dare." Thus driven to it, then, we resumed our employment. Yet, in spite of all we could do, we lagged behind Zeke and Shorty, who, breathing hard, and perspiring at every pore, toiled away without pause or cessation. I almost wickedly wished that they would load themselves down with one potato too many.

Gasping as I was with my own hamper, I could not, for the life of me, help laughing at Long Ghost. There he went:--his long neck thrust forward, his arms twisted behind him to form a shelf for his basket to rest on; and his stilts of legs every once in a while giving way under him, as if his knee-joints slipped either way.

"There! I carry no more!" he exclaimed all at once, flinging his potatoes into the boat, where the Yankee was just then stowing them away.

"Oh, then," said Zeke, quite briskly, "I guess you and Paul had better try the 'barrel-machine'--come along, I'll fix ye out in no time"; and, so saying, he waded ashore, and hurried back to the house, bidding us follow.

Wondering what upon earth the "barrel-machine" could be, and rather suspicious of it, we limped after. On arriving at the house, we found him getting ready a sort of sedan-chair. It was nothing more than an old barrel suspended by a rope from the middle of a stout oar. Quite an ingenious contrivance of the Yankee's; and his proposed arrangement with regard to mine and the doctor's shoulders was equally so.

"There now!" said he, when everything was ready, "there's no back-breaking about this; you can stand right up under it, you see: jist try it once"; and he politely rested the blade of the oar on my comrade's right shoulder, and the other end on mine, leaving the barrel between us.

"Jist the thing!" he added, standing off admiringly, while we remained in this interesting attitude.

There was no help for us; with broken hearts and backs we trudged back to the field; the doctor all the while saying masses.

Upon starting with the loaded barrel, for a few paces we got along pretty well, and were constrained to think the idea not a bad one. But we did not long think so. In less than five minutes we came to a dead halt, the springing and buckling of the clumsy oar being almost unendurable.

"Let's shift ends," cried the doctor, who did not relish the blade of the stick, which was cutting into the blade of his shoulder.

At last, by stages short and frequent, we managed to shamble down the beach, where we again dumped our cargo, in something of a pet.

"Why not make the natives help?" asked Long Ghost, rubbing his shoulder.

"Natives be dumned!" said the Yankee, "twenty on 'em ain't worth one white man. They never was meant to work any, them chaps; and they knows it, too, for dumned little work any on 'em ever does."

But, notwithstanding this abuse, Zeke was at last obliged to press a few of the bipeds into service. "Aramai!" (come here) he shouted to several, who, reclining on a bank, had hitherto been critical observers of our proceedings; and, among other things, had been particularly amused by the performance with the sedan-chair.

After making these fellows load their baskets together, the Yankee filled his own, and then drove them before him down to the beach. Probably he had seen the herds of panniered mules driven in this way by mounted Indians along the great Callao to Lima. The boat at last loaded, the Yankee, taking with him a couple of natives, at once hoisted sail, and stood across the channel for Papeetee.

The next morning at breakfast, old Tonoi ran in, and told us that the voyagers were returning. We hurried down to the beach, and saw the boat gliding toward us, with a dozing islander at the helm, and Zeke standing up in the bows, jingling a small bag of silver, the proceeds of his cargo.

CHAPTER LX.

WHAT THEY THOUGHT OF US IN MARTAIR

SEVERAL quiet days now passed away, during which we just worked sufficiently to sharpen our appetites; the planters leniently exempting us from any severe toil.

Their desire to retain us became more and more evident; which was not to be wondered at; for, beside esteeming us from the beginning a couple of civil, good-natured fellows, who would soon become quite at-home with them, they were not slow in perceiving that we were far different from the common run of rovers; and that our society was both entertaining and instructive to a couple of solitary, illiterate men like themselves.

In a literary point of view, indeed, they soon regarded us with emotions of envy and wonder; and the doctor was considered nothing short of a prodigy. The Cockney found out that he (the doctor) could read a book upside down, without even so much as spelling the big words beforehand; and the Yankee, in the twinkling of an eye, received from him the sum total of several arithmetical items, stated aloud, with the view of testing the extent of his mathematical lore.

Then, frequently, in discoursing upon men and things, my long comrade employed such imposing phrases that, upon one occasion, they actually remained uncovered while he talked.

In short, their favourable opinion of Long Ghost in particular rose higher and higher every day; and they began to indulge in all manner of dreams concerning the advantages to be derived from employing so learned a labourer. Among other projects revealed was that of building a small craft of some forty tons for the purpose of trading among the neighbouring islands. With a native crew, we would then take turns cruising over the tranquil Pacific; touching here and there, as caprice suggested, and collecting romantic articles of commerce;--beach-de-mer, the pearl-oyster, arrow-root, ambergris, sandal-wood, cocoa-nut oil, and edible birdnests.

This South Sea yachting was delightful to think of; and straightway, the doctor announced his willingness to navigate the future schooner clear of all shoals and reefs whatsoever. His impudence was audacious. He enlarged upon the science of navigation; treated us to a dissertation on Mercator's Sailing and the Azimuth compass; and went into an inexplicable explanation of the Lord only knows what plan of his for infallibly settling the longitude.

Whenever my comrade thus gave the reins to his fine fancy, it was a treat to listen, and therefore I never interfered; but, with the planters, sat in mute admiration before him. This apparent self-abasement on my part must have been considered as truly indicative of our respective merits; for, to my no small concern, I quickly perceived that, in the estimate formed of us, Long Ghost began to be rated far above myself. For aught I knew, indeed, he might have privately thrown out a hint concerning the difference in our respective stations aboard the Julia; or else the planters must have considered him some illustrious individual, for certain inscrutable reasons, going incog. With this idea of him, his undisguised disinclination for work became venial; and entertaining such views of extending their business, they counted more upon his ultimate value to them as a man of science than as a mere ditcher.

Nor did the humorous doctor forbear to foster an opinion every way so advantageous to himself; at times, for the sake of the joke, assuming airs of superiority over myself, which, though laughable enough, were sometimes annoying.

To tell the plain truth, things at last came to such a pass that I told him, up and down, that I had no notion to put up with his pretensions; if he were going to play the gentleman, I was going to follow suit; and then there would quickly be an explosion.

At this he laughed heartily; and after some mirthful chat, we resolved upon leaving the valley as soon as we could do so with a proper regard to politeness.

At supper, therefore, the same evening, the doctor hinted at our intention.

Though much surprised, and vexed, Zeke moved not a muscle. "Peter," said he at last--very gravely--and after mature deliberation, "would you like to do the cooking? It's easy work; and you needn't do anything else. Paul's heartier; he can work in the field when it suits him; and before long, we'll have ye at something more agreeable:--won't we, Shorty?"

Shorty assented.

Doubtless, the proposed arrangement was a snug one; especially the sinecure for the doctor; but I by no means relished the functions allotted to myself--they were too indefinite. Nothing final, however, was agreed upon;--our intention to leave was revealed, and that was enough for the present. But, as we said nothing further about going, the Yankee must have concluded that we might yet be induced to remain. He redoubled his endeavours to make us contented.

It was during this state of affairs that, one morning, before breakfast, we were set to weeding in a potato-patch; and the planters being engaged at the house, we were left to ourselves.

Now, though the pulling of weeds was considered by our employers an easy occupation (for which reason they had assigned it to us), and although as a garden recreation it may be pleasant enough, for those who like it--still, long persisted in, the business becomes excessively irksome.

Nevertheless, we toiled away for some time, until the doctor, who, from his height, was obliged to stoop at a very acute angle, suddenly sprang upright; and with one hand propping his spinal column, exclaimed, "Oh, that one's joints were but provided with holes to drop a little oil through!"

Vain as the aspiration was for this proposed improvement upon our species, I cordially responded thereto; for every vertebra in my spine was articulating in sympathy.

Presently, the sun rose over the mountains, inducing that deadly morning languor so fatal to early exertion in a warm climate. We could stand it no longer; but, shouldering our hoes, moved on to the house, resolved to impose no more upon the good-nature of the planters by continuing one moment longer in an occupation so extremely uncongenial.

We freely told them so. Zeke was exceedingly hurt, and said everything he could think of to alter our determination; but, finding all unavailing, he very hospitably urged us not to be in any hurry about leaving; for we might stay with him as guests until we had time to decide upon our future movements.

We thanked him sincerely; but replied that, the following morning, we must turn our backs upon the hills of Martair.

CHAPTER LXI.

PREPARING FOR THE JOURNEY

DURING the remainder of the day we loitered about, talking over our plans.

The doctor was all eagerness to visit Tamai, a solitary inland village, standing upon the banks of a considerable lake of the same name, and embosomed among groves. From Afrehitoo you went to this place by a lonely pathway leading through the wildest scenery in the world. Much, too, we had heard concerning the lake itself, which abounded in such delicious fish that, in former times, angling parties occasionally came over to it from Papeetee.

Upon its banks, moreover, grew the finest fruit of the islands, and in their greatest perfection. The "Ve," or Brazilian plum, here attained the size of an orange; and the gorgeous "Arheea," or red apple of Tahiti, blushed with deeper dyes than in any of the seaward valleys.

Beside all this, in Tamai dwelt the most beautiful and unsophisticated women in the entire Society group. In short, the village was so remote from the coast, and had been so much less affected by recent changes than other places that, in most things, Tahitian life was here seen as formerly existing in the days of young Otoo, the boy-king, in Cook's time.

After obtaining from the planters all the information which was needed, we decided upon penetrating to the village; and after a temporary sojourn there, to strike the beach again, and journey round to Taloo, a harbour on the opposite side of the island.

We at once put ourselves in travelling trim. Just previous to leaving Tahiti, having found my wardrobe reduced to two suits (frock and trousers, both much the worse for wear), I had quilted them together for mutual preservation (after a fashion peculiar to sailors); engrafting a red frock upon a blue one, and producing thereby a choice variety in the way of clothing. This was the extent of my wardrobe. Nor was the doctor by any means better off. His improvidence had at last driven him to don the nautical garb; but by this time his frock--a light cotton one--had almost given out, and he had nothing to replace it. Shorty very generously offered him one which was a little less ragged; but the alms were proudly refused; Long Ghost preferring to assume the ancient costume of Tahiti--the "Roora."

This garment, once worn as a festival dress, is now seldom met with; but Captain Bob had often shown us one which he kept as an heirloom. It was a cloak, or mantle, of yellow tappa, precisely similar to the "poncho" worn by the South-American Spaniards. The head being slipped through a slit in the middle, the robe hangs about the person in ample drapery. Tonoi obtained sufficient coarse brown tappa to make a short mantle of this description; and in five minutes the doctor was equipped. Zeke, eyeing his toga critically, reminded its proprietor that there were many streams to ford, and precipices to scale, between Martair and Tamai; and if he travelled in petticoats, he had better hold them up.

Besides other deficiencies, we were utterly shoeless. In the free and easy Pacific, sailors seldom wear shoes; mine had been tossed overboard the day we met the Trades; and except in one or two tramps ashore, I had never worn any since. In Martair, they would have been desirable: but none were to be had. For the expedition we meditated, however, they were indispensable. Zeke, being the owner of a pair of huge, dilapidated boots, hanging from a rafter like saddlebags, the doctor succeeded in exchanging for them a case-knife, the last valuable article in his possession. For myself, I made sandals from a bullock's hide, such as are worn by the Indians in California. They are made in a minute; the sole, rudely fashioned to the foot, being confined across the instep by three straps of leather.

Our headgear deserves a passing word. My comrade's was a brave old Panama hat, made of grass, almost as fine as threads of silk; and so elastic that, upon rolling it up, it sprang into perfect shape again. Set off by the jaunty slouch of this Spanish sombrero, Doctor Long Ghost, in this and his Eoora, looked like a mendicant grandee.

Nor was my own appearance in an Eastern turban less distinguished. The way I came to wear it was this. My hat having been knocked overboard a few days before reaching Papeetee, I was obliged to mount an abominable wad of parti-coloured worsted--what sailors call a Scotch cap. Everyone knows the elasticity of knit wool; and this Caledonian head-dress crowned my temples so effectually that the confined atmosphere engendered was prejudicial to my curls. In vain I tried to ventilate the cap: every gash made seemed to heal whole in no time. Then such a continual chafing as it kept up in a hot sun.

Seeing my dislike to the thing, Kooloo, my worthy friend, prevailed upon me to bestow it upon him. I did so; hinting that a good boiling might restore the original brilliancy of the colours.

It was then that I mounted the turban. Taking a new Regatta frock of the doctor's, which was of a gay calico, and winding it round my head in folds, I allowed the sleeves to droop behind--thus forming a good defence against the sun, though in a shower it was best off. The pendent sleeves adding much to the effect, the doctor called me the Bashaw with Two Tails.

Thus arrayed, we were ready for Tamai; in whose green saloons we counted upon creating no small sensation.

CHAPTER LXII.

TAMAI

LONG before sunrise the next morning my sandals were laced on, and the doctor had vaulted into Zeke's boots.

Expecting to see us again before we went to Taloo, the planters wished us a pleasant journey; and, on parting, very generously presented us with a pound or two of what sailors call "plug" tobacco; telling us to cut it up into small change; the Virginian weed being the principal circulating medium on the island.

Tamai, we were told, was not more than three or four leagues distant; so making allowances for a wild road, a few hours to rest at noon, and our determination to take the journey leisurely, we counted upon reaching the shores of the lake some time in the flush of the evening.

For several hours we went on slowly through wood and ravine, and over hill and precipice, seeing nothing but occasional herds of wild cattle, and often resting; until we found ourselves, about noon, in the very heart of the island.

It was a green, cool hollow among the mountains, into which we at last descended with a bound. The place was gushing with a hundred springs, and shaded over with great solemn trees, on whose mossy boles the moisture stood in beads. Strange to say, no traces of the bullocks ever having been here were revealed. Nor was there a sound to be heard, nor a bird to be seen, nor any breath of wind stirring the leaves. The utter solitude and silence were oppressive; and after peering about under the shades, and seeing nothing but ranks of dark, motionless trunks, we hurried across the hollow, and ascended a steep mountain opposite.

Midway up, we rested where the earth had gathered about the roots of three palms, and thus formed a pleasant lounge, from which we looked down upon the hollow, now one dark green tuft of woodland at our feet. Here we brought forth a small calabash of "poee" a parting present from Tonoi. After eating heartily, we obtained fire by two sticks, and throwing ourselves back, puffed forth our fatigue in wreaths of smoke. At last we fell asleep; nor did we waken till the sun had sunk so low that its rays darted in upon us under the foliage.

Starting up, we then continued our journey; and as we gained the mountain top--there, to our surprise, lay the lake and village of Tamai. We had thought it a good league off. Where we stood, the yellow sunset was still lingering; but over the valley below long shadows were stealing--the rippling green lake reflecting the houses and trees just as they stood along its banks. Several small canoes, moored here and there to posts in the water, were dancing upon the waves; and one solitary fisherman was paddling over to a grassy point. In front of the houses, groups of natives were seen; some thrown at full length upon the ground, and others indolently leaning against the bamboos.

With whoop and halloo, we ran down the hills, the villagers soon hurrying forth to see who were coming. As we drew near, they gathered round, all curiosity to know what brought the "karhowrees" into their quiet country. The doctor contriving to make them understand the purely social object of our visit, they gave us a true Tahitian welcome; pointing into their dwellings, and saying they were ours as long as we chose to remain.

We were struck by the appearance of these people, both men and women; so much more healthful than the inhabitants of the bays. As for the young girls, they were more retiring and modest, more tidy in their dress, and far fresher and more beautiful than the damsels of the coast. A thousand pities, thought I, that they should bury their charms in this nook of a valley.

That night we abode in the house of Rartoo, a hospitable old chief. It was right on the shore of the lake; and at supper we looked out through a rustling screen of foliage upon the surface of the starlit water.

The next day we rambled about, and found a happy little community, comparatively free from many deplorable evils to which the rest of their countrymen are subject. Their time, too, was more occupied. To my surprise, the manufacture of tappa was going on in several buildings. European calicoes were seldom seen, and not many articles of foreign origin of any description.

The people of Tamai were nominally Christians; but being so remote from ecclesiastical jurisdiction, their religion sat lightly upon them. We had been told, even, that many heathenish games and dances still secretly lingered in their valley.

Now the prospect of seeing an old-fashioned "hevar," or Tahitian reel, was one of the inducements which brought us here; and so, finding Rartoo rather liberal in his religious ideas, we disclosed our desire. At first he demurred; and shrugging his shoulders like a Frenchman, declared it could not be brought about--was a dangerous matter to attempt, and might bring all concerned into trouble. But we overcame all this, convinced him that the thing could be done, and a "hevar," a genuine pagan fandango, was arranged for that very night.

CHAPTER LXIII.

A DANCE IN THE VALLEY

THERE were some ill-natured people--tell-tales--it seemed, in Tamai; and hence there was a deal of mystery about getting up the dance.

An hour or two before midnight, Rartoo entered the house, and, throwing robes of tappa over us, bade us follow at a distance behind him; and, until out of the village, hood our faces. Keenly alive to the adventure, we obeyed. At last, after taking a wide circuit, we came out upon the farthest shore of the lake. It was a wide, dewy, space; lighted up by a full moon, and carpeted with a minute species of fern growing closely together. It swept right down to the water, showing the village opposite, glistening among the groves.

Near the trees, on one side of the clear space, was a ruinous pile of stones many rods in extent; upon which had formerly stood a temple of Oro. At present, there was nothing but a rude hut, planted on the lowermost terrace. It seemed to have been used as a "tappa herree," or house for making the native cloth.

Here we saw lights gleaming from between the bamboos, and casting long, rod-like shadows upon the ground without. Voices also were heard. We went up, and had a peep at the dancers who were getting ready for the ballet. They were some twenty in number;-waited upon by hideous old crones, who might have been duennas. Long Ghost proposed to send the latter packing; but Rartoo said it would never do, and so they were permitted to remain.

We tried to effect an entrance at the door, which was fastened; but, after a noisy discussion with one of the old witches within, our guide became fidgety, and, at last, told us to desist, or we would spoil all. He then led us off to a distance to await the performance; as the girls, he said, did not wish to be recognized. He, furthermore, made us promise to remain where we were until all was over, and the dancers had retired.

We waited impatiently; and, at last, they came forth. They were arrayed in short tunics of white tappa; with garlands of flowers on their heads. Following them were the duennas, who remained clustering about the house, while the girls advanced a few paces; and, in an instant, two of them, taller than their companions, were standing, side by side, in the middle of a ring formed by the clasped hands of the rest. This movement was made in perfect silence.

Presently the two girls join hands overhead; and, crying out, "Ahloo! ahloo!" wave them to and fro. Upon which the ring begins to circle slowly; the dancers moving sideways, with their arms a little drooping. Soon they quicken their pace; and, at last, fly round and round: bosoms heaving, hair streaming, flowers dropping, and every sparkling eye circling in what seemed a line of light.

Meanwhile, the pair within are passing and repassing each other incessantly. Inclining sideways, so that their long hair falls far over, they glide this way and that; one foot continually in the air, and their fingers thrown forth, and twirling in the moonbeams.

"Ahloo! ahloo!" again cry the dance queens; and coming together in the middle of the ring, they once more lift up the arch, and stand motionless.

"Ahloo! ahloo!" Every link of the circle is broken; and the girls, deeply breathing, stand perfectly still. They pant hard and fast a moment or two; and then, just as the deep flush is dying away from their faces, slowly recede, all round; thus enlarging the ring.

Again the two leaders wave their hands, when the rest pause; and now, far apart, stand in the still moonlight like a circle of fairies. Presently, raising a strange chant, they softly sway themselves, gradually quickening the movement, until, at length, for a few passionate moments, with throbbing bosoms and glowing cheeks, they abandon themselves to all the spirit of the dance, apparently lost to everything around. But soon subsiding again into the same languid measure as before, they become motionless; and then, reeling forward on all sides, their eyes swimming in their heads, join in one wild chorus, and sink into each other's arms.

Such is the Lory-Lory, I think they call it; the dance of the backsliding girls of Tamai.

While it was going on, we had as much as we could do to keep the doctor from rushing forward and seizing a partner.

They would give us no more "hevars" that night; and Rartoo fairly dragged us away to a canoe, hauled up on the lake shore; when we reluctantly embarked, and paddling over to the village, arrived there in time for a good nap before sunrise.

The next day, the doctor went about trying to hunt up the overnight dancers. He thought to detect them by their late rising; but never was man more mistaken; for, on first sallying out, the whole village was asleep, waking up in concert about an hour after. But, in the course of the day, he came across several whom he at once charged with taking part in the "hevar." There were some prim-looking fellows standing by (visiting elders from Afrehitoo, perhaps), and the girls looked embarrassed; but parried the charge most skilfully.

Though soft as doves, in general, the ladies of Tamai are, nevertheless, flavoured with a slight tincture of what we queerly enough call the "devil"; and they showed it on the present occasion. For when the doctor pressed one rather hard, she all at once turned round upon him, and, giving him a box on the ear, told him to "hanree perrar!" (be off with himself.)

CHAPTER LXIV.

MYSTERIOUS

THERE was a little old man of a most hideous aspect living in Tamai, who, in a coarse mantle of tappa, went about the village, dancing, and singing, and making faces. He followed us about wherever we went; and, when unobserved by others, plucked at our garments, making frightful signs for us to go along with him somewhere, and see something.

It was in vain that we tried to get rid of him. Kicks and cuffs, even, were at last resorted to; but, though he howled like one possessed, he would not go away, but still haunted us. At last, we conjured the natives to rid us of him; but they only laughed; so we were forced to endure the dispensation as well as we could.

On the fourth night of our visit, returning home late from paying a few calls through the village, we turned a dark corner of trees, and came full upon our goblin friend: as usual, chattering, and motioning with his hands. The doctor, venting a curse, hurried forward; but, from some impulse or other, I stood my ground, resolved to find out what this unaccountable object wanted of us. Seeing me pause, he crept close up to me, peered into my face, and then retreated, beckoning me to follow; which I did.

In a few moments the village was behind us; and with my guide in advance, I found myself in the shadow of the heights overlooking the farther side of the valley. Here my guide paused until I came up with him; when, side by side, and without speaking, we ascended the hill.

Presently, we came to a wretched hut, barely distinguishable in the shade cast by the neighbouring trees. Pushing aside a rude sliding door, held together with thongs, the goblin signed me to enter. Within, it looked dark as pitch; so I gave him to understand that he must strike a light, and go in before me. Without replying, he disappeared in the darkness; and, after groping about, I heard two sticks rubbing together, and directly saw a spark. A native taper was then lighted, and I stooped, and entered.

It was a mere kennel. Foul old mats, and broken cocoa-nut shells, and calabashes were strewn about the floor of earth; and overhead I caught glimpses of the stars through chinks in the roof. Here and there the thatch had fallen through, and hung down in wisps.

I now told him to set about what he was going to do, or produce whatever he had to show without delay. Looking round fearfully, as if dreading a surprise, he commenced turning over and over the rubbish in one corner. At last, he clutched a calabash, stained black, and with the neck broken off; on one side of it was a large hole. Something seemed to be stuffed away in the vessel; and after a deal of poking at the aperture, a musty old pair of sailor trousers was drawn forth; and, holding them up eagerly, he inquired how many pieces of tobacco I would give for them.

Without replying, I hurried away; the old man chasing me, and shouting as I ran, until I gained the village. Here I dodged him, and made my way home, resolved never to disclose so inglorious an adventure.

To no purpose, the next morning, my comrade besought me to enlighten him; I preserved a mysterious silence.

The occurrence served me a good turn, however, so long as we abode in Tamai; for the old clothesman never afterwards troubled me; but forever haunted the doctor, who, in vain, supplicated Heaven to be delivered from him.

CHAPTER LXV.

THE HEGIRA, OR FLIGHT

"I SAY, doctor," cried I, a few days after my adventure with the goblin, as, in the absence of our host, we were one morning lounging upon the matting in his dwelling, smoking our reed pipes, "Tamai's a thriving place; why not settle down?"

"Faith!" said he, "not a bad idea, Paul. But do you fancy they'll let us stay, though?"

"Why, certainly; they would be overjoyed to have a couple of Karhowrees for townsmen."

"Gad! you're right, my pleasant fellow. Ha! ha! I'll put up a banana-leaf as a physician from London--deliver lectures on Polynesian antiquities--teach English in five lessons, of one hour each--establish power-looms for the manufacture of tappa--lay out a public park in the middle of the village, and found a festival in honour of Captain Cook!"

"But, surely, not without stopping to take breath," observed I.

The doctor's projects, to be sure, were of a rather visionary cast; but we seriously thought, nevertheless, of prolonging our stay in the valley for an indefinite period; and, with this understanding, we were turning over various plans for spending our time pleasantly, when several women came running into the house, and hurriedly besought us to heree! heree! (make our escape), crying out something about the Mickonarees.

Thinking that we were about to be taken up under the act for the suppression of vagrancy, we flew out of the house, sprang into a canoe before the door, and paddled with might and main over to the opposite side of the lake.

Approaching Rartoo's dwelling was a great crowd, among which we perceived several natives, who, from their partly European dress, we were certain did not reside in Tamai.

Plunging into the groves, we thanked our stars that we had thus narrowly escaped being apprehended as runaway seamen, and marched off to the beach. This, at least, was what we thought we had escaped.

Having fled the village, we could not think of prowling about its vicinity, and then returning; in doing so we might be risking our liberty again. We therefore determined upon journeying back to Martair; and setting our faces thitherward, we reached the planters' house about nightfall. They gave us a cordial reception, and a hearty supper; and we sat up talking until a late hour.

We now prepared to go round to Taloo, a place from which we were not far off when at Tamai; but wishing to see as much of the island as we could, we preferred returning to Martair, and then going round by way of the beach.

Taloo, the only frequented harbour of Imeeo, lies on the western side of the island, almost directly over against Martair. Upon one shore of the bay stands the village of Partoowye, a missionary station. In its vicinity is an extensive sugar plantation--the best in the South Seas, perhaps--worked by a person from Sydney.

The patrimonial property of the husband of Pomaree, and every way a delightful retreat, Partoowye was one of the occasional residences of the court. But at the time I write of it was permanently fixed there, the queen having fled thither from Tahiti.

Partoowye, they told us, was by no means the place Papeetee was. Ships seldom touched, and very few foreigners were living ashore. A solitary whaler, however, was reported to be lying in the harbour, wooding and watering, and to be in want of men.

All things considered, I could not help looking upon Taloo as offering "a splendid opening" for us adventurers. To say nothing of the facilities presented for going to sea in the whaler, or hiring ourselves out as day labourers in the sugar plantation, there were hopes to be entertained of being promoted to some office of high trust and emolument about the person of her majesty, the queen.

Nor was this expectation altogether Quixotic. In the train of many Polynesian princes roving whites are frequently found: gentleman pensioners of state, basking in the tropical sunshine of the court, and leading the pleasantest lives in the world. Upon islands little visited by foreigners the first seaman that settles down is generally domesticated in the family of the head chief or king; where he frequently discharges the functions of various offices, elsewhere filled by as many different individuals. As historiographer, for instance, he gives the natives some account of distant countries; as commissioner of the arts and sciences, he instructs them in the use of the jack-knife, and the best way of shaping bits of iron hoop into spear-heads; and as interpreter to his majesty, he facilitates intercourse with strangers; besides instructing the people generally in the uses of the most common English phrases, civil and profane; but oftener the latter.

These men generally marry well; often--like Hardy of Hannamanoo--into the Wood royal.

Sometimes they officiate as personal attendant, or First Lord in Waiting, to the king. At Amboi, one of the Tonga Islands, a vagabond Welshman bends his knee as cupbearer to his cannibal majesty. He mixes his morning cup of "arva," and, with profound genuflections, presents it in a cocoa-nut bowl, richly carved. Upon another island of the same group, where it is customary to bestow no small pains in dressing the hair--frizzing it out by a curious process into an enormous Pope's head--an old man-of-war's-man fills the post of barber to the king. And as his majesty is not very neat, his mop is exceedingly populous; so that, when Jack is not engaged in dressing the head intrusted to his charge, he busies himself in gently titillating it--a sort of skewer being actually worn about in the patient's hair for that special purpose.

Even upon the Sandwich Islands a low rabble of foreigners is kept about the person of Tammahammaha for the purpose of ministering to his ease or enjoyment.

Billy Loon, a jolly little negro, tricked out in a soiled blue jacket, studded all over with rusty bell buttons, and garnished with shabby gold lace, is the royal drummer and pounder of the tambourine. Joe, a wooden-legged Portuguese who lost his leg by a whale, is violinist; and Mordecai, as he is called, a villainous-looking scamp, going about with his cups and balls in a side pocket, diverts the court with his jugglery. These idle rascals receive no fixed salary, being altogether dependent upon the casual bounty of their master. Now and then they run up a score at the Dance Houses in Honolulu, where the illustrious Tammahammaha III afterwards calls and settles the bill.

A few years since an auctioneer to his majesty came near being added to the retinue of state. It seems that he was the first man who had

practised his vocation in the Sandwich Islands; and delighted with
the sport of bidding upon his wares, the king was one of his best
customers. At last he besought the man to leave all and follow him,
and he should be handsomely provided for at court. But the auctioneer
refused; and so the ivory hammer lost the chance of being borne
before him on a velvet cushion when the next king went to be crowned.

But it was not as strolling players, nor as footmen out of employ,
that the doctor and myself looked forward to our approaching
introduction to the court of the Queen of Tahiti. On the contrary, as
before hinted, we expected to swell the appropriations of bread-fruit
and cocoa-nuts on the Civil List by filling some honourable office in
her gift.

We were told that, to resist the usurpation of the French, the queen
was rallying about her person all the foreigners she could. Her
partiality for the English and Americans was well known; and this was
an additional ground for our anticipating a favourable reception.
Zeke had informed us, moreover, that by the queen's counsellors at
Partoowye, a war of aggression against the invaders of Papeetee had
been seriously thought of. Should this prove true, a surgeon's
commission for the doctor, and a lieutenancy for myself, were
certainly counted upon in our sanguine expectations.

Such, then, were our views, and such our hopes in projecting a trip to
Taloo. But in our most lofty aspirations we by no means lost sight of

any minor matters which might help us to promotion. The doctor had informed me that he excelled in playing the fiddle. I now suggested that, as soon as we arrived at Partoowye, we should endeavour to borrow a violin for him; or if this could not be done, that he should manufacture some kind of a substitute, and, thus equipped, apply for an audience of the queen. Her well-known passion for music would at once secure his admittance; and so, under the most favourable auspices, bring about our introduction to her notice.

"And who knows," said my waggish comrade, throwing his head back and performing an imaginary air by briskly drawing one arm across the other, "who knows that I may not fiddle myself into her majesty's good graces so as to became a sort of Rizzio to the Tahitian princess."

CHAPTER LXVI.

HOW WE WERE TO GET TO TALOO

THE inglorious circumstances of our somewhat premature departure from Tamai filled the sagacious doctor, and myself, with sundry misgivings for the future.

Under Zeke's protection, we were secure from all impertinent interference in our concerns on the part of the natives. But as friendless wanderers over the island, we ran the risk of being apprehended as runaways, and, as such, sent back to Tahiti. The truth is that the rewards constantly offered for the apprehension of deserters from ships induce some of the natives to eye all strangers suspiciously.

A passport was therefore desirable; but such a thing had never been heard of in Imeeo. At last, Long Ghost suggested that, as the Yankee was well known and much respected all over the island, we should endeavour to obtain from him some sort of paper, not only certifying to our having been in his employ, but also to our not being highwaymen, kidnappers, nor yet runaway seamen. Even written in English, a paper like this would answer every purpose; for the unlettered natives, standing in great awe of the document, would not dare to molest us until acquainted with its purport. Then, if it came to the worst, we might repair to the nearest missionary, and have the passport explained.

Upon informing Zeke of these matters, he seemed highly flattered with the opinion we entertained of his reputation abroad; and he agreed to oblige us. The doctor at once offered to furnish him with a draught of the paper; but he refused, saying he would write it himself. With a rooster's quill, therefore, a bit of soiled paper, and a stout heart, he set to work. Evidently he was not accustomed to composition; for his literary throes were so violent that the doctor suggested that some sort of a Caesarian operation might be necessary.

The precious paper was at last finished; and a great curiosity it was. We were much diverted with his reasons for not dating it.

"In this here dummed eliminate," he observed, "a feller can't keep the run of the months, nohow; cause there's no seasons; no summer and winter, to go by. One's etarnally thinkin' it's always July, it's so pesky hot."

A passport provided, we cast about for some means of getting to Taloo.

The island of Imeeo is very nearly surrounded by a regular breakwater of coral extending within a mile or less of the shore. The smooth canal within furnishes the best means of communication with the different settlements; all of which, with the exception of Tamai, are right upon the water. And so indolent are the Imeeose that they think nothing of going twenty or thirty miles round the island in a canoe in order to reach a place not a quarter of that distance by land. But as hinted before, the fear of the bullocks has something to do with this.

The idea of journeying in a canoe struck our fancy quite pleasantly; and we at once set about chartering one, if possible. But none could we obtain. For not only did we have nothing to pay for hiring one, but we could not expect to have it loaned; inasmuch as the good-natured owner would, in all probability, have to walk along the beach as we paddled in order to bring back his property when we had no further use for it.

At last, it was decided to commence our journey on foot; trusting that we would soon fall in with a canoe going our way, in which we might take passage.

The planters said we would find no beaten path: all we had to do was to follow the beach; and however inviting it might look inland, on no account must we stray from it. In short, the longest way round was the nearest way to Taloo. At intervals, there were little hamlets along the shore, besides lonely fishermen's huts here and there, where we could get plenty to eat without pay; so there was no necessity to lay in any store.

Intending to be off before sunrise the next morning, so as to have the benefit of the coolest part of the day, we bade our kind hosts farewell overnight; and then, repairing to the beach, we launched our floating pallet, and slept away merrily till dawn.

CHAPTER LXVII.

THE JOURNEY ROUND THE BEACH

IT was on the fourth day of the first month of the Hegira, or flight from Tamai (we now reckoned our time thus), that, rising bright and early, we were up and away out of the valley of Hartair before the fishermen even were stirring.

It was the earliest dawn. The morning only showed itself along the lower edge of a bank of purple clouds pierced by the misty peaks of Tahiti. The tropical day seemed too languid to rise. Sometimes, starting fitfully, it decked the clouds with faint edgings of pink and gray, which, fading away, left all dim again. Anon, it threw out thin, pale rays, growing lighter and lighter, until at last, the golden morning sprang out of the East with a bound--darting its bright beams hither and thither, higher and higher, and sending them, broadcast, over the face of the heavens.

All balmy from the groves of Tahiti came an indolent air, cooled by its transit over the waters; and grateful underfoot was the damp and slightly yielding beach, from which the waves seemed just retired.

The doctor was in famous spirits; removing his Koora, he went splashing into the sea; and, after swimming a few yards, waded ashore, hopping, skipping, and jumping along the beach; but very careful to cut all his capers in the direction of our journey.

Say what they will of the glowing independence one feels in the saddle, give me the first morning flush of your cheery pedestrian!

Thus exhilarated, we went on, as light-hearted and care-free as we could wish.

And here I cannot refrain from lauding the very superior inducements which most intertropical countries afford, not only to mere rovers like ourselves, but to penniless people generally. In these genial regions one's wants are naturally diminished; and those which remain are easily gratified; fuel, house-shelter, and, if you please, clothing, may be entirely dispensed with.

How different our hard northern latitudes! Alas! the lot of a "poor devil," twenty degrees north of the tropic of Cancer, is indeed pitiable.

At last, the beach contracted to hardly a yard's width, and the dense thicket almost dipped into the sea. In place of the smooth sand, too, we had sharp fragments of broken coral, which made travelling exceedingly unpleasant. "Lord! my foot!" roared the doctor, fetching it up for inspection, with a galvanic fling of the limb. A sharp splinter had thrust itself into the flesh through a hole in his boot. My sandals were worse yet; their soles taking a sort of fossil impression of everything trod upon.

Turning round a bold sweep of the beach, we came upon a piece of fine, open ground, with a fisherman's dwelling in the distance, crowning a knoll which rolled off into the water.

The hut proved to be a low, rude erection, very recently thrown up; for the bamboos were still green as grass, and the thatching fresh and fragrant as meadow hay. It was open upon three sides; so that, upon drawing near, the domestic arrangements within were in plain sight. No one was stirring; and nothing was to be seen but a clumsy old chest of native workmanship, a few calabashes, and bundles of tappa hanging against a post; and a heap of something, we knew not what, in a dark corner. Upon close inspection, the doctor discovered it to be a loving old couple, locked in each other's arms, and rolled together in a tappa mantle.

"Halloa! Darby!" he cried, shaking the one with a beard. But Darby heeded him not; though Joan, a wrinkled old body, started up in affright, and yelled aloud. Neither of us attempting to gag her, she presently became quiet; and, after staring hard and asking some unintelligible questions, she proceeded to rouse her still slumbering mate.

What ailed him we could not tell; but there was no waking him. Equally in vain were all his dear spouse's cuffs, pinches, and other endearments; he lay like a log, face up, snoring away like a cavalry trumpeter.

"Here, my good woman," said Long Ghost, "just let me try"; and, taking the patient right by his nose, he so lifted him bodily into a sitting position, and held him there until his eyes opened. When this event came to pass, Darby looked round like one stupefied; and then, springing to his feet, backed away into a corner, from which place we became the objects of his earnest and respectful attention.

"Permit me, my dear Darby, to introduce to you my esteemed friend and comrade, Paul," said the doctor, gallanting me up with all the grimace and flourish imaginable. Upon this, Darby began to recover his faculties, and surprised us not a little by talking a few words of English. So far as could be understood, they were expressive of his having been aware that there were two "karhowrees" in the neighbourhood; that he was glad to see us, and would have something for us to eat in no time.

How he came by his English was explained to us before we left. Some time previous, he had been a denizen of Papeetee, where the native language is broidered over with the most classic sailor phrases. He seemed to be quite proud of his residence there; and alluded to it in the same significant way in which a provincial informs you that in his time he has resided in the capital. The old fellow was disposed to be garrulous; but being sharp-set, we told him to get breakfast;

after which we would hear his anecdotes. While employed among the calabashes, the strange, antiquated fondness between these old semi-savages was really amusing. I made no doubt that they were saying to each other, "yes, my love"--"no, my life," just in the same way that some young couples do, at home.

They gave us a hearty meal; and while we were discussing its merits, they assured us, over and over again, that they expected nothing in return for their attentions; more: we were at liberty to stay as long as we pleased; and as long as we did stay, their house and everything they had was no longer theirs, but ours; still more: they themselves were our slaves--the old lady, to a degree that was altogether superfluous. This, now, is Tahitian hospitality! Self-immolation upon one's own hearthstone for the benefit of the guest.

The Polynesians carry their hospitality to an amazing extent. Let a native of Waiurar, the westernmost part of Tahiti, make his appearance as a traveller at Partoowye, the most easterly village of Imeeo; though a perfect stranger, the inhabitants on all sides accost him at their doorways, inviting him to enter, and make himself at home. But the traveller passes on, examining every house attentively; until, at last, he pauses before one which suits him, and then exclaiming, "ah, eda maitai" (this one will do, I think), he steps in, and makes himself perfectly at ease; flinging himself upon the mats, and very probably calling for a nice young cocoa-nut, and a piece of toasted breadfruit, sliced thin, and done brown.

Curious to relate, however, should a stranger carrying it thus bravely be afterwards discovered to be without a house of his own, why, he may thenceforth go a-begging for his lodgings. The "karhowrees," or white men, are exceptions to this rule. Thus it is precisely as in civilized countries, where those who have houses and lands are incessantly bored to death with invitations to come and live in other people's houses; while many a poor gentleman who inks the seams of his coat, and to whom the like invitation would be really acceptable, may go and sue for it. But to the credit of the ancient Tahitians, it should here be observed that this blemish upon their hospitality is only of recent origin, and was wholly unknown in old times. So told me, Captain Bob.

In Polynesia it is esteemed "a great hit" if a man succeed in marrying into a family to which the best part of the community is related (Heaven knows it is otherwise with us). The reason is that, when he goes a-travelling, the greater number of houses are the more completely at his service.

Receiving a paternal benediction from old Darby and Joan, we continued our journey; resolved to stop at the very next place of attraction which offered.

Nor did we long stroll for it. A fine walk along a beach of shells, and we came to a spot where, trees here and there, the land was all meadow, sloping away to the water, which stirred a sedgy growth of reeds bordering its margin. Close by was a little cove, walled in with coral, where a fleet of canoes was dancing up and down. A few paces distant, on a natural terrace overlooking the sea, were several native dwellings, newly thatched, and peeping into view out of the foliage like summer-houses.

As we drew near, forth came a burst of voices, and, presently, three gay girls, overflowing with life, health, and youth, and full of spirits and mischief. One was arrayed in a flaunting robe of calico; and her long black hair was braided behind in two immense tresses, joined together at the ends, and wreathed with the green tendrils of a vine. From her self-possessed and forward air, I fancied she might be some young lady from Papeetee on a visit to her country relations. Her companions wore mere slips of cotton cloth; their hair was dishevelled; and though very pretty, they betrayed the reserve and embarrassment characteristic of the provinces.

The little gipsy first mentioned ran up to me with great cordiality; and, giving the Tahitian salutation, opened upon me such a fire of questions that there was no understanding, much less answering them. But our hearty welcome to Loohooloo, as she called the hamlet, was made plain enough. Meanwhile, Doctor Long Ghost gallantly presented an arm to each of the other young ladies; which, at first, they knew not what to make of; but at last, taking it for some kind of joke, accepted the civility.

The names of these three damsels were at once made known by themselves: and being so exceedingly romantic, I cannot forbear particularizing them. Upon my comrade's arms, then, were hanging Night and Morning, in the persons of Farnowar, or the Day-Born, and Earnoopoo, or the Night-Born. She with the tresses was very appropriately styled Marhar-Rarrar, the Wakeful, or Bright-Eyed.

By this time, the houses were emptied of the rest of their inmates--a few old men and women, and several strapping young fellows rubbing their eyes and yawning. All crowded round, putting questions as to whence we came. Upon being informed of our acquaintance with Zeke, they were delighted; and one of them recognized the boots worn by the doctor. "Keekee (Zeke) maitai," they cried, "nuee nuee hanna hanna portarto"--(makes plenty of potatoes).

There was now a little friendly altercation as to who should have the honour of entertaining the strangers. At last, a tall old gentleman, by name Marharvai, with a bald head and white beard, took us each by the hand, and led us into his dwelling. Once inside, Marharvai, pointing about with his staff, was so obsequious in assuring us that his house was ours that Long Ghost suggested he might as well hand over the deed.

It was drawing near noon; so after a light lunch of roasted breadfruit, a few whiffs of a pipe, and some lively chatting, our host admonished the company to lie down, and take the everlasting siesta. We complied; and had a social nap all round.

CHAPTER LXVIII.

A DINNER-PARTY IN IMEEO

IT WAS just in the middle of the merry, mellow afternoon that they ushered us to dinner, underneath a green shelter of palm boughs; open all round, and so low at the eaves that we stooped to enter.

Within, the ground was strewn over with aromatic ferns--called "nahee"--freshly gathered; which, stirred underfoot, diffused the sweetest odour. On one side was a row of yellow mats, inwrought with fibres of bark stained a bright red. Here, seated after the fashion of the Turk, we looked out, over a verdant bank, upon the mild, blue, endless Pacific. So far round had we skirted the island that the view of Tahiti was now intercepted.

Upon the ferns before us were laid several layers of broad, thick "pooroo" leaves; lapping over, one upon the other. And upon these were placed, side by side, newly-plucked banana leaves, at least two yards in length, and very wide; the stalks were withdrawn so as to make them lie flat. This green cloth was set out and garnished in the manner following:--

First, a number of "pooroo" leaves, by way of plates, were ranged along on one side; and by each was a rustic nut-bowl, half-filled with sea-water, and a Tahitian roll, or small bread-fruit, roasted brown. An immense flat calabash, placed in the centre, was heaped up with numberless small packages of moist, steaming leaves: in each was a small fish, baked in the earth, and done to a turn. This pyramid of a dish was flanked on either side by an ornamental calabash. One was brimming with the golden-hued "poee," or pudding, made from the red plantain of the mountains: the other was stacked up with cakes of the Indian turnip, previously macerated in a mortar, kneaded with the milk of the cocoa-nut, and then baked. In the spaces between the three dishes were piled young cocoa-nuts, stripped of their husks. Their eyes had been opened and enlarged; so that each was a ready-charged goblet.

There was a sort of side-cloth in one corner, upon which, in bright, buff jackets, lay the fattest of bananas; "avees," red-ripe: guavas with the shadows of their crimson pulp flushing through a transparent skin, and almost coming and going there like blushes; oranges, tinged, here and there, berry-brown; and great, jolly melons, which rolled about in very portliness. Such a heap! All ruddy, ripe, and round--bursting with the good cheer of the tropical soil from which they sprang!

"A land of orchards!" cried the doctor, in a rapture; and he snatched a morsel from a sort of fruit of which gentlemen of the sanguine temperament are remarkably fond; namely, the ripe cherry lips of Misa Day-Born, who stood looking on.

Marharvai allotted seats to his guests; and the meal began. Thinking that his hospitality needed some acknowledgment, I rose, and pledged him in the vegetable wine of the cocoa-nut; merely repeating the ordinary salutation, "Yar onor boyoee." Sensible that some compliment, after the fashion of white men, was paid him, with a smile, and a courteous flourish of the hand, he bade me be seated. No people, however refined, are more easy and graceful in their manners than the Imeeose.

The doctor, sitting next our host, now came under his special protection. Laying before his guest one of the packages of fish, Marharvai opened it; and commended its contents to his particular regards. But my comrade was one of those who, on convivial occasions, can always take care of themselves. He ate an indefinite number of "Pee-hee Lee Lees" (small fish), his own and next neighbour's bread-fruit; and helped himself, to right and left, with all the ease of an accomplished diner-out.

"Paul," said he, at last, "you don't seem to be getting along; why don't you try the pepper sauce?" and, by way of example, he steeped a morsel of food into his nutful of sea-water. On following suit, I found it quite piquant, though rather bitter; but, on the whole, a capital substitute for salt. The Imeeose invariably use sea-water in this way, deeming it quite a treat; and considering that their country is surrounded by an ocean of catsup, the luxury cannot be deemed an expensive one.

The fish were delicious; the manner of cooking them in the ground preserving all the juices, and rendering them exceedingly sweet and tender. The plantain pudding was almost cloying; the cakes of Indian turnip, quite palatable; and the roasted bread-fruit, crisp as toast.

During the meal, a native lad walked round and round the party, carrying a long staff of bamboo. This he occasionally tapped upon the cloth, before each guest; when a white clotted substance dropped forth, with a savour not unlike that of a curd. This proved to be "Lownee," an excellent relish, prepared from the grated meat of ripe cocoa-nuts, moistened with cocoa-nut milk and salt water, and kept perfectly tight until a little past the saccharine stage of fermentation.

Throughout the repast there was much lively chatting among the islanders, in which their conversational powers quite exceeded ours. The young ladies, too, showed themselves very expert in the use of their tongues, and contributed much to the gaiety which prevailed.

Nor did these lively nymphs suffer the meal to languish; for upon the doctor's throwing himself back, with an air of much satisfaction, they sprang to their feet, and pelted him with oranges and guavas. This, at last, put an end to the entertainment.

By a hundred whimsical oddities, my long friend became a great favourite with these people; and they bestowed upon him a long, comical title, expressive of his lank figure and Koora combined. The latter, by the bye, never failed to excite the remark of everybody we encountered.

The giving of nicknames is quite a passion with the people of Tahiti and Imeeo. No one with any peculiarity, whether of person or temper, is exempt; not even strangers.

A pompous captain of a man-of-war, visiting Tahiti for the second time, discovered that, among the natives, he went by the dignified title of "Atee Poee"--literally, Poee Head, or Pudding Head. Nor is the highest rank among themselves any protection. The first husband of the present queen was commonly known in the court circles as "Pot Belly." He carried the greater part of his person before him, to be sure; and so did the gentlemanly George IV.--but what a title for a king consort!

Even "Pomaree" itself, the royal patronymic, was, originally, a mere nickname; and literally signifies, one talking through his nose. The first monarch of that name, being on a war party, and sleeping overnight among the mountains, awoke one morning with a cold in his head; and some wag of a courtier had no more manners than to vulgarize him thus.

How different from the volatile Polynesian in this, as in all other respects, is our grave and decorous North American Indian. While the former bestows a name in accordance with some humorous or ignoble trait, the latter seizes upon what is deemed the most exalted or warlike: and hence, among the red tribes, we have the truly patrician appellations of "White Eagles," "Young Oaks," "Fiery Eyes," and "Bended Bows."

CHAPTER LXIX.

THE COCOA-PALM

WHILE the doctor and the natives were taking a digestive nap after dinner, I strolled forth to have a peep at the country which could produce so generous a meal.

To my surprise, a fine strip of land in the vicinity of the hamlet, and protected seaward by a grove of cocoa-nut and bread-fruit trees, was under high cultivation. Sweet potatoes, Indian turnips, and yams were growing; also melons, a few pine-apples, and other fruits. Still more pleasing was the sight of young bread-fruit and cocoa-nut trees set out with great care, as if, for once, the improvident Polynesian had thought of his posterity. But this was the only instance of native thrift which ever came under my observation. For, in all my rambles over Tahiti and Imeeo, nothing so much struck me as the comparative scarcity of these trees in many places where they ought to abound. Entire valleys, like Martair, of inexhaustible fertility are abandoned to all the rankness of untamed vegetation. Alluvial flats bordering the sea, and watered by streams from the mountains, are over-grown with a wild, scrub guava-bush, introduced by foreigners, and which spreads with such fatal rapidity that the natives, standing still while it grows, anticipate its covering the entire island. Even tracts of clear land, which, with so little pains, might be made to wave with orchards, lie wholly neglected.

When I considered their unequalled soil and climate, thus unaccountably slighted, I often turned in amazement upon the natives about Papeetee; some of whom all but starve in their gardens run to waste. Upon other islands which I have visited, of similar fertility, and wholly unreclaimed from their first-discovered condition, no spectacle of this sort was presented.

The high estimation in which many of their fruit-trees are held by the Tahitians and Imeeose--their beauty in the landscape--their manifold uses, and the facility with which they are propagated, are considerations which render the remissness alluded to still more unaccountable. The cocoa-palm is as an example; a tree by far the most important production of Nature in the Tropics. To the Polynesians it is emphatically the Tree of Life; transcending even the bread-fruit in the multifarious uses to which it is applied.

Its very aspect is imposing. Asserting its supremacy by an erect and lofty bearing, it may be said to compare with other trees as man with inferior creatures.

The blessings it confers are incalculable. Tear after year, the islander reposes beneath its shade, both eating and drinking of its fruit; he thatches his hut with its boughs, and weaves them into baskets to carry his food; he cools himself with a fan platted from the young leaflets, and shields his head from the sun by a bonnet of the leaves; sometimes he clothes himself with the cloth-like substance which wraps round the base of the stalks, whose elastic rods, strung with filberts, are used as a taper; the larger nuts, thinned and polished, furnish him with a beautiful goblet: the smaller ones, with bowls for his pipes; the dry husks kindle his fires; their fibres are twisted into fishing-lines and cords for his canoes; he heals his wounds with a balsam compounded from the juice of the nut; and with the oil extracted from its meat embalms the bodies of the dead.

The noble trunk itself is far from being valueless. Sawn into posts, it upholds the islander's dwelling; converted into charcoal, it cooks his food; and supported on blocks of stone, rails in his lands. He impels his canoe through the water with a paddle of the wood, and goes to battle with clubs and spears of the same hard material.

In pagan Tahiti a cocoa-nut branch was the symbol of regal authority. Laid upon the sacrifice in the temple, it made the offering sacred; and with it the priests chastised and put to flight the evil spirits which assailed them. The supreme majesty of Oro, the great god of their mythology, was declared in the cocoa-nut log from which his image was rudely carved. Upon one of the Tonga Islands, there stands a living tree revered itself as a deity. Even upon the Sandwich Islands, the cocoa-palm retains all its ancient reputation; the people there having thought of adopting it as the national emblem.

The cocoa-nut is planted as follows: Selecting a suitable place, you drop into the ground a fully ripe nut, and leave it. In a few days, a thin, lance-like shoot forces itself through a minute hole in the shell, pierces the husk, and soon unfolds three pale-green leaves in the air; while originating, in the same soft white sponge which now completely fills the nut, a pair of fibrous roots, pushing away the stoppers which close two holes in an opposite direction, penetrate the shell, and strike vertically into the ground. A day or two more, and the shell and husk, which, in the last and germinating stage of the nut, are so hard that a knife will scarcely make any impression, spontaneously burst by some force within; and, henceforth, the hardy young plant thrives apace; and needing no culture, pruning, or attention of any sort, rapidly advances to maturity. In four or five years it bears; in twice as many more, it begins to lift its head among the groves, where, waxing strong, it flourishes for near a century.

Thus, as some voyager has said, the man who but drops one of these nuts into the ground may be said to confer a greater and more certain benefit upon himself and posterity than many a life's toil in less genial climes.

The fruitfulness of the tree is remarkable. As long as it lives it bears, and without intermission. Two hundred nuts, besides innumerable white blossoms of others, may be seen upon it at one time; and though a whole year is required to bring any one of them to the germinating point, no two, perhaps, are at one time in precisely the same stage of growth.

The tree delights in a maritime situation. In its greatest perfection, it is perhaps found right on the seashore, where its roots are actually washed. But such instances are only met with upon islands where the swell of the sea is prevented from breaking on the beach by an encircling reef. No saline flavour is perceptible in the nut produced in such a place. Although it bears in any soil, whether upland or bottom, it does not flourish vigorously inland; and I have frequently observed that, when met with far up the valley, its tall stem inclines seaward, as if pining after a more genial region.

It is a curious fact that if you deprive the cocoa-nut tree of the verdant tuft at its head, it dies at once; and if allowed to stand thus, the trunk, which, when alive, is encased in so hard a bark as to be almost impervious to a bullet, moulders away, and, in an incredibly short period, becomes dust. This is, perhaps, partly owing to the peculiar constitution of the trunk, a mere cylinder of minute hollow reeds, closely packed, and very hard; but, when exposed at top, peculiarly fitted to convey moisture and decay through the entire stem.

The finest orchard of cocoa-palms I know, and the only plantation of them I ever saw at the islands, is one that stands right upon the southern shore of Papeetee Bay. They were set out by the first

Pomaree, almost half a century ago; and the soil being especially adapted to their growth, the noble trees now form a magnificent grove, nearly a mile in extent. No other plant, scarcely a bush, is to be seen within its precincts. The Broom Road passes through its entire length.

At noonday, this grove is one of the most beautiful, serene, witching places that ever was seen. High overhead are ranges of green rustling arches; through which the sun's rays come down to you in sparkles. You seem to be wandering through illimitable halls of pillars; everywhere you catch glimpses of stately aisles, intersecting each other at all points. A strange silence, too, reigns far and near; the air flushed with the mellow stillness of a sunset.

But after the long morning calms, the sea-breeze comes in; and creeping over the tops of these thousand trees, they nod their plumes. Soon the breeze freshens; and you hear the branches brushing against each other; and the flexible trunks begin to sway. Toward evening the whole grove is rocking to and fro; and the traveller on the Broom Road is startled by the frequent falling of the nuts, snapped from their brittle stems. They come flying through the air, ringing like jugglers' balls; and often bound along the ground for many rods.

CHAPTER LXX.

LIFE AT LOOHOOLOO

FINDING the society at Loohooloo very pleasant, the young ladies, in particular, being extremely sociable; and, moreover, in love with the famous good cheer of old Marharvai, we acquiesced in an invitation of his to tarry a few days longer. We might then, he said, join a small canoe party which was going to a place a league or two distant. So averse to all exertion are these people that they really thought the prospect of thus getting rid of a few miles' walking would prevail with us, even if there were no other inducement.

The people of the hamlet, as we soon discovered, formed a snug little community of cousins; of which our host seemed the head. Marharvai, in truth, was a petty chief who owned the neighbouring lands. And as the wealthy, in most cases, rejoice in a numerous kindred, the family footing upon which everybody visited him was, perhaps, ascribable to the fact of his being the lord of the manor. Like Captain Bob, he was, in some things, a gentleman of the old school--a stickler for the customs of a past and pagan age.

Nowhere else, except in Tamai, did we find the manners of the natives less vitiated by recent changes. The old-fashioned Tahitian dinner they gave us on the day of our arrival was a fair sample of their general mode of living.

Our time passed delightfully. The doctor went his way, and I mine. With a pleasant companion, he was forever strolling inland, ostensibly to collect botanical specimens; while I, for the most part, kept near the sea; sometimes taking the girls on an aquatic excursion in a canoe.

Often we went fishing; not dozing over stupid hooks and lines, but leaping right into the water, and chasing our prey over the coral rocks, spear in hand.

Spearing fish is glorious sport. The Imeeose, all round the island, catch them in no other way. The smooth shallows between the reef and the shore, and, at low water, the reef itself, being admirably adapted to this mode of capturing them. At almost any time of the day--save ever the sacred hour of noon--you may see the fish-hunters pursuing their sport; with loud halloos, brandishing their spears, and splashing through the water in all directions. Sometimes a solitary native is seen, far out upon a lonely shallow, wading slowly along, with eye intent and poised spear.

But the best sport of all is going out upon the great reef itself by torch-light. The natives follow this recreation with as much spirit as a gentleman of England does the chase; and take full as much delight in it.

The torch is nothing more than a bunch of dry reeds, bound firmly together: the spear, a long, light pole, with an iron head, on one side barbed.

I shall never forget the night that old Marharvai and the rest of us, paddling off to the reef, leaped at midnight upon the coral ledges with waving torches and spears. We were more than a mile from the land; the sullen ocean, thundering upon the outside of the rocks, dashed the spray in our faces, almost extinguishing the flambeaux; and, far as the eye could reach, the darkness of sky and water was streaked with a long, misty line of foam, marking the course of the coral barrier. The wild fishermen, flourishing their weapons, and yelling like so many demons to scare their prey, sprang from ledge to ledge, and sometimes darted their spears in the very midst of the breakers.

But fish-spearing was not the only sport we had at Loohooloo. Right on the beach was a mighty old cocoa-nut tree, the roots of which had been underwashed by the waves so that the trunk inclined far over its base. From the tuft of the tree a stout cord of bark depended, the end of which swept the water several yards from the shore. This was a Tahitian swing. A native lad seizes hold of the cord, and, after swinging to and fro quite leisurely, all at once sends himself fifty or sixty feet from the water, rushing through the air like a rocket. I doubt whether any of our rope-dancers would attempt the feat. For my own part, I had neither head nor heart for it; so, after sending a lad aloft with an additional cord, by way of security, I constructed a large basket of green boughs, in which I and some particular friends of mine used to swing over sea and land by the hour.

CHAPTER LXXI.

WE START FOR TALOO

BRIGHT was the morning, and brighter still the smiles of the young ladies who accompanied us, when we sprang into a sort of family canoe--wide and roomy--and bade adieu to the hospitable Marharvai and his tenantry. As we paddled away, they stood upon the beach, waving their hands, and crying out, "aroha! aroha!" (farewell! farewell!) as long as we were within hearing.

Very sad at parting with them, we endeavoured, nevertheless, to console ourselves in the society of our fellow-passengers. Among these were two old ladies; but as they said nothing to us, we will say nothing about them; nor anything about the old men who managed the canoe. But of the three mischievous, dark-eyed young witches who lounged in the stern of that comfortable old island gondola, I have a great deal to say.

In the first place, one of them was Marhar-Rarrar, the Bright-Eyed; and, in the second place, neither she nor the romps, her companions, ever dreamed of taking the voyage until the doctor and myself announced our intention; their going along was nothing more than a madcap frolic; in short, they were a parcel of wicked hoydens, bent on mischief, who laughed in your face when you looked sentimental, and only tolerated your company when making merry at your expense.

Something or other about us was perpetually awaking their mirth. Attributing this to his own remarkable figure, the doctor increased their enjoyment by assuming the part of a Merry Andrew. Yet his cap and bells never jingled but to some tune; and while playing the Tom-fool, I more than suspected that he was trying to play the rake. At home, it is deemed auspicious to go a-wooing in epaulets; but among the Polynesians, your best dress in courting is motley.

A fresh breeze springing up, we set our sail of matting, and glided along as tranquilly as if floating upon an inland stream; the white reef on one hand, and the green shore on the other.

Soon, as we turned a headland, we encountered another canoe, paddling with might and main in an opposite direction; the strangers shouting to each other, and a tall fellow in the bow dancing up and down like a crazy man. They shot by us like an arrow, though our fellow-voyagers shouted again and again for them to cease paddling.

According to the natives, this was a kind of royal mail-canoe, carrying a message from the queen to her friends in a distant part of the island.

Passing several shady bowers which looked quite inviting, we proposed touching, and diversifying the monotony of a sea-voyage by a stroll ashore. So, forcing our canoe among the bushes, behind a decayed palm lying partly in the water, we left the old folks to take a nap in the shade, and gallanted the others among the trees, which were here trellised with vines and creeping shrubs.

In the early part of the afternoon, we drew near the place to which the party were going. It was a solitary house inhabited by four or five old women, who, when we entered, were gathered in a circle about the mats, eating poee from a cracked calabash. They seemed delighted at seeing our companions, but rather drew up when introduced to ourselves. Eyeing us distrustfully, they whispered to know who we were. The answers they received were not satisfactory; for they treated us with marked coolness and reserve, and seemed desirous of breaking off our acquaintance with the girls. Unwilling, therefore, to stay where our company was disagreeable, we resolved to depart without even eating a meal.

Informed of this, Marhar-Rarrar and her companions evinced the most lively concern; and equally unmindful of their former spirits, and the remonstrances of the old ladies, broke forth into sobs and lamentations which were not to be withstood. We agreed, therefore, to tarry until they left for home; which would be at the "Aheharar," or Falling of the Sun; in other words, at sunset.

When the hour arrived, after much leave-taking, we saw them safely embarked. As the canoe turned a bluff, they seized the paddles from the hands of the old men, and waved them silently in the air. This was meant for a touching farewell, as the paddle is only waved thus when the parties separating never more expect to meet.

We now continued our journey; and, following the beach, soon came to a level and lofty overhanging bank, which, planted here and there with trees, took a broad sweep round a considerable part of the island.

A fine pathway skirted the edge of the bank; and often we paused to admire the scenery. The evening was still and fair, even for so heavenly a climate; and all round, as far as the eye could reach, was the blending blue sky and ocean.

As we went on, the reef-belt still accompanied us; turning as we turned, and thundering its distant bass upon the ear, like the unbroken roar of a cataract. Dashing forever against their coral rampart, the breakers looked, in the distance, like a line of rearing white chargers, reined in, tossing their white manes, and bridling with foam.

These great natural breakwaters are admirably designed for the protection of the land. Nearly all the Society Islands are defended by them. Were the vast swells of the Pacific to break against the soft alluvial bottoms which in many places border the sea, the soil would soon be washed away, and the natives be thus deprived of their most productive lands. As it is, the banks of no rivulet are firmer.

But the coral barriers answer another purpose. They form all the harbours of this group, including the twenty-four round about the shores of Tahiti. Curiously enough, the openings in the reefs, by which alone vessels enter to their anchorage, are invariably opposite the mouths of running streams: an advantage fully appreciated by the mariner who touches for the purpose of watering his ship.

It is said that the fresh water of the land, mixing with the salts held in solution by the sea, so acts upon the latter as to resist the formation of the coral; and hence the breaks. Here and there, these openings are sentinelled, as it were, by little fairy islets, green as emerald, and waving with palms. Strangely and beautifully diversifying the long line of breakers, no objects can strike the fancy more vividly. Pomaree II., with a taste in watering-places truly Tahitian, selected one of them as a royal retreat. We passed it on our journey.

Omitting several further adventures which befell us after leaving the party from Loohooloo, we must now hurry on to relate what happened just before reaching the place of our destination.

CHAPTER LXXII.

A DEALER IN THE CONTRABAND

IT MUST have been at least the tenth day, reckoning from the Hegira, that we found ourselves the guests of Varvy, an old hermit of an islander who kept house by himself perhaps a couple of leagues from Taloo.

A stone's-cast from the beach there was a fantastic rock, moss-grown and deep in a dell. It was insulated by a shallow brook, which, dividing its waters, flowed on both sides until united below. Twisting its roots round the rock, a gnarled "Aoa" spread itself overhead in a wilderness of foliage; the elastic branch-roots depending from the larger boughs insinuating themselves into every cleft, thus forming supports to the parent stem. In some places these pendulous branches, half-grown, had not yet reached the rock; swinging their loose fibrous ends in the air like whiplashes.

Varvy's hut, a mere coop of bamboos, was perched upon a level part of the rock, the ridge-pole resting at one end in a crotch of the "Aoa," and the other propped by a forked bough planted in a fissure.

Notwithstanding our cries as we drew near, the first hint the old hermit received of our approach was the doctor's stepping up and touching his shoulder, as he was kneeling over on a stone cleaning fish in the brook. He leaped up, and stared at us. But with a variety of uncouth gestures, he soon made us welcome; informing us, by the same means, that he was both deaf and dumb; he then motioned us into his dwelling.

Going in, we threw ourselves upon an old mat, and peered round. The soiled bamboos and calabashes looked so uninviting that the doctor was for pushing on to Taloo that night, notwithstanding it was near sunset. But at length we concluded to stay where we were.

After a good deal of bustling outside under a decrepit shed, the old man made his appearance with our supper. In one hand he held a flickering taper, and in the other, a huge, flat calabash, scantily filled with viands. His eyes were dancing in his head, and he looked from the calabash to us, and from us to the calabash, as much as to say, "Ah, my lads, what do ye think of this, eh? Pretty good cheer, eh?" But the fish and Indian turnip being none of the best, we made but a sorry meal. While discussing it, the old man tried hard to make himself understood by signs; most of which were so excessively ludicrous that we made no doubt he was perpetrating a series of pantomimic jokes.

The remnants of the feast removed, our host left us for a moment, returning with a calabash of portly dimensions and furnished with a long, hooked neck, the mouth of which was stopped with a wooden plug. It was covered with particles of earth, and looked as if just taken from some place underground.

With sundry winks and horrible giggles peculiar to the dumb, the vegetable demijohn was now tapped; the old fellow looking round cautiously, and pointing at it; as much as to intimate that it contained something which was "taboo," or forbidden.

Aware that intoxicating liquors were strictly prohibited to the natives, we now watched our entertainer with much interest. Charging a cocoa-nut shell, he tossed it off, and then filling up again, presented the goblet to me. Disliking the smell, I made faces at it; upon which he became highly excited; so much so that a miracle was wrought upon the spot. Snatching the cup from my hands, he shouted out, "Ah, karhowree sabbee lee-lee ena arva tee maitai!" in other words, what a blockhead of a white man! this is the real stuff!

We could not have been more startled had a frog leaped from his mouth. For an instant, he looked confused enough himself; and then placing a finger mysteriously upon his mouth, he contrived to make us understand that at times he was subject to a suspension of the powers of speech.

Deeming the phenomenon a remarkable one, every way, the doctor desired him to open his mouth so that he might have a look down. But he refused.

This occurrence made us rather suspicious of our host; nor could we afterward account for his conduct, except by supposing that his feigning dumbness might in some way or other assist him in the nefarious pursuits in which it afterwards turned out that he was engaged. This conclusion, however, was not altogether satisfactory.

To oblige him, we at last took a sip of his "arva tee," and found it very crude, and strong as Lucifer. Curious to know whence it was obtained, we questioned him; when, lighting up with pleasure, he seized the taper, and led us outside the hut, bidding us follow.

After going some distance through the woods, we came to a dismantled old shed of boughs, apparently abandoned to decay. Underneath, nothing was to be seen but heaps of decaying leaves and an immense, clumsy jar, wide-mouthed, and by some means, rudely hollowed out from a ponderous stone.

Here, for a while, we were left to ourselves; the old man placing the light in the jar, and then disappearing. He returned, carrying a long, large bamboo, and a crotched stick. Throwing these down, he poked under a pile of rubbish, and brought out a rough block of wood, pierced through and through with a hole, which was immediately clapped on the top of the jar. Then planting the crotched stick upright about two yards distant, and making it sustain one end of the bamboo, he inserted the other end of the latter into the hole in the block: concluding these arrangements by placing an old calabash under the farther end of the bamboo.

Coming up to us now with a sly, significant look, and pointing admiringly at his apparatus, he exclaimed, "Ah, karhowree, ena hannahanna arva tee!" as much as to say, "This, you see, is the way it's done."

His contrivance was nothing less than a native still, where he manufactured his island "poteen." The disarray in which we found it was probably intentional, as a security against detection. Before we left the shed, the old fellow toppled the whole concern over, and dragged it away piecemeal.

His disclosing his secret to us thus was characteristic of the "Tootai Owrees," or contemners of the missionaries among the natives; who, presuming that all foreigners are opposed to the ascendancy of the missionaries, take pleasure in making them confidants, whenever the enactments of their rulers are secretly set at nought.

The substance from which the liquor is produced is called "Tee," which is a large, fibrous root, something like yam, but smaller. In its green state, it is exceedingly acrid; but boiled or baked, has the sweetness of the sugar-cane. After being subjected to the fire, macerated and reduced to a certain stage of fermentation, the "Tee" is stirred up with water, and is then ready for distillation.

On returning to the hut, pipes were introduced; and, after a while, Long Ghost, who, at first, had relished the "Arva Tee" as little as myself, to my surprise, began to wax sociable over it, with Varvy; and, before long, absolutely got mellow, the old toper keeping him company.

It was a curious sight. Everyone knows that, so long as the occasion lasts, there is no stronger bond of sympathy and good feeling among men than getting tipsy together. And how earnestly, nay, movingly, a brace of worthies, thus employed, will endeavour to shed light upon, and elucidate their mystical ideas!

Fancy Varvy and the doctor, then, lovingly tippling, and brimming over with a desire to become better acquainted; the doctor politely bent upon carrying on the conversation in the language of his host, and the old hermit persisting in trying to talk English. The result was that, between the two, they made such a fricassee of vowels and consonants that it was enough to turn one's brain.

The next morning, on waking, I heard a voice from the tombs. It was the doctor solemnly pronouncing himself a dead man. He was sitting up, with both hands clasped over his forehead, and his pale face a thousand times paler than ever.

"That infernal stuff has murdered me!" he cried. "Heavens! my head's all wheels and springs, like the automaton chess-player! What's to be done, Paul? I'm poisoned."

But, after drinking a herbal draught concocted by our host, and eating a light meal, at noon, he felt much better; so much so that he declared himself ready to continue our journey.

When we came to start, the Yankee's boots were missing; and, after a diligent search, were not to be found. Enraged beyond measure, their proprietor said that Varvy must have stolen them; but, considering his hospitality, I thought this extremely improbable; though to whom else to impute the theft I knew not. The doctor maintained, however, that one who was capable of drugging an innocent traveller with "Arva Tee" was capable of anything.

But it was in vain that he stormed, and Varvy and I searched; the boots were gone.

Were it not for this mysterious occurrence, and Varvy's detestable liquors, I would here recommend all travellers going round by the beach to Partoowye to stop at the Rock, and patronize the old gentleman--the more especially as he entertains gratis.

CHAPTER LXXIII.

OUR RECEPTION IN PARTOOWYE

UPON starting, at last, I flung away my sandals--by this time quite worn out--with the view of keeping company with the doctor, now forced to go barefooted. Recovering his spirits in good time, he protested that boots were a bore after all, and going without them decidedly manly.

This was said, be it observed, while strolling along over a soft carpet of grass; a little moist, even at midday, from the shade of the wood through which we were passing.

Emerging from this we entered upon a blank, sandy tract, upon which the sun's rays fairly flashed; making the loose gravel under foot well nigh as hot as the floor of an oven. Such yelling and leaping as there was in getting over this ground would be hard to surpass. We could not have crossed at all--until toward sunset--had it not been for a few small, wiry bushes growing here and there, into which we every now and then thrust our feet to cool. There was no little judgment necessary in selecting your bush; for if not chosen judiciously, the chances were that, on springing forward again, and finding the next bush so far off that an intermediate cooling was indispensable, you would have to run hack to your old place again.

Safely passing the Sahara, or Fiery Desert, we soothed our half-blistered feet by a pleasant walk through a meadow of long grass, which soon brought us in sight of a few straggling houses, sheltered by a grove on the outskirts of the village of Partoowye.

My comrade was for entering the first one we came to; but, on drawing near, they had so much of an air of pretension, at least for native dwellings, that I hesitated; thinking they might be the residences of the higher chiefs, from whom no very extravagant welcome was to be anticipated.

While standing irresolute, a voice from the nearest house hailed us: "Aramai! aramai, karhowree!" (Come in! come in, strangers!)

We at once entered, and were warmly greeted. The master of the house was an aristocratic-looking islander, dressed in loose linen drawers, a fine white shirt, and a sash of red silk tied about the waist, after the fashion of the Spaniards in Chili. He came up to us with a free, frank air, and, striking his chest with his hand, introduced himself as Ereemear Po-Po; or, to render the Christian name back again into English--Jeremiah Po-Po.

These curious combinations of names among the people of the Society Islands originate in the following way. When a native is baptized, his patronymic often gives offence to the missionaries, and they insist upon changing to something else whatever is objectionable therein. So, when Jeremiah came to the font, and gave his name as Narmo-Nana Po-Po (something equivalent to The-Darer-of-Devils-by-Night), the reverend gentleman officiating told him that such a heathenish appellation would never do, and a substitute must be had; at least for the devil part of it. Some highly respectable Christian appellations were then submitted, from which the candidate for admission into the church was at liberty to choose. There was Adamo (Adam), Nooar (Noah), Daveedar (David), Earcobar (James), Eorna (John), Patoora (Peter), Ereemear (Jeremiah), etc. And thus did he come to be named Jeremiah Po-Po; or, Jeremiah-in-the-Dark--which he certainly was, I fancy, as to the ridiculousness of his new cognomen.

We gave our names in return; upon which he bade us be seated; and, sitting down himself, asked us a great many questions, in mixed English and Tahitian. After giving some directions to an old man to prepare food, our host's wife, a large, benevolent-looking woman, upwards of forty, also sat down by us. In our soiled and travel-stained appearance, the good lady seemed to find abundant matter for commiseration; and all the while kept looking at us piteously, and making mournful exclamations.

But Jeremiah and his spouse were not the only inmates of the mansion.

In one corner, upon a large native couch, elevated upon posts, reclined a nymph; who, half-veiled in her own long hair, had yet to make her toilet for the day. She was the daughter of Po-Po; and a very beautiful little daughter she was; not more than fourteen; with the most delightful shape--like a bud just blown; and large hazel eyes. They called her Loo; a name rather pretty and genteel, and therefore quite appropriate; for a more genteel and lady-like little damsel there was not in all Imeeo.

She was a cold and haughty young beauty though, this same little Loo, and never deigned to notice us; further than now and then to let her eyes float over our persons, with an expression of indolent indifference. With the tears of the Loohooloo girls hardly dry from their sobbing upon our shoulders, this contemptuous treatment stung us not a little.

When we first entered, Po-Po was raking smooth the carpet of dried ferns which had that morning been newly laid; and now that our meal was ready, it was spread on a banana leaf, right upon this fragrant floor. Here we lounged at our ease, eating baked pig and breadfruit off earthen plates, and using, for the first time in many a long month, real knives and forks.

These, as well as other symptoms of refinement, somewhat abated our surprise at the reserve of the little Loo; her parents, doubtless, were magnates in Partoowye, and she herself was an heiress.

After being informed of our stay in the vale of Martair, they were very curious to know on what errand we came to Taloo. We merely hinted that the ship lying in the harbour was the reason of our coming.

Arfretee, Po-Po's wife, was a right motherly body. The meal over, she recommended a nap; and upon our waking much refreshed, she led us to the doorway, and pointed down among the trees; through which we saw the gleam of water. Taking the hint, we repaired thither; and finding a deep shaded pool, bathed, and returned to the house. Our hostess now sat down by us; and after looking with great interest at the doctor's cloak, felt of my own soiled and tattered garments for the hundredth time, and exclaimed plaintively--"Ah nuee nuee olee manee! olee manee!" (Alas! they are very, very old! very old!)

When Arfretee, good soul, thus addressed us, she thought she was talking very respectable English. The word "nuee" is so familiar to foreigners throughout Polynesia, and is so often used by them in their intercourse with the natives, that the latter suppose it to be common to all mankind. "Olee manee" is the native pronunciation of "old man," which, by Society Islanders talking Saxon, is applied indiscriminately to all aged things and persons whatsoever.

Going to a chest filled with various European articles, she took out two suits of new sailor frocks and trousers; and presenting them with a gracious smile, pushed us behind a calico screen, and left us. Without any fastidious scruples, we donned the garments; and what with the meal, the nap, and the bath, we now came forth like a couple of bridegrooms.

Evening drawing on, lamps were lighted. They were very simple; the half of a green melon, about one third full of cocoa-nut oil, and a wick of twisted tappa floating on the surface. As a night lamp, this contrivance cannot be excelled; a soft dreamy light being shed through the transparent rind.

As the evening advanced, other members of the household, whom as yet we had not seen, began to drop in. There was a slender young dandy in a gay striped shirt, and whole fathoms of bright figured calico tucked about his waist, and falling to the ground. He wore a new straw hat also with three distinct ribbons tied about the crown; one black, one green, and one pink. Shoes or stockings, however, he had none.

There were a couple of delicate, olive-cheeked little girls--twins--with mild eyes and beautiful hair, who ran about the house, half-naked, like a couple of gazelles. They had a brother, somewhat younger--a fine dark boy, with an eye like a woman's. All these were the children of Po-Po, begotten in lawful wedlock.

Then there were two or three queer-looking old ladies, who wore shabby mantles of soiled sheeting, which fitted so badly, and withal had such a second-hand look that I at once put their wearers down as domestic paupers--poor relations, supported by the bounty of My Lady

Arfretee. They were sad, meek old bodies; said little and ate less; and either kept their eyes on the ground, or lifted them up deferentially. The semi-civilization of the island must have had something to do with making them what they were.

I had almost forgotten Monee, the grinning old man who prepared our meal. His head was a shining, bald globe. He had a round little paunch, and legs like a cat. He was Po-Po's factotum--cook, butler, and climber of the bread-fruit and cocoa-nut trees; and, added to all else, a mighty favourite with his mistress; with whom he would sit smoking and gossiping by the hour.

Often you saw the indefatigable Monee working away at a great rate; then dropping his employment all at once--never mind what--run off to a little distance, and after rolling himself away in a corner and taking a nap, jump up again, and fall to with fresh vigour.

From a certain something in the behaviour of Po-Po and his household, I was led to believe that he was a pillar of the church; though, from what I had seen in Tahiti, I could hardly reconcile such a supposition with his frank, cordial, unembarrassed air. But I was not wrong in my conjecture: Po-Po turned out to be a sort of elder, or deacon; he was also accounted a man of wealth, and was nearly related to a high chief.

Before retiring, the entire household gathered upon the floor; and in their midst, he read aloud a chapter from a Tahitian Bible. Then kneeling with the rest of us, he offered up a prayer. Upon its conclusion, all separated without speaking. These devotions took place regularly, every night and morning. Grace too was invariably said, by this family, both before and after eating.

After becoming familiarized with the almost utter destitution of anything like practical piety upon these islands, what I observed in our host's house astonished me much. But whatever others might have been, Po-Po was, in truth, a Christian: the only one, Arfretee excepted, whom I personally knew to be such, among all the natives of Polynesia.

CHAPTER LXXIV.

RETIRING FOR THE NIGHT--THE DOCTOR GROWS DEVOUT

THEY put us to bed very pleasantly.

Lying across the foot of Po-Po's nuptial couch was a smaller one made of Koar-wood; a thin, strong cord, twisted from the fibres of the husk of the cocoa-nut, and woven into an exceedingly light sort of network, forming its elastic body. Spread upon this was a single, fine mat, with a roll of dried ferns for a pillow, and a strip of white tappa for a sheet. This couch was mine. The doctor was provided for in another corner.

Loo reposed alone on a little settee with a taper burning by her side; the dandy, her brother, swinging overhead in a sailor's hammock The two gazelles frisked upon a mat near by; and the indigent relations borrowed a scant corner of the old butler's pallet, who snored away by the open door. After all had retired, Po-Po placed the illuminated melon in the middle of the apartment; and so, we all slumbered till morning.

Upon awaking, the sun was streaming brightly through the open bamboos, but no one was stirring. After surveying the fine attitudes into which forgetfulness had thrown at least one of the sleepers, my attention was called off to the general aspect of the dwelling, which was quite significant of the superior circumstances of our host.

The house itself was built in the simple, but tasteful native style. It was a long, regular oval, some fifty feet in length, with low sides of cane-work, and a roof thatched with palmetto-leaves. The ridgepole was, perhaps, twenty feet from the ground. There was no foundation whatever; the bare earth being merely covered with ferns; a kind of carpeting which serves very well, if frequently renewed; otherwise, it becomes dusty, and the haunt of vermin, as in the huts of the poorer natives.

Besides the couches, the furniture consisted of three or four sailor chests; in which were stored the fine wearing-apparel of the household--the ruffled linen shirts of Po-Po, the calico dresses of his wife and children, and divers odds and ends of European articles--strings of beads, ribbons, Dutch looking-glasses, knives, coarse prints, bunches of keys, bits of crockery, and metal buttons. One of these chests--used as a bandbox by Arfretee--contained several of the native hats (coal-scuttles), all of the same pattern, but trimmed with variously-coloured ribbons. Of nothing was our good hostess more proud than of these hats, and her dresses. On Sundays, she went abroad a dozen times; and every time, like Queen Elizabeth, in a different robe.

Po-Po, for some reason or other, always gave us our meals before the rest of the family were served; and the doctor, who was very discerning in such matters, declared that we fared much better than they. Certain it was that, had Ereemear's guests travelled with purses, portmanteau, and letters of introduction to the queen, they could not have been better cared for.

The day after our arrival, Monee, the old butler, brought us in for dinner a small pig, baked in the ground. All savoury, it lay in a wooden trencher, surrounded by roasted hemispheres of the breadfruit. A large calabash, filled with taro pudding, or poee, followed; and the young dandy, overcoming his customary languor, threw down our cocoa-nuts from an adjoining tree.

When all was ready, and the household looking on, Long Ghost, devoutly clasping his hands over the fated pig, implored a blessing. Hereupon, everybody present looked exceedingly pleased; Po-Po coming up and addressing the doctor with much warmth; and Arfretee, regarding him with almost maternal affection, exclaimed delightedly, "Ah! mickonaree tata matai!" in other words, "What a pious young man!"

It was just after this meal that she brought me a roll of grass sinnate (of the kind which sailors sew into the frame of their tarpaulins), and then, handing me needle and thread, bade me begin at once, and make myself the hat which I so much needed. An accomplished hand at the business, I finished it that day--merely stitching the braid together; and Arfretee, by way of rewarding my industry, with her own olive hands ornamented the crown with a band of flame-coloured ribbon; the two long ends of which streaming behind, sailor-fashion, still preserved for me the Eastern title bestowed by Long Ghost.

CHAPTER LXXV.

A RAMBLE THROUGH THE SETTLEMENT

THE following morning, making our toilets carefully, we donned our sombreros, and sallied out on a tour. Without meaning to reveal our designs upon the court, our principal object was, to learn what chances there were for white men to obtain employment under the queen. On this head, it is true, we had questioned Po-Po; but his answers had been very discouraging; so we determined to obtain further information elsewhere.

But, first, to give some little description of the village.

The settlement of Partoowye is nothing more than some eighty houses, scattered here and there, in the midst of an immense grove, where the trees have been thinned out and the underbrush cleared away. Through the grove flows a stream; and the principal avenue crosses it, over an elastic bridge of cocoa-nut trunks, laid together side by side. The avenue is broad, and serpentine; well shaded from one end to the other, and as pretty a place for a morning promenade as any lounger could wish. The houses, constructed without the slightest regard to the road, peep into view from among the trees on either side: some looking you right in the face as you pass, and others, without any manners, turning their backs. Occasionally you observe a rural retreat, inclosed by a picket of bamboos, or with a solitary pane of glass massively framed in the broadside of the dwelling, or with a rude, strange-looking door, swinging upon dislocated wooden hinges. Otherwise, the dwellings are built in the original style of the natives; and never mind how mean and filthy some of them may appear within, they all look picturesque enough without.

As we sauntered along the people we met saluted us pleasantly, and invited us into their houses; and in this way we made a good many brief morning calls. But the hour could not have been the fashionable one in Partoowye, since the ladies were invariably in dishabille. But they always gave us a cordial reception, and were particularly polite to the doctor; caressing him, and amorously hanging about his neck; wonderfully taken up, in short, with a gay handkerchief he wore there. Arfretee had that morning bestowed it upon the pious youth.

With some exceptions, the general appearance of the natives of Partoowye was far better than that of the inhabitants of Papeetee: a circumstance only to be imputed to their restricted intercourse with foreigners.

Strolling on, we turned a sweep of the road, when the doctor gave a start; and no wonder. Right before us, in the grove, was a block of houses: regular square frames, boarded over, furnished with windows and doorways, and two stories high. We ran up and found them fast going to decay: very dingy, and here and there covered with moss; no sashes, no doors; and on one side, the entire block had settled down nearly a foot. On going into the basement we looked clean up through the unbearded timbers to the roof; where rays of light, glimmering through many a chink, illuminated the cobwebs which swung all round.

The whole interior was dark and close. Burrowing among some old mats in one corner, like a parcel of gipsies in a ruin, were a few vagabond natives. They had their dwelling here.

Curious to know who on earth could have been thus trying to improve the value of real estate in Partoowye, we made inquiries; and learned that some years previous the block had been thrown up by a veritable Yankee (one might have known that), a house-carpenter by trade, and a bold, enterprising fellow by nature.

Put ashore from his ship, sick, he first went to work and got well; then sallied out with chisel and plane, and made himself generally useful. A sober, steady man, it seems, he at last obtained the confidence of several chiefs, and soon filled them with all sorts of ideas concerning the alarming want of public spirit in the people of Imeeo. More especially did he dwell upon the humiliating fact of their living in paltry huts of bamboo, when magnificent palaces of boards might so easily be mortised together.

In the end, these representations so far prevailed with one old chief that the carpenter was engaged to build a batch of these wonderful palaces. Provided with plenty of men, he at once set to work: built a saw-mill among the mountains, felled trees, and sent over to Papeetee for nails.

Presto! the castle rose; but alas, the roof was hardly on, when the Yankee's patron, having speculated beyond his means, broke all to pieces, and was absolutely unable to pay one "plug" of tobacco in the pound. His failure involved the carpenter, who sailed away from his creditors in the very next ship that touched at the harbour.

The natives despised the rickety palace of boards; and often lounged by, wagging their heads, and jeering.

We were told that the queen's residence was at the extreme end of the village; so, without waiting for the doctor to procure a fiddle, we suddenly resolved upon going thither at once, and learning whether any privy counsellorships were vacant.

Now, although there was a good deal of my waggish comrade's nonsense about what has been said concerning our expectations of court preferment, we, nevertheless, really thought that something to our advantage might turn up in that quarter.

On approaching the palace grounds, we found them rather peculiar. A broad pier of hewn coral rocks was built right out into the water; and upon this, and extending into a grove adjoining, were some eight or ten very large native houses, constructed in the handsomest style and inclosed together by a low picket of bamboos, which embraced a considerable area.

Throughout the Society Islands, the residences of the chiefs are mostly found in the immediate vicinity of the sea; a site which gives them the full benefit of a cooling breeze; nor are they so liable to the annoyance of insects; besides enjoying, when they please, the fine shade afforded by the neighbouring groves, always most luxuriant near the water.

Lounging about the grounds were some sixty or eighty handsomely-dressed natives, men and women; some reclining on the shady side of the houses, others under the trees, and a small group conversing close by the railing facing us.

We went up to the latter; and giving the usual salutation, were on the point of vaulting over the bamboos, when they turned upon us angrily, and said we could not enter. We stated our earnest desire to see the queen; hinting that we were bearers of important dispatches. But it was to no purpose; and not a little vexed, we were obliged to return to Po-Po's without effecting anything.

CHAPTER LXXVI.

AN ISLAND JILT--WE VISIT THE SHIP

UPON arriving home we fully laid open to Po-Po our motives in visiting Taloo, and begged his friendly advice. In his broken English he cheerfully gave us all the information we needed.

It was true, he said, that the queen entertained some idea of making a stand against the French; and it was currently reported also that several chiefs from Borabora, Huwyenee, Raiatair, and Tahar, the leeward islands of the group, were at that very time taking counsel with her as to the expediency of organizing a general movement throughout the entire cluster, with a view of anticipating any further encroachments on the part of the invaders. Should warlike measures be actually decided upon, it was quite certain that Pomaree would be glad to enlist all the foreigners she could; but as to her making officers of either the doctor or me, that was out of the question; because, already, a number of Europeans, well known to her, had volunteered as such. Concerning our getting immediate access to the queen, Po-Po told us it was rather doubtful; she living at that time very retired, in poor health, and spirits, and averse to receiving calls. Previous to her misfortunes, however, no one, however humble, was denied admittance to her presence; sailors, even, attended her levees.

Not at all disheartened by these things, we concluded to kill time in Partoowye until some event turned up more favourable to our projects. So that very day we sallied out on an excursion to the ship which, lying land-locked far up the bay, yet remained to be visited.

Passing on our route a long, low shed, a voice hailed us--"White men ahoy!" Turning round, who should we see but a rosy-cheeked Englishman (you could tell his country at a glance), up to his knees in shavings, and planing away at a bench. He turned out to be a runaway ship's carpenter, recently from Tahiti, and now doing a profitable business in Imeeo, by fitting up the dwellings of opulent chiefs with cupboards and other conveniences, and once in a while trying his hand at a lady's work-box. He had been in the settlement but a few months, and already possessed houses and lands.

But though blessed with prosperity and high health, there was one thing wanting--a wife. And when he came to speak of the matter, his countenance fell, and he leaned dejectedly upon his plane.

"It's too bad!" he sighed, "to wait three long years; and all the while, dear little Lullee living in the same house with that infernal chief from Tahar!"

Our curiosity was piqued; the poor carpenter, then, had been falling in love with some island coquette, who was going to jilt him.

But such was not the case. There was a law prohibiting, under a heavy penalty, the marriage of a native with a foreigner, unless the latter, after being three years a resident on the island, was willing to affirm his settled intention of remaining for life.

William was therefore in a sad way. He told us that he might have married the girl half-a-dozen times, had it not been for this odious law: but, latterly, she had become less loving and more giddy, particularly with the strangers from Tahar. Desperately smitten, and desirous of securing her at all hazards, he had proposed to the damsel's friends a nice little arrangement, introductory to marriage; but they would not hear of it; besides, if the pair were discovered living together upon such a footing, they would be liable to a degrading punishment:--sent to work making stone walls and opening roads for the queen.

Doctor Long Ghost was all sympathy. "Bill, my good fellow," said he, tremulously, "let me go and talk to her." But Bill, declining the offer, would not even inform us where his charmer lived.

Leaving the disconsolate Willie planing a plank of New Zealand pine (an importation from the Bay of Islands), and thinking the while of Lullee, we went on our way. How his suit prospered in the end we never learned.

Going from Po-Po's house toward the anchorage of the harbour of Taloo, you catch no glimpse of the water until, coming out from deep groves, you all at once find yourself upon the beach. A bay, considered by many voyagers the most beautiful in the South Seas, then lies before you. You stand upon one side of what seems a deep green river, flowing through mountain passes to the sea. Right opposite a majestic promontory divides the inlet from another, called after its discoverer, Captain Cook. The face of this promontory toward Taloo is one verdant wall; and at its base the waters lie still and fathomless. On the left hand, you just catch a peep of the widening mouth of the bay, the break in the reef by which ships enter, and, beyond, the sea. To the right, the inlet, sweeping boldly round the promontory, runs far away into the land; where, save in one direction, the hills close in on every side, knee-deep in verdure and shooting aloft in grotesque peaks. The open space lies at the head of the bay; in the distance it extends into a broad hazy plain lying at the foot of an amphitheatre of hills. Here is the large sugar plantation previously alluded to. Beyond the first range of hills, you descry the sharp pinnacles of the interior; and among these, the same silent Marling-spike which we so often admired from the other side of the island.

All alone in the harbour lay the good ship Leviathan. We jumped into the canoe, and paddled off to her. Though early in the afternoon, everything was quiet; but upon mounting the side we found four or five sailors lounging about the forecastle, under an awning. They gave us no very cordial reception; and though otherwise quite hearty in appearance, seemed to assume a look of ill-humour on purpose to honour our arrival. There was much eagerness to learn whether we wanted to "ship"; and by the unpleasant accounts they gave of the vessel, they seemed desirous to prevent such a thing if possible.

We asked where the rest of the ship's company were; a gruff old fellow made answer, "One boat's crew of 'em is gone to Davy Jones's locker:--went off after a whale, last cruise, and never come back agin. All the starboard watch ran away last night, and the skipper's ashore kitching 'em."

"And it's shipping yer after, my jewels, is it?" cried a curly-pated little Belfast sailor, coming up to us, "thin arrah! my livelies, jist be after sailing ashore in a jiffy:--the divil of a skipper will carry yees both to sea, whether or no. Be off wid ye thin, darlints, and steer clear of the likes of this ballyhoo of blazes as long as ye live. They murther us here every day, and starve us into the bargain. Here, Dick, lad, har! the poor divil's canow alongside; and paddle away wid yees for dear life."

But we loitered awhile, listening to more inducements to ship; and at last concluded to stay to supper. My sheath-knife never cut into better sea-beef than that which we found lying in the kid in the forecastle. The bread, too, was hard, dry, and brittle as glass; and there was plenty of both.

While we were below, the mate of the vessel called out for someone to come on deck. I liked his voice. Hearing it was as good as a look at his face. It betokened a true sailor, and no taskmaster.

The appearance of the Leviathan herself was quite pleasing. Like all large, comfortable old whalers, she had a sort of motherly look:--broad in the beam, flush decks, and four chubby boats hanging at the breast. Her sails were furled loosely upon the yards, as if they had been worn long, and fitted easy; her shrouds swung negligently slack; and as for the "running rigging," it never worked hard as it does in some of your "dandy ships," jamming in the sheaves of blocks, like Chinese slippers, too small to be useful: on the contrary, the ropes ran glibly through, as if they had many a time travelled the same road, and were used to it.

When evening came, we dropped into our canoe, and paddled ashore; fully convinced that the good ship never deserved the name which they gave her.

CHAPTER LXXVII.

A PARTY OF ROVERS--LITTLE LOO AND THE DOCTOR

WHILE IN Partoowye, we fell in with a band of six veteran rovers, prowling about the village and harbour, who had just come overland from another part of the island.

A few weeks previous, they had been paid off, at Papeetee, from a whaling vessel, on board of which they had, six months before, shipped for a single cruise; that is to say, to be discharged at the next port. Their cruise was a famous one; and each man stepped upon the beach at Tahiti jingling his dollars in a sock.

Weary at last of the shore, and having some money left, they clubbed, and purchased a sail-boat; proposing a visit to a certain uninhabited island, concerning which they had heard strange and golden stories. Of course, they never could think of going to sea without a medicine-chest filled with flasks of spirits, and a small cask of the same in the hold in case the chest should give out.

Away they sailed; hoisted a flag of their own, and gave three times three, as they staggered out of the bay of Papeetee with a strong breeze, and under all the "muslin" they could carry.

Evening coming on, and feeling in high spirits and no ways disposed to sleep, they concluded to make a night of it; which they did; all hands getting tipsy, and the two masts going over the side about midnight, to the tune of

  "Sailing down, sailing down, On the coast of Barbaree."

Fortunately, one worthy could stand by holding on to the tiller; and the rest managed to crawl about, and hack away the lanyards of the rigging, so as to break clear from the fallen spars. While thus employed, two sailors got tranquilly over the side, and went plumb to the bottom, under the erroneous impression that they were stepping upon an imaginary wharf to get at their work better.

After this, it blew quite a gale; and the commodore, at the helm, instinctively kept the boat before the wind; and by so doing, ran over for the opposite island of Imeeo. Crossing the channel, by almost a miracle they went straight through an opening in the reef, and shot upon a ledge of coral, where the waters were tolerably smooth. Here they lay until morning, when the natives came off to them in their canoes. By the help of the islanders, the schooner was hove over on her beam-ends; when, finding the bottom knocked to pieces, the adventurers sold the boat for a trifle to the chief of the district, and went ashore, rolling before them their precious cask of spirits. Its contents soon evaporated, and they came to Partoowye.

The day after encountering these fellows, we were strolling among the groves in the neighbourhood, when we came across several parties of natives armed with clumsy muskets, rusty cutlasses, and outlandish clubs. They were beating the bushes, shouting aloud, and apparently trying to scare somebody. They were in pursuit of the strangers, who, having in a single night set at nought all the laws of the place, had thought best to decamp.

In the daytime, Po-Po's house was as pleasant a lounge as one could wish. So, after strolling about, and seeing all there was to be seen, we spent the greater part of our mornings there; breakfasting late, and dining about two hours after noon. Sometimes we lounged on the floor of ferns, smoking, and telling stories; of which the doctor had as many as a half-pay captain in the army. Sometimes we chatted, as well as we could, with the natives; and, one day--joy to us!--Po-Po brought in three volumes of Smollett's novels, which had been found in the chest of a sailor, who some time previous had died on the island.

Amelia!--Peregrine!--you hero of rogues, Count Fathom!--what a debt do we owe you!

I know not whether it was the reading of these romances, or the want of some sentimental pastime, which led the doctor, about this period, to lay siege to the heart of the little Loo.

Now, as I have said before, the daughter of Po-Po was most cruelly reserved, and never deigned to notice us. Frequently I addressed her with a long face and an air of the profoundest and most distant respect--but in vain; she wouldn't even turn up her pretty olive nose. Ah! it's quite plain, thought I; she knows very well what graceless dogs sailors are, and won't have anything to do with us.

But thus thought not my comrade. Bent he was upon firing the cold glitter of Loo's passionless eyes.

He opened the campaign with admirable tact: making cautious approaches, and content, for three days, with ogling the nymph for about five minutes after every meal. On the fourth day, he asked her a question; on the fifth, she dropped a nut of ointment, and he picked it up and gave it to her; on the sixth, he went over and sat down within three yards of the couch where she lay; and, on the memorable morn of the seventh, he proceeded to open his batteries in form.

The damsel was reclining on the ferns; one hand supporting her cheek, and the other listlessly turning over the leaves of a Tahitian Bible. The doctor approached.

Now the chief disadvantage under which he laboured was his almost complete ignorance of the love vocabulary of the island. But French counts, they say, make love delightfully in broken English; and what hindered the doctor from doing the same in dulcet Tahitian. So at it he went.

"Ah!" said he, smiling bewitchingly, "oee mickonaree; oee ready Biblee?"

No answer; not even a look.

"Ah I matai! very goody ready Biblee mickonaree."

Loo, without stirring, began reading, in a low tone, to herself.

"Mickonaree Biblee ready goody maitai," once more observed the doctor, ingeniously transposing his words for the third time.

But all to no purpose; Loo gave no sign.

He paused, despairingly; but it would never do to give up; so he threw himself at full length beside her, and audaciously commenced turning over the leaves.

Loo gave a start, just one little start, barely perceptible, and then, fumbling something in her hand, lay perfectly motionless; the doctor rather frightened at his own temerity, and knowing not what to do next. At last, he placed one arm cautiously about her waist; almost in the same instant he bounded to his feet, with a cry; the little witch had pierced him with a thorn. But there she lay, just as quietly as ever, turning over the leaves, and reading to herself.

My long friend raised the siege incontinently, and made a disorderly retreat to the place where I reclined, looking on.

I am pretty sure that Loo must have related this occurrence to her father, who came in shortly afterward; for he looked queerly at the doctor. But he said nothing; and, in ten minutes, was quite as affable as ever. As for Loo, there was not the slightest change in her; and the doctor, of course, for ever afterwards held his peace.

CHAPTER LXXVIII.

MRS. BELL

ONE DAY, taking a pensive afternoon stroll along one of the many bridle-paths which wind among the shady groves in the neighbourhood of Taloo, I was startled by a sunny apparition. It was that of a beautiful young Englishwoman, charmingly dressed, and mounted upon a spirited little white pony. Switching a green branch, she came cantering toward me.

I looked round to see whether I could possibly be in Polynesia. There were the palm-trees; but how to account for the lady?

Stepping to one side as the apparition drew near, I made a polite obeisance. It gave me a bold, rosy look; and then, with a gay air, patted its palfrey, crying out, "Fly away, Willie!" and galloped among the trees.

I would have followed; but Willie's heels were making such a pattering among the dry leaves that pursuit would have been useless.

So I went straight home to Po-Po's, and related my adventure to the doctor.

The next day, our inquiries resulted in finding out that the stranger had been on the island about two years; that she came from Sydney; and was the wife of Mr. Bell (happy dog!), the proprietor of the sugar plantation to which I have previously referred.

To the sugar plantation we went, the same day.

The country round about was very beautiful: a level basin of verdure, surrounded by sloping hillsides. The sugar-cane--of which there was about one hundred acres, in various stages of cultivation--looked thrifty. A considerable tract of land, however, which seemed to have been formerly tilled, was now abandoned.

The place where they extracted the saccharine matter was under an immense shed of bamboos. Here we saw several clumsy pieces of machinery for breaking the cane; also great kettles for boiling the sugar. But, at present, nothing was going on. Two or three natives were lounging in one of the kettles, smoking; the other was occupied by three sailors from the Leviathan, playing cards.

While we were conversing with these worthies, a stranger approached. He was a sun-burnt, romantic-looking European, dressed in a loose suit of nankeen; his fine throat and chest were exposed, and he sported a Guayaquil hat with a brim like a Chinese umbrella. This was Mr. Bell. He was very civil; showed us the grounds, and, taking us into a sort of arbour, to our surprise, offered to treat us to some wine. People often do the like; but Mr. Bell did more: he produced the bottle. It was spicy sherry; and we drank out of the halves of fresh citron melons. Delectable goblets!

The wine was a purchase from, the French in Tahiti.

Now all this was extremely polite in Mr. Bell; still, we came to see Mrs. Bell. But she proved to be a phantom, indeed; having left the same morning for Papeetee, on a visit to one of the missionaries' wives there.

I went home, much chagrined.

To be frank, my curiosity had been wonderfully piqued concerning the lady. In the first place, she was the most beautiful white woman I ever saw in Polynesia. But this is saying nothing. She had such eyes, such moss-roses in her cheeks, such a divine air in the saddle, that, to my dying day, I shall never forget Mrs. Bell.

The sugar-planter himself was young, robust, and handsome. So, merrily may the little Bells increase, and multiply, and make music in the Land of Imeeo.

CHAPTER LXXIX.

TALOO CHAPEL--HOLDING COURT IN POLYNESIA

IN Partoowye is to be seen one of the best-constructed and handsomest chapels in the South Seas. Like the buildings of the palace, it stands upon an artificial pier, presenting a semicircular sweep to the bay. The chapel is built of hewn blocks of coral; a substance which, although extremely friable, is said to harden by exposure to the atmosphere. To a stranger, these blocks look extremely curious. Their surface is covered with strange fossil-like impressions, the seal of which must have been set before the flood. Very nearly white when hewn from the reefs, the coral darkens with age; so that several churches in Polynesia now look almost as sooty and venerable as famed St. Paul's.

In shape, the chapel is an octagon, with galleries all round. It will seat, perhaps, four hundred people. Everything within is stained a tawny red; and there being but few windows, or rather embrasures, the dusky benches and galleries, and the tall spectre of a pulpit look anything but cheerful.

On Sundays we always went to worship here. Going in the family suite of Po-Po, we, of course, maintained a most decorous exterior; and hence, by all the elderly people of the village, were doubtless regarded as pattern young men.

Po-Po's seat was in a snug corner; and it being particularly snug, in the immediate vicinity of one of the Palm pillars supporting the gallery, I invariably leaned against it: Po-Po and his lady on one side, the doctor and the dandy on the other, and the children and poor relations seated behind.

As for Loo, instead of sitting (as she ought to have done) by her good father and mother, she must needs run up into the gallery, and sit with a parcel of giddy creatures of her own age; who, all through the sermon, did nothing but look down on the congregation; pointing out, and giggling at the queer-looking old ladies in dowdy bonnets and scant tunics. But Loo, herself, was never guilty of these improprieties.

Occasionally during the week they have afternoon service in the chapel, when the natives themselves have something to say; although their auditors are but few. An introductory prayer being offered by the missionary, and a hymn sung, communicants rise in their places, and exhort in pure Tahitian, and with wonderful tone and gesture. And among them all, Deacon Po-Po, though he talked most, was the one whom you would have liked best to hear. Much would I have given to have understood some of his impassioned bursts; when he tossed his arms overhead, stamped, scowled, and glared, till he looked like the very Angel of Vengeance.

"Deluded man!" sighed the doctor, on one of these occasions, "I fear he takes the fanatical view of the subject." One thing was certain: when Po-Po spoke, all listened; a great deal more than could be said for the rest; for under the discipline of two or three I could mention, some of the audience napped; others fidgeted; a few yawned; and one irritable old gentleman, in a nightcap of cocoa-nut leaves, used to clutch his long staff in a state of excessive nervousness, and stride out of the church, making all the noise he could, to emphasize his disgust.

Right adjoining the chapel is an immense, rickety building, with windows and shutters, and a half-decayed board flooring laid upon trunks of palm-trees. They called it a school-house; but as such we never saw it occupied. It was often used as a court-room, however; and here we attended several trials; among others, that of a decayed naval officer, and a young girl of fourteen; the latter charged with having been very naughty on a particular occasion set forth in the pleadings; and the former with having aided and abetted her in her naughtiness, and with other misdemeanours.

The foreigner was a tall, military-looking fellow, with a dark cheek and black whiskers. According to his own account, he had lost a colonial armed brig on the coast of New Zealand; and since then, had been leading the life of a man about town among the islands of the Pacific.

The doctor wanted to know why he did not go home and report the loss of his brig; but Captain Crash, as they called him, had some incomprehensible reasons for not doing so, about which he could talk by the hour, and no one be any the wiser. Probably he was a discreet man, and thought it best to waive an interview with the lords of the admiralty.

For some time past, this extremely suspicious character had been carrying on the illicit trade in French wines and brandies, smuggled over from the men-of-war lately touching at Tahiti. In a grove near the anchorage he had a rustic shanty and arbour, where, in quiet times, when no ships were in Taloo, a stray native once in a while got boozy, and staggered home, catching at the cocoa-nut trees as he went. The captain himself lounged under a tree during the warm afternoons, pipe in mouth; thinking, perhaps, over old times, and occasionally feeling his shoulders for his lost epaulets.

But, sail ho! a ship is descried coming into the bay. Soon she drops her anchor in its waters; and the next day Captain Crash entertains the sailors in his grove. And rare times they have of it:--drinking and quarrelling together as sociably as you please.

Upon one of these occasions, the crew of the Leviathan made so prodigioús a tumult that the natives, indignant at the insult offered their laws, plucked up a heart, and made a dash at the rioters, one hundred strong. The sailors fought like tigers; but were at last overcome, and carried before a native tribunal; which, after a mighty clamour, dismissed everybody but Captain Crash, who was asserted to be the author of the disorders.

Upon this charge, then, he had been placed in confinement against the coming on of the assizes; the judge being expected to lounge along in the course of the afternoon. While waiting his Honour's arrival, numerous additional offences were preferred against the culprit (mostly by the old women); among others was the bit of a slip in which he stood implicated along with the young lady. Thus, in Polynesia as elsewhere;--charge a man with one misdemeanour, and all his peccadilloes are raked up and assorted before him.

Going to the school-house for the purpose of witnessing the trial, the din of it assailed our ears a long way off; and upon entering the building, we were almost stunned. About five hundred natives were present; each apparently having something to say and determined to say it. His Honour--a handsome, benevolent-looking old man--sat cross-legged on a little platform, seemingly resigned, with all Christian submission, to the uproar. He was an hereditary chief in this quarter of the island, and judge for life in the district of Partoowye.

There were several cases coming on; but the captain and girl were first tried together. They were mixing freely with the crowd; and as it afterwards turned out that everyone--no matter who--had a right to address the court, for aught we knew they might have been arguing their own case. At what precise moment the trial began it would be hard to say. There was no swearing of witnesses, and no regular jury. Now and then somebody leaped up and shouted out something which might have been evidence; the rest, meanwhile, keeping up an incessant jabbering. Presently the old judge himself began to get excited; and springing to his feet, ran in among the crowd, wagging his tongue as hard as anybody.

The tumult lasted about twenty minutes; and toward the end of it, Captain Crash might have been seen, tranquilly regarding, from his Honour's platform, the judicial uproar, in which his fate was about being decided.

The result of all this was that both he and the girl were found guilty. The latter was adjudged to make six mats for the queen; and the former, in consideration of his manifold offences, being deemed incorrigible, was sentenced to eternal banishment from the island. Both these decrees seemed to originate in the general hubbub. His Honour, however, appeared to have considerable authority, and it was quite plain that the decision received his approval.

The above penalties were by no means indiscriminately inflicted. The missionaries have prepared a sort of penal tariff to facilitate judicial proceedings. It costs so many days' labour on the Broom Road to indulge in the pleasures of the calabash; so many fathoms of stone wall to steal a musket; and so on to the end of the catalogue. The judge being provided with a book in which all these matters are cunningly arranged, the thing is vastly convenient. For instance: a crime is proved,--say bigamy; turn to letter B--and there you have it. Bigamy:--forty days on the Broom Road, and twenty mats for the queen. Read the passage aloud, and sentence is pronounced.

After taking part in the first trial, the other delinquents present were put upon their own; in which, also, the convicted culprits seemed to have quite as much to say as the rest. A rather strange proceeding; but strictly in accordance with the glorious English principle, that every man should be tried by his peers. They were all found guilty.

CHAPTER LXXX.

QUEEN POMAREE

IT is well to learn something about people before being introduced to them, and so we will here give some account of Pomaree and her family.

Every reader of Cook's Voyages must remember "Otto," who, in that navigator's time, was king of the larger peninsula of Tahiti. Subsequently, assisted by the muskets of the Bounty's men, he extended his rule over the entire island. This Otto, before his death, had his name changed into Pomaree, which has ever since been the royal patronymic.

He was succeeded by his son, Pomaree II., the most famous prince in the annals of Tahiti. Though a sad debauchee and drunkard, and even charged with unnatural crimes, he was a great friend of the missionaries, and one of their very first proselytes. During the religious wars into which he was hurried by his zeal for the new faith, he was defeated and expelled from the island. After a short exile he returned from Imeeo, with an army of eight hundred warriors, and in the battle of Narii routed the rebellious pagans with great slaughter, and reestablished himself upon the throne. Thus, by force of arms, was Christianity finally triumphant in Tahiti.

Pomaree II., dying in 1821, was succeeded by his infant son, under the title of Pomaree III. This young prince survived his father but six years; and the government then descended to his elder sister, Aimata, the present queen, who is commonly called Pomaree Vahinee I., or the first female Pomaree. Her majesty must be now upwards of thirty years of age. She has been twice married. Her first husband was a son of the old King of Tahar, an island about one hundred miles from Tahiti. This proving an unhappy alliance, the pair were soon afterwards divorced. The present husband of the queen is a chief of Imeeo.

The reputation of Pomaree is not what it ought to be. She, and also her mother, were, for a long time, excommunicated members of the Church; and the former, I believe, still is. Among other things, her conjugal fidelity is far from being unquestioned. Indeed, it was upon this ground chiefly that she was excluded from the communion of the Church.

Previous to her misfortunes she spent the greater portion of her time sailing about from one island to another, attended by a licentious court; and wherever she went all manner of games and festivities celebrated her arrival.

She was always given to display. For several years the maintenance of a regiment of household troops drew largely upon the royal exchequer. They were trouserless fellows, in a uniform of calico shirts and pasteboard hats; armed with muskets of all shapes and calibres, and commanded by a great noisy chief, strutting it in a coat of fiery red. These heroes escorted their mistress whenever she went abroad.

Some time ago, the queen received from her English sister, Victoria, a very showy, though uneasy, head-dress--a crown; probably made to order at some tinman's in London. Having no idea of reserving so pretty a bauble for coronation days, which come so seldom, her majesty sported it whenever she appeared in public; and, to show her familiarity with European customs, politely touched it to all foreigners of distinction--whaling captains, and the like--whom she happened to meet in her evening walk on the Broom Road.

The arrival and departure of royalty were always announced at the palace by the court artilleryman--a fat old gentleman who, in a prodigious hurry and perspiration, discharged minute fowling-pieces as fast as he could load and fire the same.

The Tahitian princess leads her husband a hard life. Poor fellow! he not only caught a queen, but a Tartar, when he married her. The style by which he is addressed is rather significant--"Pomaree-Tanee" (Pomaree's man). All things considered, as appropriate a title for a king-consort as could be hit upon.

If ever there were a henpecked husband, that man is the prince. One day, his carasposa giving audience to a deputation from the captains of the vessels lying in Papeetee, he ventured to make a suggestion which was very displeasing to her. She turned round and, boxing his ears, told him to go over to his beggarly island of Imeeo if he wanted to give himself airs.

Cuffed and contemned, poor Tanee flies to the bottle, or rather to the calabash, for solace. Like his wife and mistress, he drinks more than he ought.

Six or seven years ago, when an American man-of-war was lying at Papeetee, the town was thrown into the greatest commotion by a conjugal assault and battery made upon the sacred person of Pomaree by her intoxicated Tanee.

Captain Bob once told me the story. And by way of throwing more spirit into the description, as well as to make up for his oral deficiencies, the old man went through the accompanying action: myself being proxy for the Queen of Tahiti.

It seems that, on a Sunday morning, being dismissed contemptuously from the royal presence, Tanee was accosted by certain good fellows, friends and boon companions, who condoled with him on his misfortunes--railed against the queen, and finally dragged him away to an illicit vendor of spirits, in whose house the party got gloriously mellow. In this state, Pomaree Vahinee I. was the topic upon which all dilated--"A vixen of a queen," probably suggested one. "It's infamous," said another; "and I'd have satisfaction," cried a third. "And so I will!"--Tanee must have hiccoughed; for off he went; and ascertaining that his royal half was out riding, he mounted his horse and galloped after her.

Near the outskirts of the town, a cavalcade of women came cantering toward him, in the centre of which was the object of his fury. Smiting his beast right and left, he dashed in among them, completely overturning one of the party, leaving her on the field, and dispersing everybody else except Pomaree. Backing her horse dexterously, the incensed queen heaped upon him every scandalous epithet she could think of; until at last the enraged Tanee leaped out of his saddle, caught Pomaree by her dress, and dragging her to the earth struck her repeatedly in the face, holding on meanwhile by the hair of her head. He was proceeding to strangle her on the spot, when the cries of the frightened attendants brought a crowd of natives to the rescue, who bore the nearly insensible queen away.

But his frantic rage was not yet sated. He ran to the palace; and before it could be prevented, demolished a valuable supply of crockery, a recent present from abroad. In the act of perpetrating some other atrocity, he was seized from behind, and carried off with rolling eyes and foaming at the mouth.

This is a fair example of a Tahitian in a passion. Though the mildest of mortals in general, and hard to be roused, when once fairly up, he is possessed with a thousand devils.

The day following, Tanee was privately paddled over to Imeeo in a canoe; where, after remaining in banishment for a couple of weeks, he was allowed to return, and once more give in his domestic adhesion.

Though Pomaree Vahinee I. be something of a Jezebel in private life, in her public rule she is said to have been quite lenient and forbearing. This was her true policy; for an hereditary hostility to her family had always lurked in the hearts of many powerful chiefs, the descendants of the old Kings of Taiarboo, dethroned by her grandfather Otoo. Chief among these, and in fact the leader of his party, was Poofai; a bold, able man, who made no secret of his enmity to the missionaries, and the government which they controlled. But while events were occurring calculated to favour the hopes of the disaffected and turbulent, the arrival of the French gave a most unexpected turn to affairs.

During my sojourn in Tahiti, a report was rife--which I knew to originate with what is generally called the "missionary party"--that Poofai and some other chiefs of note had actually agreed, for a stipulated bribe, to acquiesce in the appropriation of their country. But subsequent events have rebutted the calumny. Several of these very men have recently died in battle against the French.

Under the sovereignty of the Pomarees, the great chiefs of Tahiti were something like the barons of King John. Holding feudal sway over their patrimonial valleys, and on account of their descent, warmly beloved by the people, they frequently cut off the royal revenues by refusing to pay the customary tribute due from them as vassals.

The truth is, that with the ascendancy of the missionaries, the regal office in Tahiti lost much of its dignity and influence. In the days of Paganism, it was supported by all the power of a numerous priesthood, and was solemnly connected with the entire superstitious idolatry of the land. The monarch claimed to be a sort of bye-blow of Tararroa, the Saturn of the Polynesian mythology, and cousin-german to inferior deities. His person was thrice holy; if he entered an ordinary dwelling, never mind for how short a time, it was demolished when he left; no common mortal being thought worthy to inhabit it afterward.

"I'm a greater man than King George," said the incorrigible young Otoo to the first missionaries; "he rides on a horse, and I on a man." Such was the case. He travelled post through his dominions on the shoulders of his subjects; and relays of mortal beings were provided in all the valleys.

But alas! how times have changed; how transient human greatness. Some years since, Pomaree Vahinee I., the granddaughter of the proud Otoo, went into the laundry business; publicly soliciting, by her agents, the washing of the linen belonging to the officers of ships touching in her harbours.

It is a significant fact, and one worthy of record, that while the influence of the English missionaries at Tahiti has tended to so great a diminution of the regal dignity there, that of the American missionaries at the Sandwich Islands has been purposely exerted to bring about a contrary result.

CHAPTER LXXXI.

WE VISIT THE COURT

IT WAS about the middle of the second month of the Hegira, and therefore some five weeks after our arrival in Partoowye, that we at last obtained admittance to the residence of the queen.

It happened thus. There was a Marquesan in the train of Pomaree who officiated as nurse to her children. According to the Tahitian custom, the royal youngsters are carried about until it requires no small degree of strength to stand up under them. But Marbonna was just the man for this--large and muscular, well made as a statue, and with an arm like a degenerate Tahitian's thigh.

Embarking at his native island as a sailor on board of a French whaler, he afterward ran away from the ship at Tahiti; where, being seen and admired by Pomaree, he had been prevailed upon to enlist in her service.

Often, when visiting the grounds, we saw him walking about in the shade, carrying two handsome boys, who encircled his neck with their arms. Marbonna's face, tattooed as it was in the ornate style of his tribe, was as good as a picture-book to these young Pomarees. They delighted to trace with their fingers the outlines of the strange shapes there delineated.

The first time my eyes lighted upon the Marquesan, I knew his country in a moment; and hailing him in his own language, he turned round, surprised that a person so speaking should be a stranger. He proved to be a native of Tior, a glen of Nukuheva. I had visited the place more than once; and so, on the island of Imeeo, we met like old friends.

In my frequent conversations with him over the bamboo picket, I found this islander a philosopher of nature--a wild heathen, moralizing upon the vices and follies of the Christian court of Tahiti--a savage, scorning the degeneracy of the people among whom fortune had thrown him.

I was amazed at the national feelings of the man. No European, when abroad, could speak of his country with more pride than Marbonna. He assured me, again and again, that so soon as he had obtained sufficient money to purchase twenty muskets, and as many bags of powder, he was going to return to a place with which Imeeo was not worthy to be compared.

It was Marbonna who, after one or two unsuccessful attempts, at last brought about our admission into the queen's grounds. Through a considerable crowd he conducted us along the pier to where an old man was sitting, to whom he introduced us as a couple of "karhowrees" of his acquaintance, anxious to see the sights of the palace. The venerable chamberlain stared at us, and shook his head: the doctor, thinking he wanted a fee, placed a plug of tobacco in his hand. This was ingratiating, and we were permitted to pass on. Upon the point of entering one of the houses, Marbonna's name was shouted in half-a-dozen different directions, and he was obliged to withdraw.

Thus left at the very threshold to shift for ourselves, my companion's assurance stood us in good stead. He stalked right in, and I followed. The place was full of women, who, instead of exhibiting the surprise we expected, accosted us as cordially as if we had called to take our Souchong with them by express invitation. In the first place, nothing would do but we must each devour a calabash of "poee," and several roasted bananas. Pipes were then lighted, and a brisk conversation ensued.

These ladies of the court, if not very polished, were surprisingly free and easy in their manners; quite as much so as King Charles's beauties. There was one of them--an arch little miss, who could converse with us pretty fluently--to whom we strove to make ourselves particularly agreeable, with the view of engaging her services as cicerone.

As such, she turned out to be everything we could desire. No one disputing her will, every place was entered without ceremony, curtains brushed aside, mats lifted, and each nook and corner explored. Whether the little damsel carried her mistress' signet, that everything opened to her thus, I know not; but Marbonna himself, the bearer of infants, could not have been half so serviceable.

Among other houses which we visited, was one of large size and fine exterior; the special residence of a European--formerly the mate of a merchant vessel,--who had done himself the honour of marrying into the Pomaree family. The lady he wedded being a near kinswoman of the queen, he became a permanent member of her majesty's household. This adventurer rose late, dressed theatrically in calico and trinkets, assumed a dictatorial tone in conversation, and was evidently upon excellent terms with himself.

We found him reclining on a mat, smoking a reed-pipe of tobacco, in the midst of an admiring circle of chiefs and ladies. He must have noticed our approach; but instead of rising and offering civilities, he went on talking and smoking, without even condescending to look at us.

"His Highness feels his 'poee,'" carelessly observed the doctor. The rest of the company gave us the ordinary salutation, our guide announcing us beforehand.

In answer to our earnest requests to see the queen, we were now conducted to an edifice, by far the most spacious, in the inclosure. It was at least one hundred and fifty feet in length, very wide, with low eaves, and an exceedingly steep roof of pandannas leaves. There were neither doors nor windows--nothing along the sides but the slight posts supporting the rafters. Between these posts, curtains of fine matting and tappa were rustling, all round; some of them were festooned, or partly withdrawn, so as to admit light and air, and afford a glimpse now and then of what was going on within.

Pushing aside one of the screens, we entered. The apartment was one immense hall; the long and lofty ridge-pole fluttering with fringed matting and tassels, full forty feet from the ground. Lounges of mats, piled one upon another, extended on either side: while here and there were slight screens, forming as many recesses, where groups of natives--all females--were reclining at their evening meal.

As we advanced, these various parties ceased their buzzing, and in explanation of our appearance among them, listened to a few cabalistic words from our guide.

The whole scene was a strange one; but what most excited our surprise was the incongruous assemblage of the most costly objects from all quarters of the globe. Cheek by jowl, they lay beside the rudest native articles, without the slightest attempt at order. Superb writing-desks of rosewood, inlaid with silver and mother-of-pearl; decanters and goblets of cut glass; embossed volumes of plates; gilded candelabra; sets of globes and mathematical instruments; the finest porcelain; richly-mounted sabres and fowling-pieces; laced hats and sumptuous garments of all sorts, with numerous other matters of

European manufacture, were strewn about among greasy calabashes half-filled with "poee," rolls of old tappa and matting, paddles and fish-spears, and the ordinary furniture of a Tahitian dwelling.

All the articles first mentioned were, doubtless, presents from foreign powers. They were more or less injured: the fowling-pieces and swords were rusted; the finest woods were scratched; and a folio volume of Hogarth lay open, with a cocoa-nut shell of some musty preparation capsized among the miscellaneous furniture of the Rake's apartment, where that inconsiderate young gentleman is being measured for a coat.

While we were amusing ourselves in this museum of curiosities, our conductor plucked us by the sleeve, and whispered, "Pomaree! Pomaree! armai kowkow."

"She is coming to sup, then," said the doctor, staring in the direction indicated. "What say you, Paul, suppose we step up?" Just then a curtain near by lifted, and from a private building a few yards distant the queen entered, unattended.

She wore a loose gown of blue silk, with two rich shawls, one red and the other yellow, tied about her neck. Her royal majesty was barefooted.

She was about the ordinary size, rather matronly; her features not very handsome; her mouth, voluptuous; but there was a care-worn expression in her face, probably attributable to her late misfortunes. From her appearance, one would judge her about forty; but she is not so old.

As the queen approached one of the recesses, her attendants hurried up, escorted her in, and smoothed the mats on which she at last reclined. Two girls soon appeared, carrying their mistress' repast; and then, surrounded by cut-glass and porcelain, and jars of sweetmeats and confections, Pomaree Vahinee I., the titular Queen of Tahiti, ate fish and "poee" out of her native calabashes, disdaining either knife or spoon.

"Come on," whispered Long Ghost, "let's have an audience at once;" and he was on the point of introducing himself, when our guide, quite alarmed, held him back and implored silence. The other natives also interfered, and, as he was pressing forward, raised such an outcry that Pomaree lifted her eyes and saw us for the first.

She seemed surprised and offended, and, issuing an order in a commanding tone to several of her women, waved us out of the house. Summary as the dismissal was, court etiquette, no doubt, required our compliance. We withdrew; making a profound inclination as we disappeared behind the tappa arras.

We departed the ground without seeing Marbonna; and previous to vaulting over the picket, feed our pretty guide after a fashion of our own. Looking round a few moments after, we saw the damsel escorted back by two men, who seemed to have been sent after her. I trust she received nothing more than a reprimand.

The next day Po-Po informed us that strict orders had been issued to admit no strangers within the palace precincts.

CHAPTER LXXXII.

WHICH ENDS THE BOOK

DISAPPOINTED in going to court, we determined upon going to sea. It would never do, longer to trespass on Po-Po's hospitality; and then, weary somewhat of life in Imeeo, like all sailors ashore, I at last pined for the billows.

Now, if her crew were to be credited, the Leviathan was not the craft to our mind. But I had seen the captain, and liked him. He was an uncommonly tall, robust, fine-looking man, in the prime of life. There was a deep crimson spot in the middle of each sunburnt cheek, doubtless the effect of his sea-potations. He was a Vineyarder, or native of the island of Martha's Vineyard (adjoining Nantucket), and--I would have sworn it--a sailor, and no tyrant.

Previous to this, we had rather avoided the Leviathan's men, when they came ashore; but now, we purposely threw ourselves in their way, in order to learn more of the vessel.

We became acquainted with the third mate, a Prussian, and an old merchant-seaman--a right jolly fellow, with a face like a ruby. We took him to Po-Po's, and gave him a dinner of baked pig and breadfruit; with pipes and tobacco for dessert. The account he gave us of the ship agreed with my own surmises. A cosier old craft never floated; and the captain was the finest man in the world. There was plenty to eat, too; and, at sea, nothing to do but sit on the windlass and sail. The only bad trait about the vessel was this: she had been launched under some baleful star; and so was a luckless ship in the fishery. She dropped her boats into the brine often enough, and they frequently got fast to the whales; but lance and harpoon almost invariably "drew" when darted by the men of the Leviathan. But what of that? We would have all the sport of chasing the monsters, with none of the detestable work which follows their capture. So, hurrah for the coast of Japan! Thither the ship was bound.

A word now about the hard stories we heard the first time we visited the ship. They were nothing but idle fictions, got up by the sailors for the purpose of frightening us away, so as to oblige the captain, who was in want of more hands, to lie the longer in a pleasant harbour.

The next time the Vineyarder came ashore, we flung ourselves in his path. When informed of our desire to sail with him, he wanted to know our history; and, above all, what countrymen we were. We said that we had left a whaler in Tahiti, some time previous; and, since then, had been--in the most praiseworthy manner--employed upon a plantation. As for our country, sailors belong to no nation in particular; we were, on this occasion, both Yankees. Upon this he looked decidedly incredulous; and freely told us that he verily believed we were both from Sydney.

Be it known here that American sea captains, in the Pacific, are mortally afraid of these Sydney gentry; who, to tell the truth, wherever known, are in excessively bad odour. Is there a mutiny on board a ship in the South Seas, ten to one a Sydney man is the ringleader. Ashore, these fellows are equally riotous.

It was on this account that we were anxious to conceal the fact of our having belonged to the Julia, though it annoyed me much, thus to deny the dashing little craft. For the same reason, also, the doctor fibbed about his birthplace.

Unfortunately, one part of our raiment--Arfretee's blue frocks--we deemed a sort of collateral evidence against us. For, curiously enough, an American sailor is generally distinguished by his red frock; and an English tar by his blue one: thus reversing the national colours. The circumstance was pointed out by the captain; and we quickly explained the anomaly. But, in vain: he seemed inveterately prejudiced against us; and, in particular, eyed the doctor most distrustfully.

By way of propping the tatter's pretensions, I was throwing out a hint concerning Kentucky, as a land of tall men, when our Vine-yarder turned away abruptly, and desired to hear nothing more. It was evident that he took Long Ghost for an exceedingly problematical character.

Perceiving this, I resolved to see what a private interview would do. So, one afternoon, I found the captain smoking a pipe in the dwelling of a portly old native--one Mai-Mai--who, for a reasonable compensation, did the honours of Partoowye to illustrious strangers.

His guest had just risen from a sumptuous meal of baked pig and taro pudding; and the remnants of the repast were still visible. Two reeking bottles, also, with their necks wrenched off, lay upon the mat. All this was encouraging; for, after a good dinner, one feels affluent and amiable, and peculiarly open to conviction. So, at all events, I found the noble Vineyarder.

I began by saying that I called for the purpose of setting him right touching certain opinions of his concerning the place of my nativity:--I was an American--thank heaven!--and wanted to convince him of the fact.

After looking me in the eye for some time, and, by so doing, revealing an obvious unsteadiness in his own visual organs, he begged me to reach forth my arm. I did so; wondering what upon earth that useful member had to do with the matter in hand.

He placed his fingers upon my wrist; and holding them there for a moment, sprang to his feet, and, with much enthusiasm, pronounced me a Yankee, every beat of my pulse!

"Here, Mai-Mai!" he cried, "another bottle!" And, when it came, with one stroke of a knife, he summarily beheaded it, and commanded me to drain it to the bottom. He then told me that if I would come on board his vessel the following morning, I would find the ship's articles on the cabin transom.

This was getting along famously. But what was to become of the doctor?

I forthwith made an adroit allusion to my long friend. But it was worse than useless. The Vineyarder swore he would have nothing to do with him--he (my long friend) was a "bird" from Sydney, and nothing would make him (the man of little faith) believe otherwise.

I could not help loving the free-hearted captain; but indignant at this most unaccountable prejudice against my comrade, I abruptly took leave.

Upon informing the doctor of the result of the interview, he was greatly amused; and laughingly declared that the Vineyarder must be a penetrating fellow. He then insisted upon my going to sea in the ship, since he well knew how anxious I was to leave. As for himself, on second thoughts, he was no sailor; and although "lands--' men" very often compose part of a whaler's crew, he did not quite relish the idea of occupying a position so humble. In short, he had made up his mind to tarry awhile in Imeeo.

I turned the matter over; and at last decided upon quitting the island. The impulse urging me to sea once more, and the prospect of eventually reaching home, were too much to be resisted; especially as the Leviathan, so comfortable a craft, was now bound on her last whaling cruise, and, in little more than a year's time, would be going round Cape Horn.

I did not, however, covenant to remain in the vessel for the residue of the voyage; which would have been needlessly binding myself. I merely stipulated for the coming cruise, leaving my subsequent movements unrestrained; for there was no knowing that I might not change my mind, and prefer journeying home by short and easy stages.

The next day I paddled off to the ship, signed and sealed, and stepped ashore with my "advance"--fifteen Spanish dollars--tasseling the ends of my neck-handkerchief.

I forced half of the silver on Long Ghost; and having little use for the remainder, would have given it to Po-Po as some small return for his kindness; but, although he well knew the value of the coin, not a dollar would he accept.

In three days' time the Prussian came to Po-Po's, and told us that the captain, having made good the number of his crew by shipping several islanders, had determined upon sailing with the land breeze at dawn the following morning. These tidings were received in the afternoon. The doctor immediately disappeared, returning soon after with a couple of flasks of wine concealed in the folds of his frock. Through the agency of the Marquesan, he had purchased them from an understrapper of the court.

I prevailed upon Po-Po to drink a parting shell; and even little Loo, actually looking conscious that one of her hopeless admirers was about leaving Partoowye for ever, sipped a few drops from a folded leaf. As for the warm-hearted Arfretee, her grief was unbounded. She even besought me to spend my last night under her own palm-thatch; and then, in the morning, she would herself paddle me off to the ship.

But this I would not consent to; and so, as something to remember her by, she presented me with a roll of fine matting, and another of tappa. These gifts placed in my hammock, I afterward found very agreeable in the warm latitudes to which we were bound; nor did they fail to awaken most grateful remembrances.

About nightfall, we broke away from this generous-hearted household, and hurried down to the water.

It was a mad, merry night among the sailors; they had on tap a small cask of wine, procured in the same way as the doctor's flasks.

An hour or two after midnight, everything was noiseless; but when the first streak of the dawn showed itself over the mountains, a sharp voice hailed the forecastle, and ordered the ship unmoored.

The anchors came up cheerily; the sails were soon set; and with the early breath of the tropical morning, fresh and fragrant from the hillsides, we slowly glided down the bay, and were swept through the opening in the reef. Presently we "hove to," and the canoes came alongside to take off the islanders who had accompanied us thus far. As he stepped over the side, I shook the doctor long and heartily by the hand. I have never seen or heard of him since.

Crowding all sail, we braced the yards square; and, the breeze freshening, bowled straight away from the land. Once more the sailor's cradle rocked under me, and I found myself rolling in my gait.

By noon, the island had gone down in the horizon; and all before us was the wide Pacific.